Electric Vehicle Technologies: Trends, Control, and Charging Solutions

Edited by

Nitesh Tiwari
Department of Electrical Engineering
KIPM College of Engineering and Technology
Gorakhpur (UP), India

Shekhar Yadav
Department of Electrical Engineering
Madan Mohan Malaviya University of Technology
Gorakhpur (UP), India

&

Sabha Raj Arya
Department of Electrical Engineering, Sardar Vallabhbhai
National Institute of Technology, Surat, Gujarat, India

Electric Vehicle Technologies: Trends, Control, and Charging Solutions

Editors: Nitesh Tiwari, Shekhar Yadav & Sabha Raj Arya

ISBN (Online): 978-981-5324-87-7

ISBN (Print): 978-981-5324-88-4

ISBN (Paperback): 978-981-5324-89-1

need for a court order if at any point you breach any terms of this License Agreement. In no event will any delay or failure by Bentham Science Publishers in enforcing your compliance with this License Agreement constitute a waiver of any of its rights.

3. You acknowledge that you have read this License Agreement, and agree to be bound by its terms and conditions. To the extent that any other terms and conditions presented on any website of Bentham Science Publishers conflict with, or are inconsistent with, the terms and conditions set out in this License Agreement, you acknowledge that the terms and conditions set out in this License Agreement shall prevail.

Bentham Science Publishers Pte. Ltd.
80 Robinson Road #02-00
Singapore 068898
Singapore
Email: subscriptions@benthamscience.net

BENTHAM SCIENCE

CONTENTS

FOREWORD

The transition to electric vehicles (EVs) represents one of the most significant shifts in modern transportation, driven by the urgent need to reduce carbon emissions and reliance on fossil fuels. As governments and industries across the globe strive to address climate change and promote sustainable mobility, innovative technologies have become essential to the development and success of EVs. This collection of chapters delves into the core areas of research and development that are poised to shape the future of electric vehicles. From solar energy integration to advanced control systems, these chapters provide a comprehensive and forward-thinking perspective on the technologies that will drive the next generation of electric mobility.

Chapter 1, "A Review of Emerging Research Trends and Opportunities in Harnessing Solar Energy for Electric Vehicles," explores the growing importance of solar energy as a sustainable power source for EVs. This chapter presents an overview of the promising opportunities and challenges involved in integrating solar energy with electric vehicles, an area that continues to receive increasing attention in the research community. As solar technology matures, its potential to support and enhance the energy needs of EVs becomes increasingly significant.

In Chapter 2, "Introduction to EV Motors," the fundamental components of electric vehicle propulsion are examined. Understanding the operation and control of electric motors is critical to optimizing the performance of EVs. This chapter serves as an essential introduction to the various motor types, including their characteristics, advantages, and applications, providing readers with a solid foundation in EV motor technology.

Chapter 3, "Introduction to Power Electronics Converters," addresses the crucial role that power electronics play in the efficient operation of EV systems. These converters manage the flow of electrical energy between the battery, motor, and charging system. The chapter discusses the key converter technologies that facilitate the smooth and reliable operation of electric vehicles, and how these systems contribute to their overall performance and energy efficiency.

The discussion progresses with Chapter 4, "Field Oriented Speed Control of BLDC Motor for Practical Drive Cycle," which focuses on an advanced motor control strategy for electric vehicles. Field Oriented Control (FOC) of BLDC motors is a key method for enhancing performance and efficiency in real-world driving conditions. This chapter explains how this technique optimizes motor operation, allowing EVs to achieve higher levels of efficiency and performance during dynamic driving cycles.

In Chapter 5, "Phase Shifted Full Bridge Converter-based Battery Charger for Fast Charging of Electric Vehicles," the need for fast and efficient charging solutions is explored. This chapter introduces phase-shifted full bridge converters as a solution for rapid battery charging in EVs. By focusing on the optimization of charging times, this chapter addresses one of the most critical challenges faced by the EV industry—ensuring that electric vehicles are ready for use with minimal downtime.

Chapter 6, "An Adaptive Passivity-based Controller for Battery Charging Application: The Lagrangian Framework," presents an innovative approach to battery charging using a passivity-based controller. This chapter introduces the Lagrangian framework to optimize the charging process, ensuring that EV batteries are charged efficiently and safely, thereby extending their lifespan and improving overall vehicle performance.

In Chapter 7, "Vehicle-to-Grid (V2G) Battery Charging System for Electric Vehicles," we look at the bidirectional energy flow that allows electric vehicles to not only draw power from the grid but also return energy. The Vehicle-to-Grid (V2G) concept is a promising development in the integration of EVs with the broader energy grid. This chapter highlights the technical, economic, and regulatory aspects of V2G systems, and how they can support grid stability and energy sustainability.

Chapter 8, "IoT Based Floor Cleaning Electric Vehicle Robot with Live Streaming Camera," introduces the integration of Internet of Things (IoT) technologies with electric vehicles, specifically in the context of autonomous cleaning robots. This chapter highlights the application of advanced sensors, IoT connectivity, and robotics in the development of intelligent EV systems, extending the use of EV technologies beyond traditional transportation.

In Chapter 9, "Hardware Design and Modelling of Solar-Based Wireless Electric Vehicle Charging Station," the design and modeling of solar-powered wireless charging stations are explored. This chapter discusses the intersection of solar energy, wireless power transfer, and EV charging, providing insights into how these technologies can be integrated to create efficient, sustainable charging infrastructure for electric vehicles.

Finally, Chapter 10, "Hardware Design of Electric Bicycle with Solar Panel," closes the collection by addressing the design and development of solar-powered electric bicycles. This chapter emphasizes the growing trend of integrating renewable energy with lightweight personal transportation options, offering a glimpse into the future of urban mobility and clean, accessible transportation.

Prof. S. K. Srivastava
Madan Mohan Malaviya University of Technology
Gorakhpur (UP), India

PREFACE

The rapid evolution of electric vehicles (EVs) and the increasing emphasis on sustainability have driven research in various fields, including solar energy integration, power electronics, and autonomous systems. This compilation of chapters offers a comprehensive review of the emerging technologies and methods that are shaping the future of electric vehicle (EV) systems. From advancements in solar energy harnessing to innovative control techniques for motor drives, this book explores the diverse landscape of research and development in EV technology, providing insights into both current trends and future opportunities.

Chapter 1, "A Review of Emerging Research Trends and Opportunities in Harnessing Solar Energy for Electric Vehicles," sets the stage by discussing the growing role of solar energy in powering electric vehicles. This chapter outlines the potential benefits, challenges, and opportunities of integrating solar power with EV systems to create a more sustainable transportation solution.

In Chapter 2, "Introduction to EV Motors," readers are introduced to the various types of motors used in electric vehicles, including their construction, operation, and performance characteristics. Understanding these motors is crucial to developing efficient EV systems that can meet the increasing demands for performance and energy efficiency.

Chapter 3, "Introduction to Power Electronics Converters," explores the critical role that power electronics play in the operation of electric vehicles. This chapter provides an overview of the key converter technologies used in EVs, which are essential for controlling the power flow between the battery, motor, and other components.

The focus shifts to motor control in Chapter 4, "Field Oriented Speed Control of BLDC Motor for Practical Drive Cycle," where advanced techniques for controlling Brushless Direct Current (BLDC) motors are discussed. This chapter emphasizes how these techniques contribute to the efficiency and performance of EVs during real-world driving cycles.

Chapter 5, "Phase Shifted Full Bridge Converter-based Battery Charger for Fast Charging of Electric Vehicles," addresses the importance of fast and efficient charging solutions for EVs. The chapter delves into phase-shifted full bridge converters and their application in optimizing battery charging times without compromising system safety or longevity.

In Chapter 6, "An Adaptive Passivity-based Controller for Battery Charging Application: The Lagrangian Framework," a novel controller is introduced that improves the adaptive charging of EV batteries. The chapter emphasizes the benefits of the Lagrangian framework in enhancing battery performance and overall energy management.

Chapter 7, "Vehicle-to-Grid (V2G) Battery Charging System for Electric Vehicles," explores the potential of bidirectional charging systems, enabling EVs to not only charge from the grid but also contribute energy back to it. This chapter discusses the technological, economic, and regulatory challenges and opportunities of V2G systems in supporting grid stability and energy sustainability.

In Chapter 8, "IoT Based Floor Cleaning Electric Vehicle Robot with Live Streaming Camera," the application of IoT and robotics in EV technology is highlighted. This chapter presents the design and operation of an autonomous floor-cleaning robot, showcasing how these innovations can be integrated into the broader field of electric vehicle development.

Chapter 9, "Hardware Design and Modelling of Solar-Based Wireless Electric Vehicle Charging Station," focuses on the integration of solar energy and wireless charging technologies. The chapter presents a hardware design for a solar-based charging station, demonstrating how these technologies can be combined to offer more sustainable and efficient EV charging solutions.

Lastly, Chapter 10, "Hardware Design of Electric Bicycle with Solar Panel," examines the design considerations and challenges in developing solar-powered electric bicycles. This chapter underscores the importance of solar energy in supporting the growing demand for sustainable urban mobility solutions.

Together, these chapters provide a holistic view of the current state and future directions of electric vehicle research, emphasizing innovative approaches to energy generation, storage, and management. As the world moves toward cleaner, more efficient transportation solutions, the research presented here offers valuable insights into the technologies that will shape the future of electric mobility.

Nitesh Tiwari
Department of Electrical Engineering
KIPM College of Engineering and Technology
Gorakhpur (UP), India

Shekhar Yadav
Department of Electrical Engineering
Madan Mohan Malaviya University of Technology
Gorakhpur (UP), India

&

Sabha Raj Arya
Department of Electrical Engineering
Sardar Vallabhbhai National Institute of Technology
Surat, Gujarat, India

List of Contributors

Aishvarya Narain	United College of Engineering and Research, Prayagraj, Uttar Pradesh, India
Aditi Saxena	Indian Institute of Technology, Kanpur, India
Arun Kumar Yadav	Department of Electrical Engineering, Bansal Institute of Engineering & Technology, Lucknow, Uttar Pradesh, India
Anurag Dwivedi	Department of Electrical Engineering, Bansal Institute of Engineering & Technology, Lucknow, Uttar Pradesh, India
Anuradha Tiwari	Department of Electrical Engineering, Bansal Institute of Engineering & Technology, Lucknow, Uttar Pradesh, India
Ajay Kumar Maurya	Department of Electrical Engineering, KIPM College of Engineering and Technology, Gida, Gorakhpur (UP), India
Ankesh Kumar Mishra	Department of Electrical Engineering, KIPM College of Engineering and Technology, Gida, Gorakhpur (UP), India
Aditya Chaurasia	Department of Electrical Engineering, KIPM College of Engineering and Technology, Gida, Gorakhpur (UP), India
Chandra Mohan Chaurasiya	Department of Electrical Engineering, KIPM College of Engineering and Technology, Gorakhpur (UP), India
Kumari Shipra	Department of Electrical Engineering, Noida International University, Greater Noida-201312, India
Neha Gupta	Amity School of Engineering and Technology, Amity University, Uttar Pradesh, Lucknow Campus, Lucknow, India
Nitesh Tiwari	Department of Electrical Engineering, KIPM College of Engineering and Technology, Gorakhpur (UP), India
Paritosh Kumar Rai	Department of Electrical Engineering, Bansal Institute of Engineering & Technology, Lucknow, Uttar Pradesh, India
Palak Gaur	Department of Electrical Engineering, Bansal Institute of Engineering & Technology, Lucknow, Uttar Pradesh, India
Rakesh Maurya	Department of Electrical Engineering, Sardar Vallabhbhai National Institute of Technology, Surat-395007, Gujarat, India
Rachit Srivastava	Department of Electrical Engineering, Bansal Institute of Engineering & Technology, Lucknow, Uttar Pradesh, India
Shaniya Ashraf	Department of Electrical Engineering, Madan Mohan Malaviya University of Technology, Gorakhpur (UP), India
Shekhar Yadav	Department of Electrical Engineering, Madan Mohan Malaviya University of Technology, Gorakhpur (UP), India
Sahil Ramazan	Department of Electrical Engineering, Bansal Institute of Engineering & Technology, Lucknow, Uttar Pradesh, India
Shubham Gupta	Department of Electrical Engineering, KIPM College of Engineering and Technology, Gorakhpur (UP), India

Shivangi Agrawal   Department of Electrical Engineering, KIPM College of Engineering and Technology, Gorakhpur (UP), India

Sumit Patel   Department of Electrical Engineering, KIPM College of Engineering and Technology, Gorakhpur (UP), India

S. Karmakar   Department of Electrical Engineering, National Institute of Technology Durgapur, Durgapur, India

S. Sen   Department of Electrical Engineering, National Institute of Technology Durgapur, Durgapur, India

T.K. Saha   Department of Electrical Engineering, National Institute of Technology Durgapur, Durgapur, India

Vidhi Dubey   Department of Electrical Engineering, Bansal Institute of Engineering and Technology, Lucknow, Uttar Pradesh, India

Vaibhav Tripath   Department of Electrical Engineering, Bansal Institute of Engineering and Technology, Lucknow, Uttar Pradesh, India

Electric Vehicle Technologies, 2025, 1-22

CHAPTER 1

Comprehensive Review of Technological Advances in Solar EV Charging Systems and the Impact of Shading

Aishvarya Narain[1,*]

[1] *United College of Engineering and Research, Prayagraj, Uttar Pradesh, India*

Abstract: This review provides a comprehensive overview of the technological advancements in solar Electric Vehicle (EV) charging systems, with a particular focus on the challenges posed by Partial Shading Conditions (PSC). As the adoption of electric vehicles grows globally, the integration of solar power for EV charging offers significant potential in reducing carbon emissions and optimizing energy efficiency. The review delves into the evolution of solar PV-EV charging systems, highlighting innovations in system designs, energy management strategies, and Vehicle-to-Grid (V2G) technologies. A key focus is placed on the impact of shading on Photovoltaic (PV) module performance, with an exploration of various mitigation strategies such as advanced optimization algorithms, hybrid PV systems, and battery storage solutions. Through a review of recent studies, it outlines the effectiveness of solar-powered charging infrastructure, including grid-connected and off-grid systems, in diverse environmental conditions. Despite the progress, challenges related to battery performance, system costs, and the feasibility of large-scale deployment are discussed. Furthermore, the review investigates the economic and environmental benefits of solar-assisted EV charging, with a focus on sustainability, cost reduction, and the integration of renewable energy sources. The chapter concludes by identifying future research directions to address the unresolved issues surrounding partial shading, battery degradation, and the optimization of solar charging systems for widespread adoption. Ultimately, it emphasizes the importance of overcoming shading effects to enhance the efficiency, reliability, and sustainability of solar EV charging systems, contributing to the broader goals of sustainable transportation and clean energy.

Keywords: Electrical vehicle, Partial shading, PV array, Solar power, Sustainable transportation.

---

* **Corresponding author Aishvarya Narain:** United College of Engineering and Research, Prayagraj, Uttar Pradesh, India; E-mail: aishvaryanarain@united.ac.in

Nitesh Tiwari, Shekhar Yadav and Sabha Raj Arya (Eds.)

INTRODUCTION

Electric Vehicles (EVs) running on solar power combine sustainable transportation with renewable energy. Even though modern EV solar panels cannot fully power the car, they can be used as additional sources of charging. By using sunlight to generate electricity, these panels extend the driving range and aid in battery charging. Nonetheless, there are still issues with panel integration and efficiency. The idea of an EV that runs entirely on solar power may become a reality as technology evolves. Engineers and researchers are working hard to optimize solar energy integration into electric vehicles. Innovative features encompass solar coatings that adapt to various surfaces and flexible solar panels that conform to the car's contours. Additionally, EVs can maximize solar charging based on sunlight availability and weather conditions thanks to smart charging systems. Even though completely solar-powered cars are still a way off, these developments bring us closer to a more sustainable and eco-friendly future.

The loss in power output from a partially shaded solar panel is not always proportional to the shaded area. In fact, partial shading can result in unbalanced energy losses. It is surprising to learn that a solar panel can drop to zero watts of output power from just a 10% shade. This occurs as a result of the dark cells having a substantial impact on the total current and power output. Fig. (**1**) shows the different conditions that cause partial shading, *i.e.*, dust, snow, clouds, self-shading, trees, bird droppings, buildings, *etc*. The characteristic curve shows that when partial shading occurs, the maximum point is low with multiple peaks. The shading causes multiple peaks, *i.e.*, global maxima along with local maxima in the current and power curve. The loss of power, *i.e.*, mismatched power losses, and the loss of current, *i.e.*, current loss, are shown in Fig. (**1**).

Solar panels in EVs currently serve as an auxiliary charging source, extending driving range and reducing reliance on grid power, though fully solar-powered EVs are not yet feasible. Technological advancements like flexible panels and smart charging systems are improving solar integration. Partial shading significantly reduces panel efficiency, causing mismatched power losses and multiple peaks in the current-power curve, which are influenced by the above factors. Section 2 discusses the technological advancement in SPV for EVs.

TECHNOLOGICAL ADVANCES IN PV ARRAYS FOR EV CHARGING IN SHADED ENVIRONMENTS (2014-2024)

A case study to highlight the technical, economic, and regulatory challenges of the integration of solar energy systems into EV charging infrastructure has been presented [1]. Key technical issues include the design and optimization of solar PV systems, site suitability, panel efficiency, and grid integration. Regulatory barriers include interconnection standards, utility rules, and permitting processes. The study's analysis shows that solar-powered EV charging is feasible, with solar power generation and EV charging patterns well aligned. The findings provide valuable guidance for promoting sustainable energy and transportation electrification.

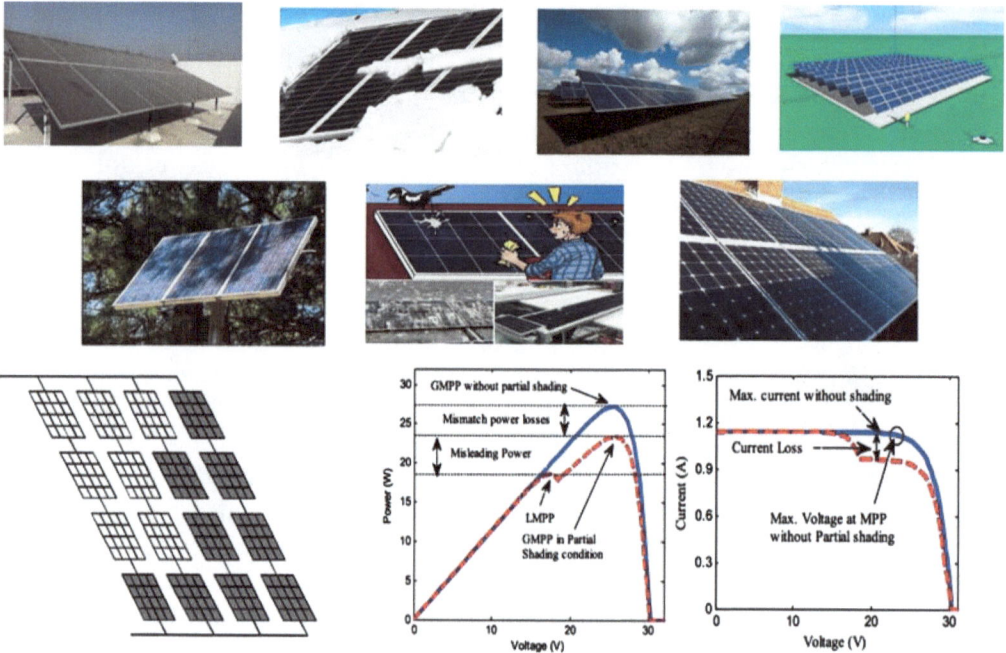

Fig. (1). Different conditions of partial shading.

A paper [2] explores using solar energy to charge EVs at workplaces for maximum energy yield and analyzes solar insolation variations to determine energy availability and the need for grid connection in the Netherlands. The study compares different EV charging profiles to minimize grid dependence and maximize solar power utilization, considering only weekday and daily charging scenarios. In addition to assessing the viability of incorporating local storage to cut grid dependence by 25%, a priority approach for managing several EVs charging from the same EV-PV charger is proposed. The study also investigates the design of a solar-powered EV charging station with a double-axis solar tracker, which enhances the energy yield by 17%, mainly in summer, and presents a storage size methodology adapted to different locations.

A new approach has been introduced to assess the effects of the full-battery effect and calculate the associated CO_2 reductions when conventional vehicles are charged with onboard solar power [3]. Using solar radiation and driver mobility data, the methodology uniquely quantifies full-battery impact through normalized real-world solar radiation and specific vehicle and solar system parameters. The study examines a 12V vehicle battery charged *via* a horizontally mounted photovoltaic roof, utilizing sub-hourly resolution models to accurately reflect system dynamics during brief driving periods. The study highlights minimal CO_2 savings during these events but does not include potential driving-pattern adjustments that can optimize the use of solar rooftop PV systems, such as optimizing for maximizing usable solar radiation.

A study [4] offers insights into electromobility powered by renewable energy sources based on real-world data. It provides estimates of Battery Electric Vehicle (BEV) energy consumption and evaluates the roles of both PV panels and the grid in the vehicle's charging process under real driving conditions. The study also presents guidelines for designing solar charging stations to meet the annual energy demands of a typical BEV. Future research directions include examining the relationship between BEV charging time and charge levels, as well as the effects of shading, orientation, tilt, and dust on PV output in urban solar carports.

The study investigates the impact of partial shading on the solar roofs of Hybrid Electric Vehicles (HEVs) using MATLAB/Simulink simulation models, exploring different shading scenarios and their effects on output power [5]. It evaluates the performance of solar panels under shading conditions by analyzing I-V and P-V measurements and comparing half-cell and full-cell solar panel configurations. The research indicates that half-cell solar panels can significantly reduce power losses compared to full-cell panels under partial shading, with various degrees of shadowing simulated to validate this finding. The study recommends the adoption of half-cell module designs to mitigate shading effects in HEVs. Future research directions include optimizing vehicle dimensions and exploring the use of thin-film solar panels on additional window surfaces. Additionally, the Maximum Power Point Tracking (MPPT) algorithm is used to enhance power extraction efficiency in the presence of partial shading.

Another study [6] examines the combined benefits of integrating solar and wind resources in vulnerable low-voltage distribution grids. It demonstrates that combining these renewable sources can mitigate challenges arising from their stochastic nature. The study also evaluates the performance of power distribution grids at the common coupling point (PCC) when influenced by photovoltaic generators, wind power, and electric vehicles. Additionally, it investigates the transient stability of the grids under various fault conditions. Simulations are carried out using DIgSILENT PowerFactory software, utilizing a DSL model with foundational formulas and state equations. The paper details the formulation of these models and presents the simulation results in tabular form.

PV array systems and EVs work in perfect harmony to provide sustainable energy and mobility options. EVs significantly reduce greenhouse gas emissions and reliance on non-renewable resources because they run on electricity rather than fossil fuels. The environmental benefits are further enhanced when the battery is charged using electricity produced by photovoltaic panels, which directly convert sunlight into electrical energy. The carbon footprint of energy production and consumption can be reduced by using PV arrays, providing a clean, renewable energy source that can be used to power EVs. In keeping with international efforts to combat climate change, this combination not only encourages energy independence but also facilitates the transition to a more sustainable and environmentally friendly energy ecology. PV array configuration in different PSCs is reviewed in Table **1**. The objective, performance, and PV array configuration sizing under different PSC conditions of the last 10 years have been considered. The test environment, like OFF grid, ON grid, and laboratory-based, is considered for bifurcation.

Table 1. Types of PV configurations under PSC with the publications in the time span of 2014- 2024.

Authors, Year [ref]	Objective	Performance Parameters	PSC Condition	PV Array Configuration Size	Grid Connected
2014 [7]	Global maximum power point (GMPP)	MPP error, GMPP	PSC Considered	46 PV module (1000 W)	No (Laboratory based)
2014 [8]	Study of PV system connected to the grid	GMPP, Current	Climate condition Considered	4 PV module (130.72 W)	No(Off-grid)
2014 [9]	Identification of MPP location	GMPP, Current	PSC not Considered	3x3 PV module (40 W)	No(Off-grid)
2014 [10]	Optimized string proposed	GMPP, Current	PSC Considered	2x3, 3x3 PV module (1.34 KW)	No(Off-grid)
2014 [11]	Different module investigated	GMPP, Current, mismatch losses (ML), fill factor (FF)	PSC not Considered	10x3 PV module (290.5 W)	No(Off-grid)
2015 [12]	Power and current curve w.r.t voltage analysis	GMPP, Current	PSC not Considered	60 PV cells module (90 W)	No(Off-grid)
2015 [13]	Investigation of solar configuration	GMPP, FF, power losses (PL)	PSC not Considered	24 PV module (1446 W)	No(Off-grid)
2015 [14]	Study of conventional solar configuration	Power, Voltage	PSC Considered	3x3 PV module (353 W)	No(Off-grid)

(Table 1) cont.....

Authors, Year [ref]	Objective	Performance Parameters	PSC Condition	PV Array Configuration Size	Grid Connected
2015 [15]	Analysis of shade dispersion	GMPP, Utilization factor	PSC Considered	3x3, 6x4 PV module (708.57 W)	No(Off-grid)
2015 [16]	Optimization used to obtain GMPP	Maximize Power	PSC Considered	10x100 PV module (40.5 KW)	No(Off-grid)
2015 [17]	Study of different configuration	Maximum power, voltage, and current	PSC Considered	30 PV module (5000 W)	No(Off-grid)
2016 [18]	Study on solar configuration	Power, voltage, current, efficiency	PSC not Considered	3 PV module (375 W)	No(Off-grid)
2016 [19]	Study under different partial shading conditions	GMPP, PL, FF	Two different PSCs Considered	4x4 PV cells module (8 W)	No (Laboratory based)
2016 [20]	Study for power enhancement (PE)	Maximum power, PE	PSC Considered	4x4 PV module (960 W)	No(Off-grid)
2016 [21]	Study of optimal total-cross-tied configuration	GMPP, PL, FF, PE, ML, (performance ratio)PR	PSC Considered	4x3 PV module (567 W)	No(Off-grid)
2017 [22]	Study on different solar configuration	GMPP	PSC Considered	3 PV module (581 W)	No(Off-grid)
2017 [23]	Investigation of different configuration	GMPP, FF, PL, PR	PSC Considered	6x4 PV module (3419 W)	No(Off-grid)
2018 [24]	Experimental configuration	GMPP	PSC Considered	3x3 PV module (400 W)	No(Off-grid)
2018 [25]	Study of column index method-based Dominance Square configuration	GMPP, ML, PL, FF	PSC Considered	9x9 PV module (8000 W)	No(Off-grid)
2019 [26]	Relay control-based switch configuration	GMPP, FF	PSC not Considered	3x3 PV module (30 W)	No(Off-grid)
2019 [27]	Su-Du-Ku configuration result analysis	GMPP, FF, ML, and efficiency	Shade dispersion	9x9 PV module (2280 W)	No(Off-grid)
2019 [28]	Skyscraper puzzle used in solar configuration	ML, FF, PL, GMPP	PSC Considered	9x9, 5x5 PV module (5658 W)	No(Off-grid)
2020 [29]	Alter PV module configuration	GMPP	PSC Considered	6x6 PV module (9000 W)	No(Off-grid)

(Table 1) cont.....

Authors, Year [ref]	Objective	Performance Parameters	PSC Condition	PV Array Configuration Size	Grid Connected
2020 [30]	Ladder solar configuration investigation	GMPP, FF, ML	PSC Considered	4x4 PV module (3200 W)	No(Off-grid)
2020 [31]	Switch matrix approach configuration analysis	GMPP, FF, ML	PSC not Considered	4x4 PV module (140 W)	No(Off-grid)
2021 [32]	ANN-based system performance analysis	Efficiency comparison, Power	environmental effects	Solar cell PV module (7000 W)	No(Off-grid)
2021 [33]	Tracking of GMPP	Voltage at MPP,	PSC Considered	6x6 PV module (20 W)	No (Laboratory based)
2021 [34]	Obtaining the different cell interconnections topologies.	Maximum Power, Voltage at MPP	PSC Considered	4x4 PV module (3158.2 W)	No (Laboratory based)
2022 [35]	Optimization based analysis	GMPP, FF, PL, PE	PSC Considered	6x6 PV module (3766 W)	No(Off-grid)
2022 [36]	GMPP using 8-Queen's technique	GMPP, FF, ML, PE	PSC Considered	6x6, 9x9, 10x12, 20x20, 4x4 PV module	No(Off-grid)
2022 [37]	Investigation of output power using different configuration.	MPP, Current, Voltage at MPP	PSC Considered	7x3 PV module (5000 W)	No(Off-grid)
2023 [38]	Analysis of panel positions Roof-mounted PV system.	MPP, Energy loss	PSC and orientation of Cells Considered	72 cells PV module (325 W) and 9 PV module (3000 W)	Yes(On-grid)
2023 [39]	Loss reduction using arbitrary array size	Power, Efficiency, PL	PSC Considered	4x4 PV module (5000 W)	No(Off-grid)
2023 [40]	The driving training-based optimization (DTBO) method to find GMPP.	Power, MPP	PSC Considered	4x1 PV module	No (Laboratory based)
2024 [41]	Grey Wolf Algorithm Based Global Maximum Power Point Tracking	GMPP, Speed, Efficiency, Runtime, Power, Voltage	PSC Considered	Single PV panel module	No (Laboratory based)

(Table 1) cont.....

Authors, Year [ref]	Objective	Performance Parameters	PSC Condition	PV Array Configuration Size	Grid Connected
2024 [42]	Competence square technique for PV array reconfiguration.	Power, FF, ML	PSC Considered	6x6 PV module	No(Off-grid)
2024 [43]	The effects of partial shading mitigation	GMPP, ML, FF, Efficiency, Shade Dispersion Ratio (SDR)	PSC Considered	9x9 and 6x6 PV module	No (Laboratory based)
2024 [44]	Investigate power, dynamic response, steady state distortions	MPP, Power, Settling time	PSC Considered	Triple diode PV cell module	No (Off-grid)

ANALYSIS OF SOLAR EV CHARGING SYSTEMS, THEIR CHARACTERISTICS, AND PERFORMANCE

Many manufacturers are investing in this technology because EVs have several essential properties that distinguish them from regular internal combustion engine vehicles. Due to their zero tailpipe emissions, EVs are renowned for enhancing air quality and reducing greenhouse gas emissions. Due to their electric motors, they provide instant torque and smooth acceleration. This results in a different driving experience with fewer moving parts, thereby reducing maintenance costs. Major automakers such as Tesla, Nissan, and Chevrolet have created a variety of electric vehicle models with varying emphasis on features, including price, performance, luxury, and range. For example, Nissan's Leaf model promotes affordability and everyday utility, while Tesla focuses on high performance and cutting-edge technology. Additionally, newcomers like Lucid Motors and Rivian are setting the bar in terms of luxury features and battery technology advancements. Global EV adoption is increasing as a result of different approaches from manufacturers catering to different consumer demands and tastes. Fig. (**2**) bifurcated the EV according to its characteristics and manufacturers.

In a paper [45], a model is introduced that leverages Vehicle-to-Grid (V2G) technology and smart EV charging to enhance PV power consumption. Three control algorithms, including linear optimization or real-time strategies, manage the charging profiles of multiple Electric Vehicles (EVs). The study evaluates the impact on PV self-consumption and peak demand reduction through a simulation using one year of data on PV power generation, EV usage patterns, and energy demand. Additionally, based on many indicators, qualitative information about battery degeneration brought on by these charging procedures is given. Changes to the microgrid structure, such as the inclusion of more EVs, were simulated, illustrating the advantages of using PV power for smart charging. The results show how different charging strategies and microgrid structures affect the balance between demand and supply. The study highlights that smart charging and V2G can significantly contribute to a well-balanced demand and supply system and reduce negative impacts on existing energy infrastructure. Despite some model limitations, the findings support the integration of sustainable energy and transportation technologies for better energy management.

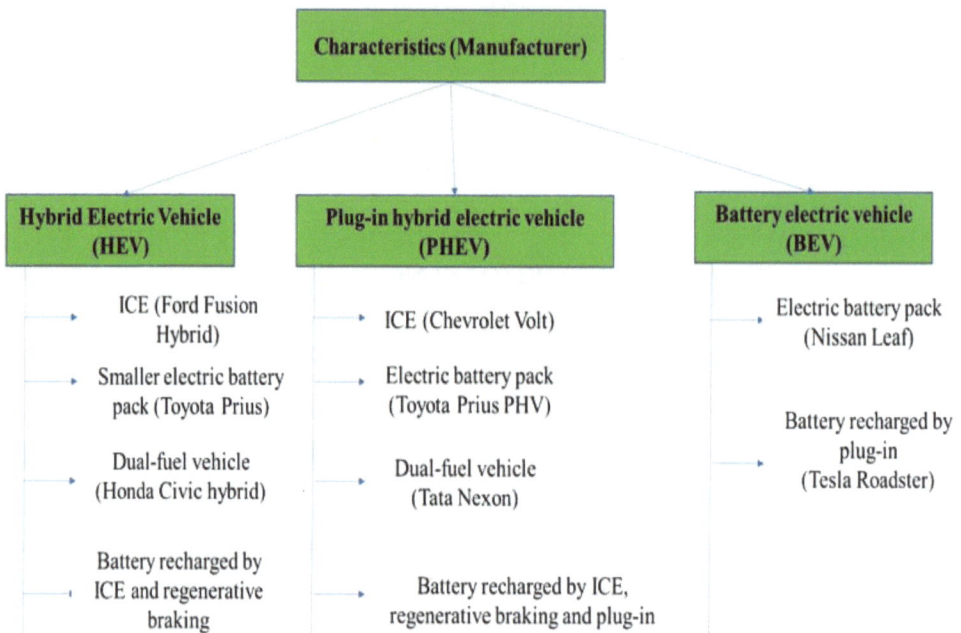

Fig. (2). Type of EV characteristics and technologies.

In a paper [46], a thorough analysis of solar PV-EV charging systems and their global deployment is provided. It introduces analytical methods aimed at gathering insights into the behavior of EV charging, charging station operational modes, and geographical distribution of charging stations, emphasizing their efficiency in terms of time and cost. The review covers various aspects of solar-powered EV systems, including charging infrastructure, methodology, and EV energy management strategies. Despite the progress discussed, many challenges remain unresolved, particularly related to the cost and performance of battery storage systems, which currently limit their economic feasibility. The paper suggests that installing globally distributed solar PV-EV charging stations represents the most optimal and viable approach, highlighting various methods outlined within the study to achieve this goal.

Table **2** summarizes key studies on solar-powered electric vehicle (EV) charging systems, highlighting objectives, performance parameters, and the impact of partial shading conditions. It provides insights into the integration of photovoltaic arrays, grid connectivity, and EV-related aspects to optimize charging efficiency.

Table 2. Key findings on solar-powered EV systems and performance metrics.

Refs.	Objective	Performance Parameters	PSC Condition	PV Array Configuration	Grid Connected	EV Related Aspects
[47]	Assessing in-room tech amenities' impact on guest satisfaction.	Guest satisfaction, impact of tech amenities	N/A	N/A	N/A	Focus on tech impact in 5-star hotels, not EV-related.
[48]	Studying Housekeeping services on customer satisfaction.	Housekeeping quality, cleanliness	N/A	N/A	N/A	Focus on customer satisfaction in multiplexes, not EV-related.
[49]	Analyzing the impact of solar PV on EV charging.	PV energy generation for EVs, cost, CO_2 reduction	Partial shading	Fixed rooftop PV arrays	Yes (grid-connected charging)	Evaluates solar energy for charging EVs, energy savings, and environmental benefits.
[50]	Feasibility study of PV-EV integration.	Energy efficiency, cost reduction	Partial shading	Rooftop PV systems	Yes (grid and EV charging interaction)	Assesses economic and technical feasibility of PV for EVs.
[51]	Grid interaction of solar-powered charging stations.	Efficiency of solar charging stations for EVs.	Partial shading	Grid-connected solar panels	Yes (grid-connected)	Focus on optimizing solar-powered charging infrastructure for EVs.
[52]	Techno-economic analysis of PV-EV charging systems.	PV energy efficiency, cost, solar energy utilization	Partial shading	Building-integrated PV systems	Yes (grid-integrated charging)	Studies solar charging systems for EVs and cost-efficiency.
[53]	Evaluating PV-EV integration and optimization.	Power generation, shading effects, system efficiency	Partial shading	Rooftop integrated PV	Yes (grid interaction)	Focus on optimizing power collection from PV systems for EV charging.

(Table 2) cont.....

Refs.	Objective	Performance Parameters	PSC Condition	PV Array Configuration	Grid Connected	EV Related Aspects
[54]	Investigating PV performance under partial shading.	Shading effects on PV module performance	Partial shading	Rooftop PV array	Yes (grid-connected)	Impact of shading on solar efficiency for EV charging.
[55]	Business model for solar-assisted EV charging stations.	Financial analysis, system reliability, environmental impact	Partial shading	Solar-assisted charging stations	Yes (grid-connected)	Investigates business models for solar-assisted EV charging.
[56]	Hybrid PV systems for EV charging under shading.	PV power output, EV charging time, cost	Partial shading	Hybrid PV system with battery storage	Yes (grid-integrated)	Focus on hybrid PV solutions to power EVs under shading conditions.
[57]	Techno-economic assessment of solar-powered EV stations.	Cost-effectiveness, environmental impact	Partial shading	Integrated rooftop PV arrays	Yes (grid-connected)	Evaluates the cost and feasibility of solar charging stations for EVs.
[58]	Shading analysis for urban roads.	Shading metrics, shadow analysis	Urban shading, trees/buildings	3D model, fisheye images	N/A	No direct EV focus but provides insights into shading analysis for future EV charging infrastructure.
[59]	Feasibility of PV systems for EVs and households in Northern Cyprus.	Solar energy potential, cost-benefit analysis	Seasonal shading	Ground-mounted PV	Yes (grid-connected)	Focus on PV systems for both households and EVs in Northern Cyprus.
[60]	Designing grid-interactive solar PV systems for EVs.	Energy generation, load flow analysis, shading effects	Partial shading	Rooftop PV systems for EV charging	Yes (grid-connected)	Focus on solar PV systems for real-time EV charging.
[61]	Impact of partial shading on PV in Sudanese-Sahelian climate.	Efficiency reduction, shading impact on PV	Partial shading	Ground-mounted PV systems	Yes (grid-connected)	Focuses on PV performance under shading for EV charging in specific climates.

(Table 2) cont.....

Refs.	Objective	Performance Parameters	PSC Condition	PV Array Configuration	Grid Connected	EV Related Aspects
[62]	Adaptive PV/battery system for solar EVs.	Charging efficiency, PV array flexibility	Dynamic shading	Adaptive PV/battery system	Yes (solar and battery storage)	Enhances charging efficiency for solar electric vehicles (SEVs).
[63]	Improving performance of PV systems under shading.	Power extraction, efficiency, MPPT	Partial shading	PV with full-bridge inverter	Yes (grid-integrated)	Focus on improving PV performance for EV charging under shading conditions.
[64]	Advances in high-speed vehicles and their power grid impacts.	High-speed vehicle grid interaction, PV system efficiency	Partial shading	Compact PV systems	Yes (for high-speed vehicles)	Focus on high-speed vehicle integration with the grid and PV systems for EVs.
[65]	Techno-economic analysis of solar-based charging for e-rickshaws.	System reliability, cost-benefit, CO_2 reduction	Partial shading	Integrated PV panels for e-rickshaw charging	Yes (grid-integrated)	Focus on solar charging for e-rickshaws, an EV category.
[66]	Solar-integrated charging for EVs.	Solar energy utilization, PV array placement, charging efficiency	Partial shading	Solar-powered charging system	Yes (grid-integrated)	Focus on solar charging and energy storage for EVs.
[67]	Designing modern solar-assisted EV charging stations.	Charging station efficiency, power factor correction	Partial shading	Solar-assisted EV chargers	Yes (grid-connected)	Focus on efficient and solar-assisted EV charging station designs.
[68]	Bidirectional DC-DC converter for solar EV charging.	Energy efficiency, system stability	Partial shading	Bidirectional DC-DC converters with PV system	Yes (grid-interactive)	Focus on improving solar-powered charging for EVs through efficient energy management.

(Table 2) cont.....

Refs.	Objective	Performance Parameters	PSC Condition	PV Array Configuration	Grid Connected	EV Related Aspects
[69]	Solar radiation impact on PV for hybrid/EVs.	MPPT efficiency, solar radiation impact	Variable shading	PV system integrated with EVs	Yes (grid-integrated)	Examines solar radiation's impact on MPPT algorithms for hybrid/EV charging.
[70]	Optimization of SPHEV charging scheduling using MILP.	Charging cost reduction, scheduling optimization	Shading effects	PV-based charging system	Yes (grid-integrated)	Focuses on scheduling solar-based charging for SPHEVs.
[71]	Optimizing PV panel orientation for EV charging.	PV energy production, cost reduction	Partial shading	Optimized PV array orientation	Yes (grid-integrated)	Focus on cost-effective PV orientation to power EVs.
[72]	Optimizing solar-assisted EV charging station placement.	Site selection, charging station sizing	Shading conditions	Distributed solar PV charging stations	Yes (grid-connected)	Focus on optimizing the location and size of solar-powered charging stations.
[73]	EV adoption trends and power grid integration.	EV market trends, grid interaction challenges	N/A	N/A	Yes (grid interaction)	Reviews the challenges of EV grid integration and technological advancements.
[74]	Solar energy for extending EV range.	Energy efficiency, battery charging time	N/A	PV panels on EV roofs	No grid connection	Focus on using solar panels on EVs to extend range and reduce reliance on the grid.
[75]	Solar recharging for EVs at commuter workplaces.	Solar power generation, EV charging efficiency	Daytime shading	Large solar arrays in parking lots	Yes (grid-connected)	Focus on solar charging for EVs at workplaces, reducing grid dependence.
[76]	Solar power-assisted battery balancing for EVs.	Battery optimization, charging efficiency	Partial shading	Solar power-assisted battery system	No grid connection	Focuses on solar-assisted battery balancing systems for EVs.

(Table 2) cont.....

Refs.	Objective	Performance Parameters	PSC Condition	PV Array Configuration	Grid Connected	EV Related Aspects
[77]	Review of business models for solar-powered charging stations.	Customer adoption, cost reduction strategies	N/A	N/A	Yes (grid integration discussed)	Focus on creating sustainable business models for solar-powered EV charging.
[78]	Shading analysis for SPEV charging efficiency.	Shading impact, optimal parking location	Partial shading	N/A (focus on parking location)	No direct grid focus	Uses shading metrics for optimizing solar charging of SPEVs.
[79]	Fuzzy logic and optimization for PV energy collection under PSC.	Power extraction efficiency, optimization under PSC	Partial shading	PV system with optimization algorithms.	Yes (grid-connected)	Optimizes PV energy collection for EVs under partial shading.
[80]	Evaluating PV systems for PHEV charging.	Energy self-consumption, grid electricity minimization	Partial shading	PV carport integrated with charging stations.	Yes (grid interaction)	Focuses on optimizing PV systems for efficient PHEV charging.

CONCLUSION AND FUTURE SCOPE

Ongoing research is crucial in addressing the remaining challenges and optimizing the integration of PV systems with EVs. While significant progress has been made in exploring various PV structures and their performance under partial shading conditions, further advancements are required to enhance the overall efficiency, sustainability, and cost-effectiveness of these systems. The challenge of mitigating shading effects on PV array performance remains a critical area of focus, with continued innovation needed to develop more resilient systems capable of maximizing energy output in diverse environmental conditions.

Similarly, as EV technology continues to evolve, further research is essential to enhance key components, such as battery technology, energy management systems, and charging infrastructure. The exploration of alternative battery chemistries, such as solid-state batteries, holds promise for reducing charging times, improving safety, and increasing energy density. Moreover, the development of ultra-fast and wireless charging technologies will help reduce range anxiety, further accelerating the adoption of EVs.

In the realm of solar-PV integration with EVs, ongoing research into V2G technology represents a promising avenue. By enabling EVs to serve as mobile energy storage units, V2G systems can contribute to grid stabilization, reducing pressure on existing energy infrastructure during peak demand periods. The future success of such integration will depend on the development of sophisticated energy management systems and smart grid solutions that ensure the reliable, efficient exchange of energy between EVs and the grid.

Looking ahead, the future of solar EV charging systems lies in the convergence of PV technology, EV advancements, and smart grid systems. The development of next-generation PV materials, such as perovskite solar cells, promises lower production costs and higher efficiency, which could significantly enhance the feasibility of large-scale solar charging systems. Additionally, optimizing PV system designs to better handle partial shading conditions will increase the viability of solar-powered EV charging in real-world scenarios.

The future scope of solar-powered Electric Vehicles (EVs) and their integration with Photovoltaic (PV) systems holds immense potential for advancing both energy and transportation sectors. As technology continues to evolve, there are several critical areas where further research and innovation can drive progress:

• **Advanced battery technologies**: The development of more efficient and long-lasting batteries remains a pivotal challenge. Future research can focus on improving energy density, reducing charging times, and enhancing the lifecycle of batteries. This will contribute significantly to the overall performance and reliability of solar-powered EVs, making them more competitive with conventional vehicles.

• **Optimized charging infrastructure**: The integration of solar-powered charging stations must be explored further, especially in terms of scalability and cost-effectiveness. Research can be directed toward developing smart charging systems that not only optimize the use of renewable energy but also enable seamless interaction between the grid and EVs through V2G technologies. Additionally, standardizing charging interfaces and improving the efficiency of solar PV systems will be essential.

• **Energy storage solutions**: To address intermittent solar energy production, advancements in energy storage technologies are crucial. Investigating novel storage methods such as solid-state batteries or flow batteries can help balance energy supply and demand, ensuring that solar energy collected during the day can be effectively used for EV charging at night or during cloudy weather.

• **Hybrid and multifunctional systems**: Exploring hybrid systems that combine solar energy with other renewable sources, such as wind or grid power, could enhance the reliability of PV-EV charging. Moreover, vehicle-integrated photovoltaics, where solar panels are integrated into the vehicle body itself, could reduce dependency on external charging stations and further promote energy autonomy for EVs.

• **Energy efficiency and optimization models**: Future research should focus on developing more sophisticated energy management and optimization models. These models can account for factors like partial shading, weather patterns, and driving conditions to optimize the solar energy harnessed and its distribution for EV charging, ultimately enhancing the overall energy efficiency of the system.

• **Policy and regulatory support**: The role of government policies and regulations will become increasingly critical in fostering the growth of solar-powered EVs. Future efforts can focus on creating incentives for the development and deployment of PV-EV infrastructure, as well as standardizing international regulations to ensure the compatibility of solar charging stations and vehicles across regions.

• **Environmental impact assessment**: While the integration of solar power with EVs offers significant environmental benefits, it will be important to continuously assess and optimize the lifecycle environmental impact. Research into sustainable manufacturing practices for solar panels, batteries, and EV components can help reduce the overall carbon footprint of solar-powered EVs.

AUTHORS' CONTRIBUTION

The author conceived, researched, and wrote the entirety of this book chapter. All data collection, analysis, and interpretation, as well as drafting and revision of the manuscript, were performed solely by the author.

REFERENCES

[1]   M.U. Nawaz, M.S. Qureshi, and S. Umar, "Integration of Solar Energy Systems with Electric Vehicle Charging Infrastructure: Challenges and opportunity", *Rev. Esp. Doc. Cient.,* vol. 18, no. 02, pp. 1-18, 2024.

[2]   G.R. Chandra Mouli, P. Bauer, and M. Zeman, "System design for a solar powered electric vehicle charging station for workplaces", *Appl. Energy,* vol. 168, pp. 434-443, 2016.
[http://dx.doi.org/10.1016/j.apenergy.2016.01.110]

[3]   C. Lodi, S. Gil-Sayas, D. Currò, S. Serra, and Y. Drossinos, "Full-battery effect during on-board solar charging of conventional vehicles", *Transp. Res. Part D Transp. Environ.,* vol. 96, p. 102862, 2021.
[http://dx.doi.org/10.1016/j.trd.2021.102862]

[4]   E. Kostopoulos, G. Spyropoulos, K. Christopoulos, and J.K. Kaldellis, "Solar energy contribution to an electric vehicle needs on the basis of long-term measurements", *Procedia Struct. Integr.,* vol. 10,

pp. 203-210, 2018.
[http://dx.doi.org/10.1016/j.prostr.2018.09.029]

[5]   O. Attia, H. Souissi, M. Khalil, and C.B. Salah, "Functioning of the Half-Cells Photovoltaic Module in hybrid EV under Partial Shading", *18th International Multi-Conference on Systems, Signals & Devices (SSD),* pp. 1252-1257, 2021.
[http://dx.doi.org/10.1109/SSD52085.2021.9429410]

[6]   M. Eidiani, and A. Ghavami, "Impact of Electric Vehicles and Photovoltaic and Wind Generators on Distribution Grid", *Majlesi Journal of Energy Management,* vol. 7, no. 4, pp. 33-42, 2018.

[7]   E.I. Batzelis, I.A. Routsolias, and S.A. Papathanassiou, "An explicit PV string model based on the lambert $ W $ function and simplified MPP expressions for operation under partial shading", *IEEE Trans. Sustain. Energy,* vol. 5, no. 1, pp. 301-312, 2014.
[http://dx.doi.org/10.1109/TSTE.2013.2282168]

[8]   T. Ma, H. Yang, and L. Lu, "Development of a model to simulate the performance characteristics of crystalline silicon photovoltaic modules/strings/arrays", *Sol. Energy,* vol. 100, pp. 31-41, 2014.
[http://dx.doi.org/10.1016/j.solener.2013.12.003]

[9]   J. Qi, Y. Zhang, and Y. Chen, "Modeling and maximum power point tracking (MPPT) method for PV array under partial shade conditions", *Renew. Energy,* vol. 66, pp. 337-345, 2014.
[http://dx.doi.org/10.1016/j.renene.2013.12.018]

[10]   J. Storey, P.R. Wilson, and D. Bagnall, "The optimized-string dynamic photovoltaic array", *IEEE Trans. Power Electron.,* vol. 29, no. 4, pp. 1768-1776, 2014.
[http://dx.doi.org/10.1109/TPEL.2013.2265497]

[11]   11. Vijayalekshmy, S., Rama Iyer, S., & Beevi, B. Comparative analysis on the performance of a short string of series-connected and parallel-connected photovoltaic array under partial shading. *Journal of The Institution of Engineers (India)*: Series B, 96, 217-226, 2015.

[12]   J. Bai, Y. Cao, Y. Hao, Z. Zhang, S. Liu, and F. Cao, "Characteristic output of PV systems under partial shading or mismatch conditions", *Sol. Energy,* vol. 112, pp. 41-54, 2015.
[http://dx.doi.org/10.1016/j.solener.2014.09.048]

[13]   F. Belhachat, and C. Larbes, "Modeling, analysis and comparison of solar photovoltaic array configurations under partial shading conditions", *Sol. Energy,* vol. 120, pp. 399-418, 2015.
[http://dx.doi.org/10.1016/j.solener.2015.07.039]

[14]   L.A. Trejos-Grisales, C.A. Ramos-Paja, and A.J. Saavedra-Montes, "Equivalent circuits for simulating irregular PV arrays under partial shading conditions", *TecnoLógicas,* vol. 18, no. 35, pp. 57-69, 2015.
[http://dx.doi.org/10.22430/22565337.187]

[15]   S. Malathy, and R. Ramaprabha, "A static PV array architecture to enhance power generation under partial shaded conditions", *IEEE 11th International Conference on Power Electronics and Drive Systems,* pp. 341-346, 2015.
[http://dx.doi.org/10.1109/PEDS.2015.7203505]

[16]   G. Shankar, and V. Mukherjee, "MPP detection of a partially shaded PV array by continuous GA and hybrid PSO", *Ain Shams Eng. J.,* vol. 6, no. 2, pp. 471-479, 2015.
[http://dx.doi.org/10.1016/j.asej.2014.10.017]

[17]   Xueye, Z. J. W., & Tianlong, Z. Research on the output characteristics of photovoltaic array under the non-uniform light. *International Journal of control and automation*, 8(10), 431-444, 2015.

[18]   M. Forcan, Ž. Đurišić, and J. Mikulović, "An algorithm for elimination of partial shading effect based on a Theory of Reference PV String", *Sol. Energy,* vol. 132, pp. 51-63, 2016.
[http://dx.doi.org/10.1016/j.solener.2016.03.003]

[19]   19. Kumar, A., Pachauri, R. K., & Chauhan, Y. K. Experimental analysis of SP/TCT PV array configurations under partial shading conditions. *IEEE 1st international conference on power electronics, intelligent control and energy systems (ICPEICES),* pp. 1-6, 2016.

[20]   N. Rakesh, and T.V. Madhavaram, "Performance enhancement of partially shaded solar PV array using novel shade dispersion technique", *Front. Energy,* vol. 10, no. 2, pp. 227-239, 2016.
[http://dx.doi.org/10.1007/s11708-016-0405-y]

[21]   S. Vijayalekshmy, G.R. Bindu, and S. Rama Iyer, "A novel Zig-Zag scheme for power enhancement of partially shaded solar arrays", *Sol. Energy,* vol. 135, pp. 92-102, 2016.
[http://dx.doi.org/10.1016/j.solener.2016.05.045]

[22]   R.P. Vengatesh, and S.E. Rajan, "Analysis of PV module connected in different configurations under uniform and non-uniform solar radiations", *Int. J. Green Energy,* vol. 13, no. 14, pp. 1507-1516, 2016.
[http://dx.doi.org/10.1080/15435075.2016.1207078]

[23]   N. Mishra, A.S. Yadav, R. Pachauri, Y.K. Chauhan, and V.K. Yadav, "Performance enhancement of PV system using proposed array topologies under various shadow patterns", *Sol. Energy,* vol. 157, pp. 641-656, 2017.
[http://dx.doi.org/10.1016/j.solener.2017.08.021]

[24]   J.D. Bastidas-Rodríguez, L.A. Trejos-Grisales, D. González-Montoya, C.A. Ramos-Paja, G. Petrone, and G. Spagnuolo, "General modeling procedure for photovoltaic arrays", *Electr. Power Syst. Res.,* vol. 155, pp. 67-79, 2018.
[http://dx.doi.org/10.1016/j.epsr.2017.09.023]

[25]   D.S. Pillai, J. Prasanth Ram, M. Siva Sai Nihanth, and N. Rajasekar, "A simple, sensorless and fixed reconfiguration scheme for maximum power enhancement in PV systems", *Energy Convers. Manage.,* vol. 172, pp. 402-417, 2018.
[http://dx.doi.org/10.1016/j.enconman.2018.07.016]

[26]   R. Pachauri, R. Singh, A. Gehlot, R. Samakaria, and S. Choudhury, "Experimental analysis to extract maximum power from PV array reconfiguration under partial shading conditions," *Engineering Science and Technology, an International Journal* , vol. 22, no. 1, pp. 109–130, 2019..

[27]   G. Sai Krishna, and T. Moger, "Improved SuDoKu reconfiguration technique for total-cross-tied PV array to enhance maximum power under partial shading conditions", *Renew. Sustain. Energy Rev.,* vol. 109, pp. 333-348, 2019.
[http://dx.doi.org/10.1016/j.rser.2019.04.037]

[28]   M.S.S. Nihanth, J.P. Ram, D.S. Pillai, A.M.Y.M. Ghias, A. Garg, and N. Rajasekar, "Enhanced power production in PV arrays using a new skyscraper puzzle based one-time reconfiguration procedure under partial shade conditions (PSCs)", *Sol. Energy,* vol. 194, pp. 209-224, 2019.
[http://dx.doi.org/10.1016/j.solener.2019.10.020]

[29]   A. Ul-Haq, R. Alammari, A. Iqbal, M. Jalal, and S. Gul, "Computation of power extraction from photovoltaic arrays under various fault conditions", *IEEE Access,* vol. 8, pp. 47619-47639, 2020.
[http://dx.doi.org/10.1109/ACCESS.2020.2978621]

[30]   M. Premkumar, U. Subramaniam, T. Babu, R. Elavarasan, and L. Mihet-Popa, "Evaluation of mathematical model to characterize the performance of conventional and hybrid PV array topologies under static and dynamic shading patterns", *Energies,* vol. 13, no. 12, p. 3216, 2020.
[http://dx.doi.org/10.3390/en13123216]

[31]   A. Srinivasan, S. Devakirubakaran, and B. Meenakshi Sundaram, "Mitigation of mismatch losses in solar PV system – Two-step reconfiguration approach", *Sol. Energy,* vol. 206, pp. 640-654, 2020.
[http://dx.doi.org/10.1016/j.solener.2020.06.004]

[32]   H.F. Hashim, M.M. Kareem, W.K. Al-Azzawi, and A.H. Ali, "Improving the performance of photovoltaic module during partial shading using ANN", *International Journal of Power Electronics and Drive Systems (IJPEDS),* vol. 12, no. 4, p. 2435, 2021.
[http://dx.doi.org/10.11591/ijpeds.v12.i4.pp2435-2442]

[33]   A. Chalh, A. El Hammoumi, S. Motahhir, A. El Ghzizal, A. Derouich, M. Masud, and M.A. AlZain, "Investigation of partial shading scenarios on a photovoltaic array's characteristics", *Electronics*

(Basel), vol. 11, no. 1, p. 96, 2021.
[http://dx.doi.org/10.3390/electronics11010096]

[34]　T. Alves, and N. Torres, "Different techniques to mitigate partial shading in photovoltaic panels", *Energies,* vol. 14, no. 13, p. 3863, 2021.
[http://dx.doi.org/10.3390/en14133863]

[35]　A. Fathy, Butterfly optimization algorithm based methodology for enhancing the shaded photovoltaic array extracted power *via* reconfiguration process., *Energy Convers. Manage.,* vol. 220, p. 113115, 2020.
[http://dx.doi.org/10.1016/j.enconman.2020.113115]

[36]　S. Rezazadeh, A. Moradzadeh, K. Pourhossein, M. Akrami, B. Mohammadi-Ivatloo, and A. Anvari-Moghaddam, "Photovoltaic array reconfiguration under partial shading conditions for maximum power extraction: A state-of-the-art review and new solution method", *Energy Convers. Manage.,* vol. 258, p. 115468, 2022.
[http://dx.doi.org/10.1016/j.enconman.2022.115468]

[37]　K. Abdulmawjood, S. Alsadi, S.S. Refaat, and W.G. Morsi, "Characteristic study of solar photovoltaic array under different partial shading conditions", *IEEE Access,* vol. 10, pp. 6856-6866, 2022.
[http://dx.doi.org/10.1109/ACCESS.2022.3142168]

[38]　H. Oufettoul, N. Lamdihine, S. Motahhir, N. Lamrini, I.A. Abdelmoula, and G. Aniba, "Comparative performance analysis of PV module positions in a solar PV array under partial shading conditions", *IEEE Access,* vol. 11, pp. 12176-12194, 2023.
[http://dx.doi.org/10.1109/ACCESS.2023.3237250]

[39]　B. Aljafari, P.R. Satpathy, S.B. Thanikanti, and H. Haes Alhelou, "A zero switch and sensorless reconfiguration approach for sustainable operation of roof-top photovoltaic system during partial shading", *IET Renew. Power Gener.,* vol. 17, no. 6, pp. 1385-1412, 2023.
[http://dx.doi.org/10.1049/rpg2.12683]

[40]　H. Rehman, I. Sajid, A. Sarwar, M. Tariq, F.I. Bakhsh, S. Ahmad, H.A. Mahmoud, and A. Aziz, "Driving training-based optimization (DTBO) for global maximum power point tracking for a photovoltaic system under partial shading condition", *IET Renew. Power Gener.,* vol. 17, no. 10, pp. 2542-2562, 2023.
[http://dx.doi.org/10.1049/rpg2.12768]

[41]　H. Gundogdu, A. Demirci, S.M. Tercan, and U. Cali, "A novel improved grey wolf algorithm based global maximum power point tracker method considering partial shading", *IEEE Access,* vol. 12, pp. 6148-6159, 2024.
[http://dx.doi.org/10.1109/ACCESS.2024.3350269]

[42]　D. Kumar, and R. Raushan, "An innovative competence square technique for PV array reconfiguration under partial shading conditions", *International Journal of Modelling and Simulation,* vol. 44, no. 3, pp. 156-171, 2024.
[http://dx.doi.org/10.1080/02286203.2022.2163027]

[43]　D. Ramesh, and K. Anbalagan, "Modified Odd–Even–Prime pattern for effective dispersion of shade over the PV array under partial shading conditions", *Sol. Energy,* vol. 269, p. 112303, 2024.
[http://dx.doi.org/10.1016/j.solener.2023.112303]

[44]　C. Hussaian Basha, M. Palati, C. Dhanamjayulu, S.M. Muyeen, and P. Venkatareddy, "A novel on design and implementation of hybrid MPPT controllers for solar PV systems under various partial shading conditions", *Sci. Rep.,* vol. 14, no. 1, p. 1609, 2024.
[http://dx.doi.org/10.1038/s41598-023-49278-9] [PMID: 38238374]

[45]　M. van der Kam, and W. van Sark, "Smart charging of electric vehicles with photovoltaic power and vehicle-to-grid technology in a microgrid; a case study", *Appl. Energy,* vol. 152, pp. 20-30, 2015.
[http://dx.doi.org/10.1016/j.apenergy.2015.04.092]

[46]　S. Khan, A. Ahmad, F. Ahmad, M. Shafaati Shemami, M. Saad Alam, and S. Khateeb, "A

comprehensive review on solar-powered electric vehicle charging system", *Smart Science,* vol. 6, no. 1, pp. 54-79, 2018.
[http://dx.doi.org/10.1080/23080477.2017.1419054]

[47]   Mouli, G. R. C., Leendertse, M., Prasanth, V., Bauer, P., Silvester, S., van de Geer, S., & Zeman, M. Economic and CO2 emission benefits of a solar powered electric vehicle charging station for workplaces in the Netherlands. *IEEE Transportation Electrification Conference and Expo (ITEC)*, pp. 1-7, 2016.
[http://dx.doi.org/10.1109/ITEC.2016.7520273]

[48]   A.R. Bhatti, Z. Salam, M.J.B.A. Aziz, and K.P. Yee, "A critical review of electric vehicle charging using solar photovoltaic", *Int. J. Energy Res.,* vol. 40, no. 4, pp. 439-461, 2016.
[http://dx.doi.org/10.1002/er.3472]

[49]   M. Abdelhamid, S. Pilla, R. Singh, I. Haque, and Z. Filipi, "A comprehensive optimized model for on-board solar photovoltaic system for plug-in electric vehicles: energy and economic impacts", *Int. J. Energy Res.,* vol. 40, no. 11, pp. 1489-1508, 2016.
[http://dx.doi.org/10.1002/er.3534]

[50]   C. Park, H. Park, H. Jeon, K. Choi, and J. Suh, "Evaluation and validation of photovoltaic potential based on time and pathway of solar-powered electric vehicle", *Appl. Sci. (Basel),* vol. 13, no. 2, p. 1025, 2023.
[http://dx.doi.org/10.3390/app13021025] [PMID: 38282829]

[51]   M. Shepero, J. Munkhammar, J. Widén, J.D.K. Bishop, and T. Boström, "Modeling of photovoltaic power generation and electric vehicles charging on city-scale: A review", *Renew. Sustain. Energy Rev.,* vol. 89, pp. 61-71, 2018.
[http://dx.doi.org/10.1016/j.rser.2018.02.034]

[52]   K. Araki, L. Ji, G. Kelly, and M. Yamaguchi, "To do list for research and development and international standardization to achieve the goal of running a majority of electric vehicles on solar energy", *Coatings,* vol. 8, no. 7, p. 251, 2018.
[http://dx.doi.org/10.3390/coatings8070251]

[53]   E.S. Percis, M. S, and N. A, "Electric vehicle as an energy storage for grid connected solar power system", *International Journal of Power Electronics and Drive Systems (IJPEDS),* vol. 6, no. 3, pp. 567-575, 2015.
[http://dx.doi.org/10.11591/ijpeds.v6.i3.pp567-575]

[54]   Arun, P. S., & Mohanrajan, S. R. Effect of partial shading on vehicle integrated PV system. *3rd international conference on electronics, communication and aerospace technology (ICECA)*, pp. 1262-1267, 2019.
[http://dx.doi.org/10.1109/ICECA.2019.8821888]

[55]   B. Ye, J. Jiang, L. Miao, P. Yang, J. Li, and B. Shen, "Feasibility study of a solar-powered electric vehicle charging station model", *Energies,* vol. 8, no. 11, pp. 13265-13283, 2015.
[http://dx.doi.org/10.3390/en81112368]

[56]   G. Badea, R.A. Felseghi, M. Varlam, C. Filote, M. Culcer, M. Iliescu, and M.S. Răboacă, "Design and simulation of romanian solar energy charging station for electric vehicles", *Energies,* vol. 12, no. 1, p. 74, 2018.
[http://dx.doi.org/10.3390/en12010074]

[57]   O. Kanz, A. Reinders, J. May, and K. Ding, "Environmental impacts of integrated photovoltaic modules in light utility electric vehicles", *Energies,* vol. 13, no. 19, p. 5120, 2020.
[http://dx.doi.org/10.3390/en13195120]

[58]   J. Baek, and Y. Choi, "Comparative study on shading database construction for urban roads using 3d models and fisheye images for efficient operation of solar-powered electric vehicles", *Energies,* vol. 15, no. 21, p. 8228, 2022.
[http://dx.doi.org/10.3390/en15218228]

[59] Y. Kassem, H. Gokcekus, and A. Aljatlawe, "Utilization of solar energy for electric vehicle charging and the energy consumption of residential buildings in Northern Cyprus: A case study," *Engineering, Technology & Applied Science Research,* vol. 13, no. 5, pp. 11598–11607, 2023.,

[60] M. Thulasingam, A.D.V. Raj Periyanayagam, and M. Krishnamoorthy, "Feasibility analysis and modeling of a solar hybrid system for residential electric vehicle charging", *International Journal of Electrical and Computer Engineering (IJECE),* vol. 14, no. 2, pp. 1251-1262, 2024. [IJECE]. [http://dx.doi.org/10.11591/ijece.v14i2.pp1251-1262]

[61] B. Yaouba, M. Bajaj, C. Welba, K. Bernard, Kitmo, S. Kamel, and M.F. El-Naggar, "An experimental and case study on the evaluation of the partial shading impact on PV module performance operating under the sudano-sahelian climate of Cameroon", *Front. Energy Res.,* vol. 10, p. 924285, 2022. [http://dx.doi.org/10.3389/fenrg.2022.924285]

[62] M. Alahmad, M. A. Chaaban, and L. Chaar, "A novel photovoltaic/battery structure for solar electrical vehicles (PVBS for SEV)," in Proc. *IEEE Vehicle Power and Propulsion Conf.,* pp. 1–4, 2011.,

[63] P. Geetha, and S. Usha, "Design and Analysis of Partial shading of the PV System Integrated with High-Frequency Inverter and Rectifier Operation for the Electric Vehicle", *J. Phys. Conf. Ser.,* vol. 2335, no. 1, p. 012045, 2022. [http://dx.doi.org/10.1088/1742-6596/2335/1/012045]

[64] S. Conti, S. Di Mauro, A. Raciti, S.A. Rizzo, G. Susinni, S. Musumeci, and A. Tenconi, "Solar electric vehicles: state-of-the-art and perspectives", *AEIT International Annual Conference,* pp. 1-6, 2018.

[65] P. Shrivastava, M.S. Alam, and M.S.J. Asghar, "Design and techno-economic analysis of plug-in electric vehicle-integrated solar PV charging system for India", *IET Smart Grid,* vol. 2, no. 2, pp. 224-232, 2019. [http://dx.doi.org/10.1049/iet-stg.2018.0079]

[66] M. Umair, N.M. Hidayat, A. Sukri Ahmad, N.H. Nik Ali, M.I.M. Mawardi, and E. Abdullah, "A renewable approach to electric vehicle charging through solar energy storage", *PLoS One,* vol. 19, no. 2, p. e0297376, 2024. [http://dx.doi.org/10.1371/journal.pone.0297376] [PMID: 38422065]

[67] S.M. Shariff, M.S. Alam, F. Ahmad, Y. Rafat, M.S.J. Asghar, and S. Khan, "System design and realization of a solar-powered electric vehicle charging station", *IEEE Syst. J.,* vol. 14, no. 2, pp. 2748-2758, 2020. [http://dx.doi.org/10.1109/JSYST.2019.2931880]

[68] J. Traube, F. Lu, D. Maksimovic, J. Mossoba, M. Kromer, P. Faill, S. Katz, B. Borowy, S. Nichols, and L. Casey, "Mitigation of solar irradiance intermittency in photovoltaic power systems with integrated electric-vehicle charging functionality", *IEEE Trans. Power Electron.,* vol. 28, no. 6, pp. 3058-3067, 2013. [http://dx.doi.org/10.1109/TPEL.2012.2217354]

[69] C. Schuss, B. Eichberger, and T. Rahkonen, "Impact of solar radiation on the output power of moving photovoltaic (PV) installations", *IEEE International Instrumentation and Measurement Technology Conference (I2MTC),* pp. 1-6, 2018. [http://dx.doi.org/10.1109/I2MTC.2018.8409696]

[70] Aliakbari, A., & Vahidinasab, V. Optimal charging scheduling of solar plugin hybrid electric vehicles considering on-the-road solar energy harvesting. *10th Smart Grid Conference (SGC),* pp. 1-6, 2020. [http://dx.doi.org/10.1109/SGC52076.2020.9335773]

[71] Mouli, G. R. C., & Bauer, P. Optimal system design for a solar powered EV charging station. *IEEE Transportation Electrification Conference and Expo (ITEC),* pp. 1094-1099, 2018. [http://dx.doi.org/10.1109/ITEC.2018.8450083]

[72] D. Ji, M. Lv, J. Yang, and W. Yi, "Optimizing the locations and sizes of solar assisted electric vehicle charging stations in an urban area", *IEEE Access,* vol. 8, pp. 112772-112782, 2020.

[http://dx.doi.org/10.1109/ACCESS.2020.3003071]

[73]   R. Verma, S.K. Srivastava, and A. Narain, *Proceedings of 6th International Conference on Advanced Production and Industrial Engineering (ICAPIE)*, pp. 387-396, 2022.

[74]   I. Diahovchenko, L. Petrichenko, I. Borzenkov, and M. Kolcun, "Application of photovoltaic panels in electric vehicles to enhance the range", *Heliyon,* vol. 8, no. 12, p. e12425, 2022.
[http://dx.doi.org/10.1016/j.heliyon.2022.e12425] [PMID: 36590513]

[75]   D.P. Birnie III, "Solar-to-vehicle (S2V) systems for powering commuters of the future", *J. Power Sources,* vol. 186, no. 2, pp. 539-542, 2009.
[http://dx.doi.org/10.1016/j.jpowsour.2008.09.118]

[76]   C. Duan, C. Wang, Z. Li, J. Chen, S. Wang, A. Snyder, and C. Jiang, "A solar power-assisted battery balancing system for electric vehicles", *IEEE Trans. Transp. Electrif.,* vol. 4, no. 2, pp. 432-443, 2018.
[http://dx.doi.org/10.1109/TTE.2018.2817123]

[77]   Robinson, J., Brase, G., Griswold, W., Jackson, C., & Erickson, L. Business models for solar powered charging stations to develop infrastructure for electric vehicles. *Sustainability*, 6(10), 7358-7387, 2014.
[http://dx.doi.org/10.3390/su6107358]

[78]   J. Baek, and Y. Choi, "An Experimental Study on Performance Evaluation of Shading Matrix to Select Optimal Parking Space for Solar-Powered Electric Vehicles", *Sustainability (Basel),* vol. 14, no. 22, p. 14922, 2022.
[http://dx.doi.org/10.3390/su142214922]

[79]   S.S. Kumar, and K. Balakrishna, "A novel design and analysis of hybrid fuzzy logic MPPT controller for solar PV system under partial shading conditions", *Sci. Rep.,* vol. 14, no. 1, p. 10256, 2024.
[http://dx.doi.org/10.1038/s41598-024-60870-5] [PMID: 38704401]

[80]   M. Brenna, A. Dolara, F. Foiadelli, S. Leva, and M. Longo, "Urban scale photovoltaic charging stations for electric vehicles", *IEEE Trans. Sustain. Energy,* vol. 5, no. 4, pp. 1234-1241, 2014.
[http://dx.doi.org/10.1109/TSTE.2014.2341954]

CHAPTER 2

Introduction to EV Motors

Aditi Saxena[1,*], **Shaniya Ashraf**[2] and **Shekhar Yadav**[2]

[1] *Indian Institute of Technology, Kanpur, India*

[2] *Department of Electrical Engineering, Madan Mohan Malaviya University of Technology, Gorakhpur (UP), India*

Abstract: This chapter provides a background of the study on Electric Vehicles (EVs), focusing on motor drive technologies that are still evolving. The need to optimize EV applications and performance is taken into account. EVs have been promising technologies for achieving a sustainable transport sector in the future due to their minimized carbon emissions, low noise, high efficiency, flexibility in grid operation, and integration. The future of EVs holds significant promise as advancements in technology and infrastructure converge. In general, Direct Current Motors (DCMs), Induction Motors (IMs), and Permanent Magnet Motors (PMMs) can generally be found in trading centers, whereas Reluctance Motors (RMs) have been utilized eventually and are approached towards commercial availability. This chapter briefly introduces various types of electric motors and their usage in electric vehicles. The reader will certainly have a basic understanding of motor mechanisms used in various applications of electric drives.

In the interest of the share market, let's analyze some figures to verify the usage and importance of electric vehicles in society. The annual EV sales crossed 12 lakh vehicles in FY2023, with more than 60% of the share accounted for by registered Electric two-Wheelers (E2W) followed by passenger Electric three-Wheelers (E3WP) with approximately 29% market share. The data also says that 13% of the new cars sold in 2022 were electric ones. The growth in CO_2 emissions should also be reduced in order to meet Net Zero Emissions by 2050. The share of sales of EVs increased by 4% in 2021. The global sales of battery electric vehicles (BEVs) and Plug-in Hybrid EVs (PHEVs) exceeded six million units in 2020.

Keywords: Battery pack, Charging infrastructure, Die-cast rotors, Electric car, Electric vehicles, Electric current, Electric motors, Electric traction systems, Greenhouse gas emissions, Induction motors, Internal combustion engine, Lorentz force, Net Zero Emissions, Permanent magnet motors, Power electronic converters, Reluctance motors, Rechargeable batteries, Switched reluctance machine, Two wheelers.

---

[*] **Corresponding author Aditi Saxena:** Indian Institute of Technology, Kanpur, India;
E-mail: aditisaxena131@gmail.com

Nitesh Tiwari, Shekhar Yadav and Sabha Raj Arya (Eds.)

INTRODUCTION

EVs identify a transformative shift in the automotive industry, determined by a global journey of eco-friendly transportation. These vehicles rely on rechargeable batteries to store and supply electricity to electric motors, which drive the wheels. The aim is to reduce greenhouse gas emissions and mitigate environmental impact and dependence on fossil fuels. EVs include Hybrid Electric Vehicles (HEVs), Plug-in Hybrid Electric Vehicles (PHEVs), and many more, depending on the electrification level of the vehicle [1]. Fig. (**1**) shows the components of an electric car.

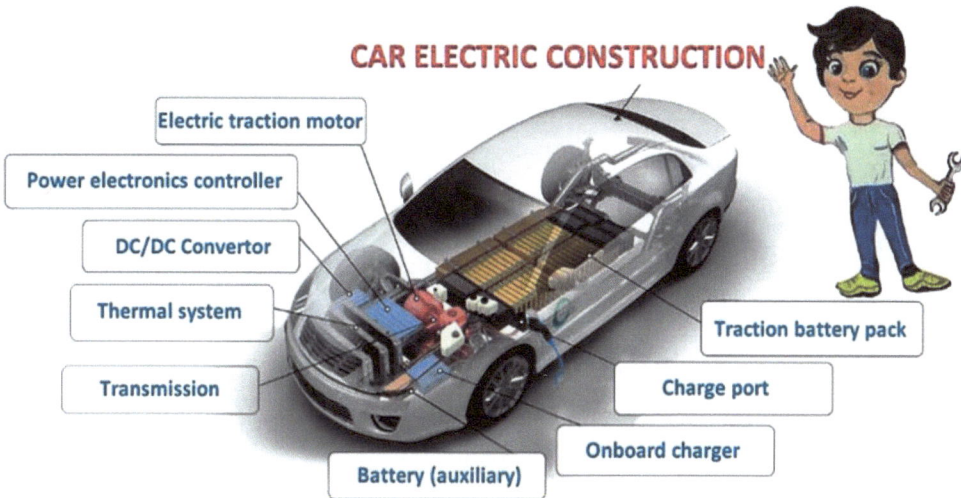

Fig. (1). Components of an electric car [3].

Components of electric vehicles include the battery pack, which serves as the energy storage unit, the electric motor, which serves as a contrast to combustion engines and delivers instant torque, resulting in responsive acceleration, and power electronic converters, which manage the flow of electrical energy between the battery and the electric motor. Ensuring optimal efficiency and charging plays a role in supporting worldwide adoption by addressing concerns related to range anxiety, convenience, and accessibility. Here is how charging infrastructure contributes to the widespread adoption of EVs. Advancement in fast charging technologies aims to reduce charging time and increase convenience for users. The oil crisis helped to conserve profit and funding for EV development. The insufficient energy density and increase in the cost of batteries made EVs less feasible in comparison with Internal Combustion (IC) engine automobiles. In urban areas, passenger vehicles have been the major source of air pollution. Therefore, we focus on this by introducing the pros of EVs. Electric traction systems are equipped with advanced capabilities such as increased fuel efficiency, quick charging options, and extended range [2].

The path to electrification is driven not only by environmental concerns but also by changing societal values. There is a growing consensus among governments, companies, and consumers regarding the necessity of shifting toward low-carbon technologies. Various measures, such as the European Union's Green Deal and China's New Energy Vehicle (NEV) program, have expedited the uptake of Electric Vehicles (EVs) through tax breaks, subsidies, and investments in infrastructure. In the U.S., the Inflation Reduction Act has played a crucial role in enhancing the EV market by fostering domestic battery manufacturing and developing extensive charging networks [3].

Electric Vehicles (EVs) also transform the driving experience by providing features like immediate acceleration, quiet operation, and reduced maintenance costs due to their less complex mechanical systems. These factors, along with their increasing affordability, make EVs attractive to a growing number of consumers. Additionally, as electricity grids evolve to include more renewable energy sources, the overall carbon footprint of EVs continues to decrease, further strengthening their sustainability appeal [4].

CONCEPT OF EV MOTORS

Basically, the principle of Electric Vehicle (EV) motors revolves around electromagnetic induction, where electrical energy is converted into mechanical energy to drive the vehicle. Here is a breakdown of the fundamental principles involved in detail:

- Electromagnetic Induction: EV motors operate on the principle of electromagnetic induction, discovered by Michael Faraday in the 19th century. When an electric current flows through a conductor, it generates a magnetic field around the conductor. Conversely, when a magnetic field moves relative to a conductor, it induces an electric current in the conductor. This phenomenon is the basis of how electric motors work.
- Magnetic Fields and Coils: EV motors consist of coils of wire wound around a core, typically made of ferromagnetic material like iron. These coils, also known as windings, create magnetic fields when electric current flows through them. In a basic DC (Direct Current) motor, a permanent magnet provides the magnetic field, while in more advanced AC (Alternating Current) motors, the magnetic field is generated by electromagnets within the motor [5].
- Lorentz Force: When an electric current flows through the coils of an EV motor, it interacts with the magnetic field to produce a force known as the Lorentz force. This force causes the coils to experience a torque, resulting in rotational

motion. The direction of the torque depends on the direction of the current and the orientation of the magnetic field.

- Rotor and Stator: EV motors typically have two main components: the rotor and the stator. The rotor is the rotating part of the motor, usually located at the center, while the stator is the stationary part surrounding the rotor. The coils are mounted on either the rotor or the stator, depending on the motor design. Fig. (2) shows the stator and rotor in a motor:
- Commutation (for DC Motors): In DC motors, the direction of the electric current in the coils needs to be reversed periodically to maintain continuous rotation. This process, known as commutation, is typically achieved using a commutator—a segmented ring that reverses the direction of current flow in the coils as the rotor rotates.
- Control and Power Electronics: In modern EVs, sophisticated control and power electronics regulate the flow of electric current to the motor, ensuring optimal performance and efficiency. These systems may include inverters to convert DC power from the battery into AC power for AC motors, as well as sensors and feedback mechanisms to monitor motor speed, torque, and temperature [6].

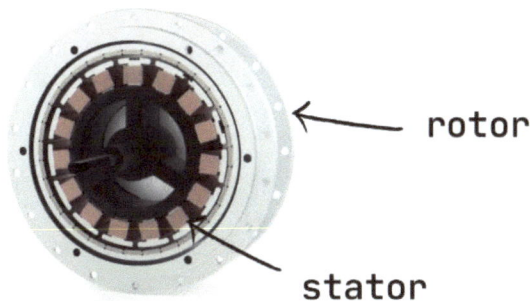

Fig. (2). Stator and rotor [8].

In summary, the basic principle of EV motors involves the conversion of electrical energy into mechanical energy through electromagnetic induction. By harnessing the interaction between magnetic fields and electric currents, EV motors provide the motive force necessary to propel electric vehicles, offering a clean, efficient, and sustainable alternative to traditional internal combustion engines.

CLASSIFICATION OF EV MOTORS

There are various types of electrical motor drives, each designed for specific applications and performance requirements. The features of each candidate motor drive are further described as follows:

DC Motors: DC motors have generally been utilized in EVs, especially in the early stages of electric vehicle advancement. DC motors have played a crucial role in the development of electric (EVs) from the outset due to their efficiency in converting electrical energy into mechanical energy. These motors are often chosen for tasks that necessitate high starting torque, such as lifting heavy loads or operating robust machinery. One of the primary benefits of DC motors is their accurate speed control, making them suitable for situations that demand precise adjustments. Their compact size and relatively straightforward design also lead to easier maintenance [7].

On the other hand, conventional brushed DC motors require frequent upkeep because the brushes and commutators tend to wear out. While this maintenance is manageable in less demanding scenarios, it renders these motors less ideal for contemporary EVs, which need low-maintenance options for sustained performance. Furthermore, DC motors can produce Electromagnetic Interference (EMI) that may disrupt nearby electronic devices, a factor that designers must consider when developing EVs [8]. Fig. (**3**) shows the DC Motor.

Fig. (3). DC Motor [9].

Besides, in modern EVs, a more common choice is the use of Alternating Current (AC) motors, specifically brushless DC or induction motors. These AC motors provide advantages such as higher efficiency, better power density, and simpler maintenance compared to traditional brushed DC motors [9].

Induction motors (IMs): Induction motors (IMs) are widely utilized in electric vehicles (EVs) because of their strong performance, efficiency, and dependability. Often referred to as asynchronous motors, these machines function based on the concept of electromagnetic induction. When Alternating Current (AC) is fed into the stator, it generates a rotating magnetic field. This, in turn, induces a current within the rotor, producing a magnetic field that interacts with the stator's magnetic field to generate torque and facilitate vehicle movement.

IMs are specified with three-phase AC windings present on the stator and short-circuited copper windings (or cast aluminum bars) on the rotor. Basically, any electrical machines with brushes or commutators are not used because of the requirement of high maintenance. The preferred choice for many industrial applications is the squirrel cage induction machine [10]. It is known for its simplicity, reliability, ruggedness, cheapness, and widespread use in various industrial and commercial applications [11]. Eliminating the brush friction allows the motors to push the maximum speed boundary further, while their increased speed rating enables them to deliver high output. Speed adjustments in induction motors are accomplished by altering the voltage frequency [12]. Field weakening allows the decoupling of the field vector from the torque vector through vector control. This results in high efficiency at high speed and low torque, as copper and core losses are reduced. However, efficiency decreases in the low-speed, high-torque range due to increased rotor losses. Die-casting techniques have made copper rotors more cost-effective, providing a significant advantage to these machines. Compared to aluminum die-cast rotors, copper rotors boast a 60% increase in electrical conductivity, resulting in a reduction of overall motor losses by approximately 15–20% [13]. A graphical representation of torque and power in an induction motor is represented in Fig. (**4**).

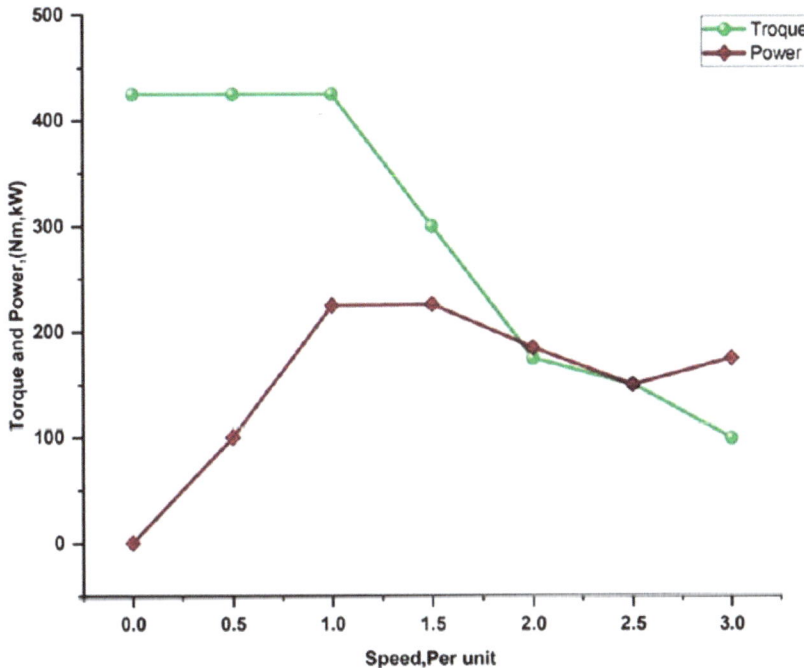

Fig. (4). Torque-speed characteristics [2].

Induction motors are preferred for EV propulsion due to their affordability, reliability, and established manufacturing and power converter technologies. Nonetheless, they suffer from drawbacks such as low efficiency and poor power factor, constraining their application in larger motor drives and high-speed EV inverters [14].

Permanent Magnet Motors (PMMs)

Permanent Magnet Motors (PMMs) are commonly utilized in Electric Vehicles (EVs) because of their high efficiency and excellent performance. These motors operate with permanent magnets rather than electromagnets to create a magnetic field, enabling them to produce greater torque at lower speeds. This feature is particularly beneficial for EVs, as it improves acceleration and driving dynamics, which are essential aspects of contemporary electric mobility. One major benefit of Permanent Magnet Motors (PMMs) is their energy efficiency [15].

PMMs exhibit a distinguishing capability to generate a continuous magnetic field autonomously. This inherent magnetism, which remains consistently active, positions them as the most efficient method for propelling electrified vehicles [16]. The rare-earth neodymium magnet, specifically neodymium-iron-boron (NdFeB), is frequently employed in high-performance Permanent Magnet (PM) motors [17].

The inherent efficiency of a permanent magnet motor surpasses that of an induction motor due to the absence of the inherent lag between the applied and induced magnetic fields. Permanent magnet motors operate synchronously with the applied frequency, enabling them to run at speeds determined by the frequency drive. As the frequency is increased, the total losses in induction motors escalate significantly compared to those in permanent magnet motors, which can achieve efficiencies of up to 97.5%. The main types of permanent magnet motors are surface permanent magnet motors (SPM) and Internal Permanent Magnet (IPM) motors. The primary distinction lies in the positioning of the magnets relative to the rotor: SPM motors feature magnets on the external surface of the rotor, whereas IPM motors embed their magnets within the rotor structure. Permanent-magnet motors find their primary application in variable-speed drives, where the stator is powered by an electronically controlled source with variable frequency and variable voltage capabilities. These drives enable precise control over speed and position. Permanent magnet machines are widely used in modern automotive vehicles, including cars and trucks [18]. The permanent magnet motor is shown in Fig. (**5**).

Fig. (5). Permanent magnet motor [11].

Advancements in control systems like Field-Oriented Control (FOC) and Model Predictive Control (MPC) have improved the performance and efficiency of Permanent Magnet Motors (PMMs). These techniques allow for real-time modifications of motor parameters, enhancing both torque and energy efficiency, which leads to better vehicle dynamics and longer battery life. As the electric vehicle sector continues to expand, PMMs are anticipated to play a more significant role, largely due to their effectiveness and capacity to satisfy the increasing demand for high-performance, low-maintenance electric drivetrains.

Permanent magnet motors offer significant advantages over traditional motors in terms of energy efficiency and power density. One key benefit is their reduced energy loss due to lower heat generation and friction during operation, leading to overall higher efficiency. This means less wasted energy and potentially lower operating costs. Additionally, permanent magnet motors have a higher power density, meaning they can deliver more power relative to their size and weight compared to conventional motors. This characteristic makes them particularly advantageous in applications where space and weight constraints are critical factors, allowing for more compact and efficient motor designs. Overall, the combination of improved energy efficiency and higher power density makes permanent magnet motors a compelling choice for various industrial and commercial applications seeking to optimize performance and minimize energy consumption [19].

Reluctance Motors (RM)

Reluctance Notors (RMs) represent a promising technology for Electric Vehicles (EVs), offering various benefits regarding performance and cost-effectiveness. These motors operate on the principle of reluctance, causing the rotor to align in a position that reduces the reluctance of the magnetic circuit.

Reluctance motors are valued for their simplicity, making them easier to maintain and less costly to produce. The simplicity does not compromise efficiency; these motors boast high-efficiency levels, especially in applications requiring variable speed control. Despite their straightforward design, reluctance motors offer impressive torque density, making them ideal for space-constrained environments where high torque output is essential. Their controllability over a wide speed range is another advantage, making them suitable for applications demanding precise speed control. Reluctance motors are robust performers, capable of withstanding harsh conditions and temperature variations without sacrificing performance. Their relatively low cost, combined with high power density and suitability for high-speed applications, further enhances their appeal. Moreover, they are energy-efficient, particularly when paired with advanced control techniques like vector control. With few moving parts and sturdy construction, reluctance motors require minimal maintenance, ensuring reduced downtime and lower operating costs in the long run. The classification of these motors will be discussed further.

Synchronous Reluctance Machines (SyRMs) and switched reluctance machines (SRMs) are indeed significant machine architectures that leverage the reluctance principle to generate torque. In SyRMs, the rotor design typically has salient poles with no windings or magnets, and the stator is wound with three-phase windings to produce a rotating magnetic field. The rotor aligns itself with the stator magnetic field due to the tendency of magnetic flux to flow through the path of least reluctance [20]. SyRMs can be controlled using Field-Oriented Control (FOC) techniques similar to those used in PMSMs. This allows precise control of torque and flux, optimizing efficiency and performance. By varying the current in the stator windings, the torque output of SyRMs can be adjusted to meet the requirements of different applications.

The rotor and stator of an SRM are designed with salient poles to facilitate the generation of torque through the controlled switching of current in the stator windings. The switching sequence is crucial in determining the direction and magnitude of torque output. SRMs often require complex control strategies compared to SyRMs or other motors due to the necessity of precise current switching to achieve optimal torque production. However, advancements in power electronics and control algorithms have made SRMs more viable for various applications, including electric vehicles and industrial machinery. The growing interest in SRM drives for EV applications is driven by their inherent advantages in simplicity, reliability, torque density, wide speed range, fault tolerance, efficiency, and environmental compatibility. Recent research and advancements indicate that reluctance motors may play a crucial role in the future of vehicles, especially as manufacturers aim to minimize their dependence on rare earth elements and reduce the overall expenses associated with EV production. These motors are a significant focus area for research, with efforts ongoing to enhance their torque density and efficiency and to lessen noise in electric vehicle applications [21].

COMPARISON OF ELECTRIC MOTORS FOR EV APPLICATIONS

Examining the progress and prototype demonstrations of electric and hybrid electric vehicles during the past decade has revealed the utilization of various types of machines: Induction Machine (IM), Permanent Magnet excited Synchronous Machine (PMSM), and the switched reluctance machine (SRM). The incorporation of these machines indicates that each possesses unique advantages and disadvantages, making them suitable for different hybrid vehicle concepts. Consequently, these machine types are evaluated further in the subsequent section for comparison. The induction machine stands out for its reliability and cost-effectiveness, particularly in terms of low production expenses. However, achieving high power and dynamics requires complex and costly field-oriented control methods. While it boasts the best average efficiency across various speeds, it falls short of the peak efficiency achieved by a PMSM. Therefore, the induction machine proves advantageous when consistent efficiency over a wide speed range is essential, and space constraints are not a concern, albeit offering moderate power density. Consequently, these machines are used in electric vehicles or series Hybrid Electric Vehicles (HEVs).

Comparatively, the switched reluctance machine shares similar power density and efficiency levels with the induction machine but lags behind in other aspects. Its notable drawbacks, historically rendering it unsuitable, include pronounced torque fluctuations at low speeds and notable acoustic noise emissions. In contrast, the permanent magnet synchronous machine excels in power density, enabling the creation of high-power machines with minimal weight. Additionally, it achieves optimal efficiency within a specific range of speeds. Consequently, the PMSM emerges as the best for realizing fuel-efficient hybrid electric vehicles. Nonetheless, its reliance on rare-earth magnets makes it the most expensive machine. Machines used for EVs are shown in Fig. (**6**).

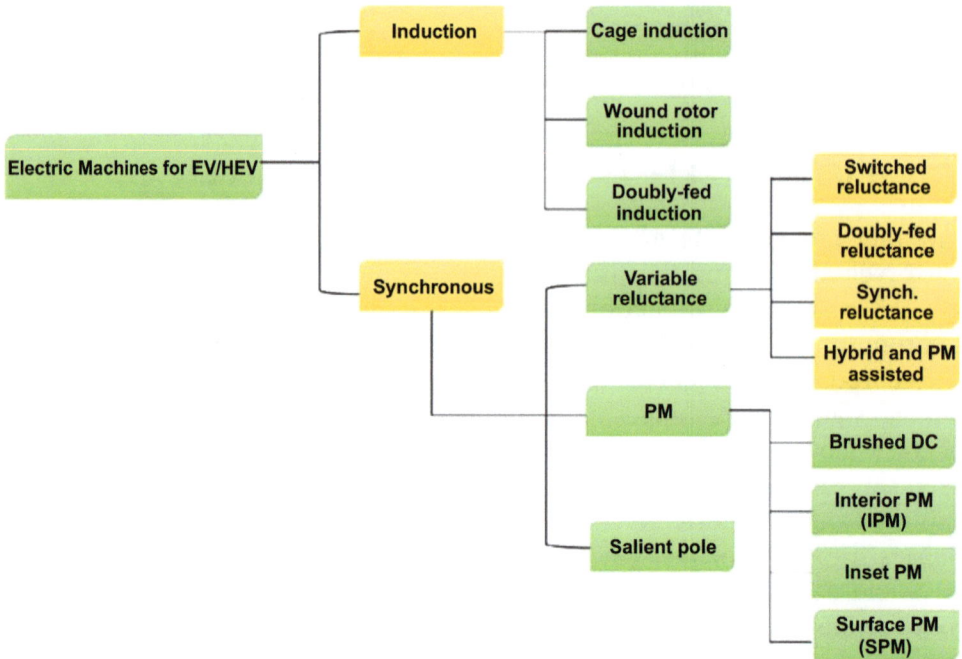

Fig. (6). Machines used for EVs [2].

CASE STUDY: ADOPTION OF ELECTRIC VEHICLES IN CITY X

Background

City X, a bustling metropolis with a population of over 2 million, faces significant challenges related to air pollution and traffic congestion. In response to these issues and a growing global emphasis on sustainable transportation, the city government launched an ambitious initiative to promote the adoption of Electric Vehicles (EVs) among its residents and businesses.

Goals

- Reduce Air Pollution: The primary objective of the initiative is to decrease harmful emissions from vehicles, thereby improving air quality and public health in City X.
- Alleviate Traffic Congestion: By encouraging the use of EVs, the city aims to reduce traffic congestion on the roads, leading to smoother traffic flow and shorter commute times.
- Promote Sustainability: City X aims to establish itself as a leader in sustainable transportation by promoting the use of clean energy vehicles and reducing its carbon footprint.

Implementation

- Infrastructure Development: City X invested in the development of a comprehensive charging infrastructure to support EV adoption. This includes installing public charging stations in strategic locations such as parking lots, shopping centers, and residential areas.
- Incentive Programs: To encourage the transition to EVs, the city introduced various incentive programs, including tax credits, rebates, and subsidies for EV purchases. Additionally, EV owners were offered discounted or free parking and access to carpool lanes.
- Public Awareness Campaigns: City X launched a series of public awareness campaigns to educate residents and businesses about the benefits of EVs. These campaigns include informational workshops, community events, and advertising campaigns highlighting the environmental and economic advantages of electric transportation.

CONCLUDING REMARKS

Selecting the appropriate electric motor simplifies the design and packaging for powertrain components, primarily due to its compact size and reduced thermal limitations. In-wheel motors contribute to weight reduction in vehicles and create additional interior space, thereby enabling the exploration of innovative body styles. In the ongoing development of inverters and motors to enhance the efficiency and affordability of future electric vehicles, several challenges remain to be addressed. The primary objective is to attain high power density, which contributes to the seamless integration of the electric drive with the battery system. This necessitates the refinement of more advanced and integrated designs.

ACKNOWLEDGMENTS

We would like to express our sincere gratitude to the reviewers for their invaluable feedback, which greatly contributed to the improvement of the manuscript. We are deeply appreciative of their time, expertise, and dedication to advancing scientific knowledge in our field.

AUTHORS' CONTRIBUTION

Aditi Saxena: Preparation of manuscript, conceptualization of the study, data analysis, and interpretation.

Shaniya Ashraf: Reviewing of the literature, formal analysis, initial draft of the manuscript.

Shekhar Yadav: Reviewed the final draft for accuracy and provided feedback on key technical aspects, critical insights, and revisions to the manuscript.

REFERENCES

[1]   W. Cao, A.A. Bukhari, and L. Aarniovuori, "Review of electrical motor drives for electric vehicle applications", *Mehran University Research Journal of Engineering & Technology.,* vol. 38, no. 3, pp. 525-540, 2019.

[2]   Kosuru VS, Kavasseri Venkitaraman A. Trends and challenges in electric vehicle motor drivelines-A review. *International journal of electrical and computer engineering systems*, 14(4): 485-95, 2023.

[3]   G. Patil, G. Pode, B. Diouf, and R. Pode, "Sustainable Decarbonization of Road Transport: Policies, Current Status, and Challenges of Electric Vehicles", *Sustainability (Basel),* vol. 16, no. 18, p. 8058, 2024.
[http://dx.doi.org/10.3390/su16188058]

[4]   J.A. Sanguesa, V. Torres-Sanz, P. Garrido, F.J. Martinez, and J.M. Marquez-Barja, "A review on electric vehicles: Technologies and challenges", *Smart Cities,* vol. 4, no. 1, pp. 372-404, 2021.
[http://dx.doi.org/10.3390/smartcities4010022]

[5]   N. Tiwari, S. Yadav, and S.R. Arya, "Battery and super capacitor powered energy management scheme for EV/HEV using fuzzy logic controller and PID controller", *International Journal of Power Electronics,* vol. 15, no. 3/4, pp. 309-333, 2022.
[http://dx.doi.org/10.1504/IJPELEC.2022.122411]

[6]   Xue XD, Cheng KW, Cheung NC. Selection of electric motor drives for electric vehicles. *Australasian Universities Power Engineering Conference*, pp. 1-6, 2008.

[7]   Sen, P. C. Electric motor drives and control-past, present, and future. *Transactions on Industrial Electronics*, 37(6), 562-575, 1990.

[9]   B. K. Bose, Power Electronics and Motor Drives: Advances and Trends. Academic Press, 2020.,

[10]   N. Tiwari, S. Yadav, and S.R. Arya, "PI gain optimisation and artificial intelligence based direct torque control of induction motor equipped electric vehicle drives", *International Journal of Electric and Hybrid Vehicles,* vol. 15, no. 2, pp. 151-182, 2023.
[http://dx.doi.org/10.1504/IJEHV.2023.132034]

[11]   Khaleel M, Ahmed AA, Alsharif A. Technology challenges and trends of electric motor and drive in electric vehicle. *Int. J. Electr. Eng. and Sustain*, 8: 41-8, 2023.

[12]   Finken T, Hameyer K. Design of electric motors for hybrid-and electric-vehicle applications. *ICEMS*, 2009.

[13]   J. Wu, Z. Luo, N. Zhang, and Y. Zhang, "A new uncertain analysis method and its application in vehicle dynamics", *Mech. Syst. Signal Process.,* vol. 50-51, pp. 659-675, 2015.
[http://dx.doi.org/10.1016/j.ymssp.2014.05.036]

[14]   N. Tiwari, S. Yadav, and S.R. Arya, "Artificial intelligence and PI gain optimisation for sensorless indirect vector control of induction motor-based electric vehicle drives", *International Journal of Ambient Energy,* vol. 45, no. 1, p. 2315485, 2024.
[http://dx.doi.org/10.1080/01430750.2024.2315485]

[15]   N. Tiwari, S. Yadav, and S.R. Arya, "Multi-objective metaheuristic optimised PI gains of model reference adaptive controlled induction motor drive for electric vehicle", *International Journal of Vehicle Performance,* vol. 9, no. 3, pp. 272-289, 2023.
[http://dx.doi.org/10.1504/IJVP.2023.131973]

[16]   Saxena A, Gupta A, Tiwari N. Design and Implementation of Adaptive and Artificial Intelligence Controller for Brushless Motor Drive Electric Vehicle. *SAE Technical Paper*, 2023.

[17]   I. Szénásy, and D. Csikor, "Induction Motor Energy Efficiency Investigation", *Engineering Proceedings,* vol. 79, no. 1, p. 75, 2024.

[18]   A. Loganayaki and R. B. Kumar, "Permanent Magnet Synchronous Motor for Electric Vehicle Applications," *5th International Conference on Advanced Computing & Communication Systems (ICACCS), Coimbatore, India*, pp. 1064-1069, 2019.
[http://dx.doi.org/10.1109/ICACCS.2019.8728442]

[19]   A.V. Khachane, and S.S. Dhamse, "Switched Reluctance Motor Drive for Electric Vehicle Applications Based on Speed Characteristics", *2020 IEEE International Conference for Innovation in Technology (INOCON),* pp. 1-6, 2020.
[http://dx.doi.org/10.1109/INOCON50539.2020.9298271]

[20]   H. Heidari, A. Rassõlkin, A. Kallaste, T. Vaimann, E. Andriushchenko, A. Belahcen, and D.V. Lukichev, "A review of synchronous reluctance motor-drive advancements", *Sustainability (Basel),* vol. 13, no. 2, p. 729, 2021.
[http://dx.doi.org/10.3390/su13020729]

[21]   X. Sun, L. Chen, and Z. Yang, "Overview of bearingless permanent-magnet synchronous motors", *IEEE Trans. Ind. Electron.,* vol. 60, no. 12, pp. 5528-5538, 2013.
[http://dx.doi.org/10.1109/TIE.2012.2232253]

Introduction to Power Electronics Converters

Neha Gupta[1,*]

[1] *Amity School of Engineering and Technology, Amity University, Uttar Pradesh, Lucknow Campus, India*

Abstract: This chapter has been written keeping in mind that the electric vehicle is a multidisciplinary subject mainly involving electrical and mechanical engineering. So, the chapter begins by briefly discussing the basics of various semiconductor devices mainly used in the power electronic converters used for electric vehicles. This chapter clearly explains the requirement of power electronic converters to turn the electricity derived from an electric battery into a suitable form for an electric drive. It discusses the suitability of various semiconductor devices in different applications of drives based on switching and conduction losses. This chapter gives a comprehensive review of various power electronic converters used for electric drives. The former part of the chapter is dedicated to a detailed discussion of various configurations of DC-DC converters for electric drives with schematic diagrams, mathematical equations, and waveforms. In the later part of the chapter, a detailed discussion of various configurations of DC-AC converters for electric drives with schematic diagrams, mathematical equations, and waveforms is provided. This chapter also includes a comparison of various configurations to suit a particular kind of electric vehicle. For better understanding, the chapter also discusses speed control of induction motor drives using power electronic converters. A case study of the design and development of a bidirectional charger for electric vehicles is discussed on the MATLAB Simulink platform. Bidirectional chargers, which enable power flow in both directions from the grid to the vehicle (G2V) and from the vehicle to the grid (V2G), are at the forefront of this technological evolution.

Keywords: Bidirectional charger, Converters, Electric drive, Electric vehicle, Induction motor, Semiconductor devices.

INTRODUCTION

The electrical energy readily available is of fixed frequency and fixed voltage type. For domestic and small commercial uses, mostly single-phase supply is available whereas industrial users draw supply from three-phase lines. Electric Vehicle charging and control requires a flexible power supply, wherein variable

---

* **Corresponding author Neha Gupta:** Amity School of Engineering and Technology, Amity University, Uttar Pradesh, Lucknow Campus, India; E-mail: ngupta1@lko.amity.edu

Nitesh Tiwari, Shekhar Yadav and Sabha Raj Arya (Eds.)

frequency and variable voltage may be available as per the various application-based requirements. To fulfil such industrial demands of conditioned power, power electronics converters are required. Power conditioning is an integrated term used for power conversion (from AC-DC and DC-AC) as well as power control [1].

Power converters are electrical networks consisting of a combination of semiconductor devices. Depending on the type of semiconductor device used, the converter can be uncontrolled, semi-controlled, or fully controlled. These semiconductor devices act as a controlled or uncontrolled switch in the power electronic converter. Power electronic converters can give the desired output by designing a proper switching strategy. In this way, with the use of these converters, the required input for industrial applications can be obtained [2].

In this chapter, a brief introduction to the most popular semiconductor devices has been given. The chapter gives a comprehensive review of power electronic converters used for electric drives. For a better understanding of the concept, a simulation of a converter for electric vehicle charging using MATLAB Simulink has also been included [3].

Basics of Semiconductor Devices

In this section, we will give a brief overview of the most commonly used semiconductor devices to give an understanding of the selection of semiconductor switches for a particular application [1, 2]. There are a number of switches available in the market for different merits and demerits they offer, like Power Diodes, Bipolar Junction Transistor (BJT), Metal-oxide Semiconductor Field Effect Transistor (MOSFET), Insulated Gate Bipolar Transistor (IGBT), Silicon Controlled Rectifier (SCR), Gate turnoff switches (GTO), MOS controlled Thyristors (MCT), *etc* [4].

In this chapter, we will discuss the most popular semiconductor switches: 1) Silicon Controlled Rectifier (SCR), 2) Power-Metal-oxide Semiconductor Field Effect transistor (Power MOSFET), 3) Insulated Gate Bipolar Transistor (IGBT), *etc*. The focus of the chapter will be power electronic converters [5].

Silicon Controlled Rectifier (SCR)

SCR is a 4-layer, 3-junction, 3-terminal pnpn semiconductor device, as shown in Fig. (**1**). The terminal connected to the exterior p layer is denoted as the anode (A), the terminal connected to the exterior n layer is denoted as the cathode (K), and the terminal connected to interior p layer is denoted as Gate (G). Fig. **(2)** shows VI characteristics of an SCR. The working of an SCR can be split into 3 modes of operation [6].

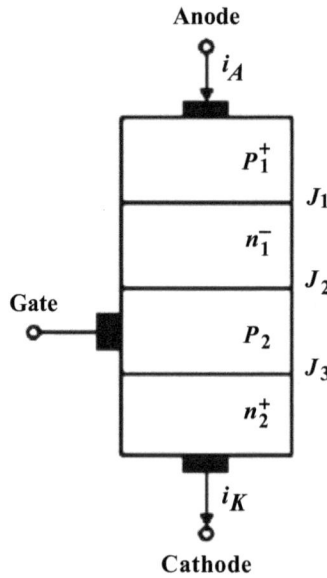

Fig. (1). Pnpn junction.

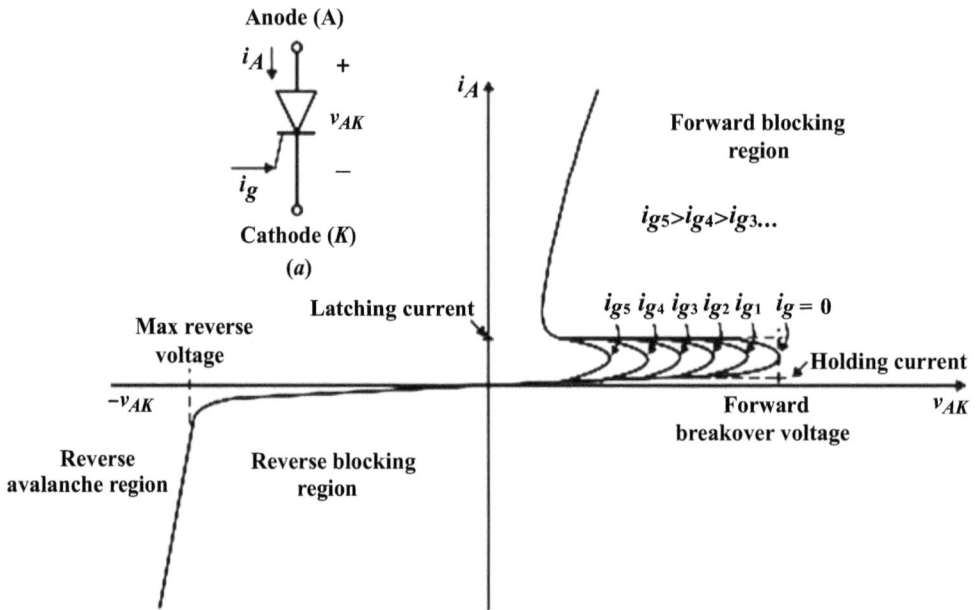

Fig. (2). (**a**) Symbol of an SCR (**b**)VI characteristics of an SCR.

Forward Blocking Mode

When the anode terminal is positive and the cathode terminal is negative, the junction J_1, J_3 are forward-biased, but conduction is not possible since the junction J_2 is reverse-biased and offers a very high resistance. If the forward bias is increased, junction J_2 undergoes an avalanche breakdown. The voltage at which breakdown occurs is known as the forward breakover voltage V_{BO}. Before forward breakover voltage, the SCR is in the blocking mode.

Forward Conduction Mode

When the anode terminal is positive, the cathode terminal is negative, and the gate terminal is supplied with a separate positive supply, junctions J_1 and J_3 are forward-biased and J_2 is also forward-biased, and current flows from the anode to the cathode.

Reverse Blocking Mode

When the anode terminal is negative and the cathode terminal is positive, junctions J_1 and J_3 are reverse-biased and junction J_2 is forward-biased. In this mode, a small leakage current flows. If the reverse bias is increased, junctions J_1 and J_3 undergo an avalanche breakdown. The voltage at which breakdown occurs is known as reverse breakover voltage V_{BR}. A very large current flows through the thyristor, which gives rise to losses and should, therefore, be avoided.

The current at which the conduction starts is known as the latching current. Once the SCR is in conduction mode, it remains in the conduction mode even if the Gate terminal voltage is withdrawn. If the anode current falls below a current value, the SCR will turn off. The anode current below which SCR enters the blocking mode is known as the Holding Current [7].

The characteristics of SCR make it suitable for high-voltage applications. Also, the switching control of SCR switches is simple. Hence, they are found suitable for applications like speed control, camera flashes, *etc*.

Power MOSFET

Power MOSFET is a 3-terminal device containing Drain (D), Source (S), and Gate (G), as shown in Fig. (**3**). Fig. (**3**) shows the symbol MOSFET, where the arrow indicates the direction flow of electrons. MOSFET is a voltage-controlled device. The current flow in MOSFET is due to the movement of the majority of carriers only, which makes it a unipolar device. It is known for its high switching speed, which is more than 1MHz. The output characteristics of a power MOSFET, which is a graph plotted between drain current (I_D and drain to source voltage

(V_{DS}), are shown in Fig. (**4**). For smaller voltages, the graph is approximately linear. For a given gate-to-source voltage, if drain-to-source voltage is further increased, the drain current is almost constant. Thus, MOSFET works as a switch if operated either in the cut-off region or saturation region. In the cut-off region, MOSFET behaves as a closed switch, and in the saturation region, it behaves as

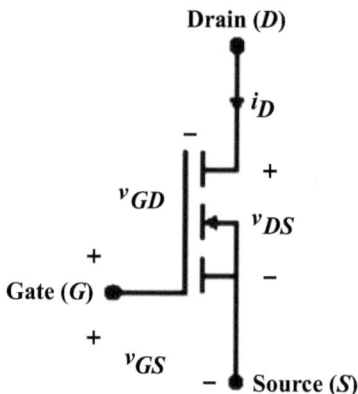

Fig. (3). Power MOSFET symbol.

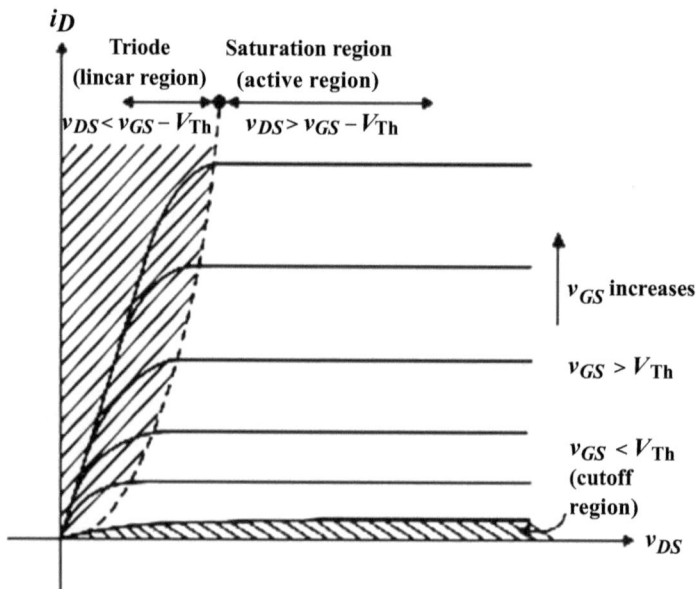

Fig. (4). Output Characteristics of power MOSFET.

an open switch. In the converters, we use power MOSFET as a switch. Further, the cut-off and saturation points depend on the gate-to-source voltage applied to the power MOSFET [8].

Power MOSFET is known for its low switching losses, high conduction losses, and high on-state resistance, which makes it suitable for high-frequency applications.

Insulated Gate Bipolar Transistor (IGBT)

Like MOSFET, IGBT is a device based on MOS technology. IGBT is a device that has positive characteristics of MOSFET and Bipolar Junction Transistor (BJT). It has high input impedance and low on-state resistance. Fig. (5). shows an electrical equivalent circuit of IGBT, a two-transistor model, and a symbol of IGBT. The output characteristics of IGBT are shown in Fig. (6). It is a graph between the collector current I_C and collector-emitter voltage V_{CE} for various gate emitter voltage V_{GE}. The characteristics of an IGBT are like BJT. The IGBT is a controlled switch whose control parameter is various gate emitter voltage V_{GE}. In this way, IGBT is a voltage-controlled device [9].

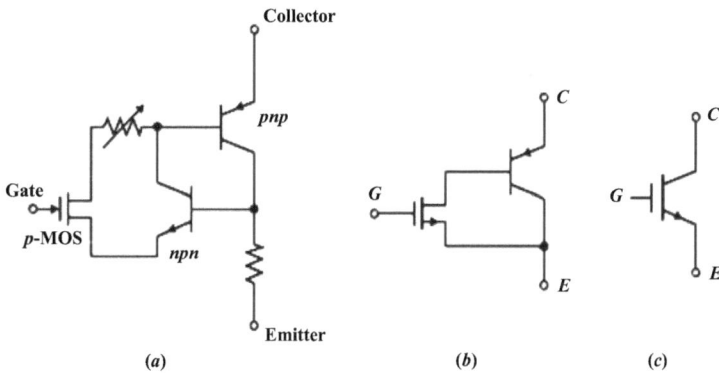

Fig. (5). IGBT**(a)** Equivalent Circuit, **(b)** Two-transistor model, **(c)** Symbol.

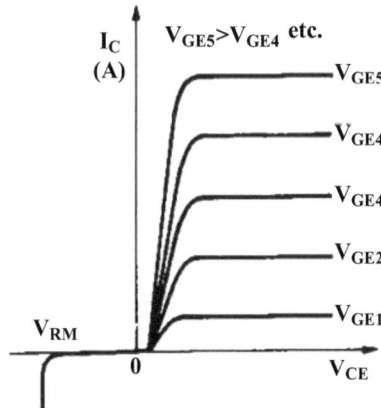

Fig. (6). Output Characteristics of IGBT.

The lower switching losses, lower gate drive requirements, and small snubber circuit requirements make an IGBT a compact as well as cost-effective device that is found to be more suitable for AC-DC drives, UPS systems, *etc.* A brief discussion on popular semiconductor switches has been done in this section to form a basis for a power converter study. Detailed study construction and characteristics of switches is beyond the scope of this particular book chapter.

DC-DC Converters for Electric Drives

The most used DC-DC converters are known as Choppers. The main function of choppers in DC drives is to provide a DC voltage input to the drive [1, 2]. To achieve this, variable input DC-DC converters are designed with the help of semiconductor switches explained in the previous chapter. For the design of the DC-DC converter, we preferably use MOSFET or IGBT over SCR. Because MOSFET and IGBT offer low switching losses and are self-commuted devices, *i.e.*, they do not have external commutation circuitry. The advantage of low switching loss makes them suitable for high-frequency operation, thereby reducing current ripple and eliminating discontinuous conduction. The advantage of feeding DC drives through DC-DC converters is to achieve regenerative braking at low speeds with the help of variable DC supply achieved through fixed DC-fed choppers [10].

DC-DC- Converter Fed Separately Excited DC Motor Control

Any DC motor has three modes of operation: 1) Generating Mode, 2) Motoring Mode, and 3) Braking mode. Since here we are discussing speed control of electric vehicles, our focus will be on motoring mode only.

The Schematic diagram of the DC-DC converter fed separately excited DC motor is shown in Fig. (**7**). In this diagram, MOSFET has been used as the switching device whose on-off period may be decided as per the requirement of the drive. The switch is operated at regular intervals with time Period T with t_{on} as the on-time duration. MOSFET has been used as a switch to ensure low switching losses and continuous conduction.

The waveforms of terminal voltage and armature current are shown in Fig. (**8**). When the MOSFET switch is closed, the KVL equation is given by Eq. (**1**).

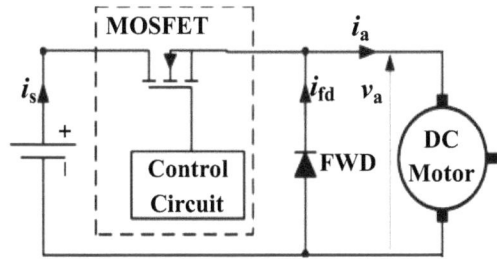

Fig. (7). DC-DC converter fed separately excited DC Motor.

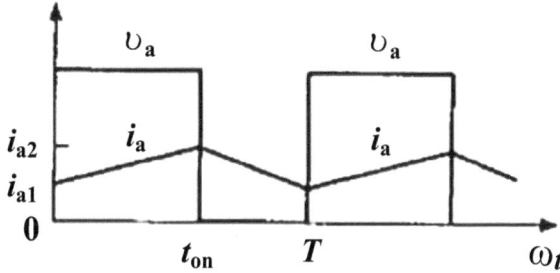

Fig. (8). Waveforms of DC-DC converter fed separately excited DC Motor.

$$V = R_a i_a + L_a \frac{di_a}{dt} + E \qquad (1)$$

When the MOSFET switch is open, the motor current freewheels through the freewheeling diode (FWD). KVL equation is given by Eq. (**2**).

$$0 = R_a i_a + L_a \frac{di_a}{dt} + E \qquad (2)$$

When the switch is closed, the motor is connected to the supply through a DC-DC converter; the armature current rises from ia1 to ia2. When the switch is open, the motor is disconnected from the supply and freewheels through FWD; the armature current falls from ia2 to ia1. The ratio of the switch to the time-period of one cycle is represented as the duty cycle α, given by Eq. (**3**).

$$\alpha = \frac{t_{on}}{T} \qquad (3)$$

The average value of terminal voltage shown in Fig. (**8**) can be calculated as given by Eq. (**4**).

$$V_a = \frac{1}{T} \int_0^{t_{on}} V \, dt \qquad (4)$$

By solving Eq. (**4**), we get Eq. (**5**).

$$V_a = \alpha V \tag{5}$$

The voltage drop across the inductance is because of the DC component of the armature current, given by Eqs. (**6**)and **7**).

$$V_a = R_a i_a + E \tag{6}$$

$$I_a = \frac{\alpha V - E}{R_a} \tag{7}$$

As we know, the speed of the DC motor varies with the armature current; with proper switching, we can achieve the desired armature current for speed control of the DC motor.

DC-DC Converter Fed DC Series Motor Control

The schematic diagram for DC-DC converter fed DC series motor control is the same as shown in Fig. (**7**). The expression for V_a is given by Eq. (**4**). But in the case of the DC series motor, back emf (e) is not constant but varies proportional to the armature current (I_a) non-linearly due to magnetic saturation [11].

When the MOSFET switch is closed, the KVL equation is given by Eq. (**8**).

$$V = R_a i_a + L_a \frac{di_a}{dt} + f(i_a)\omega_m \tag{8}$$

ω_m = angular speed of the motor

When the MOSFET switch is open, the KVL equation is given by Eq. (**9**).

$$0 = R_a i_a + L_a \frac{di_a}{dt} + f(i_a)\omega_m \tag{9}$$

The dependency of the back emf of the DC series motor on the armature current makes Eqs. (**8** and **9**) non-linear. To solve this equation, we replace e by the average value E_a given by Eqs. (**10** and **11**).

$$E_a = K_a \omega_m \tag{10}$$

$$K_a = f(i_a) \tag{11}$$

From Eq. (**12**).

$$\omega_m = \frac{V_a - I_a R_a}{K_a} \tag{12}$$

From Eq. (**12**), it is evident that speed control can be achieved by varying the armature current. By designing a proper switching strategy, we can get the desired speed control.

DC-AC Converter for Electric Vehicle

DC to AC converter is commonly known as an inverter. The main function of an inverter in an electric vehicle is to convert DC battery power to a suitable AC supply for the propulsion of the vehicle as well as for other devices in the vehicle that are powered by AC supply. In the case of AC supply, there are two main parameters that can be varied to get the desired speed control of an electric vehicle: 1) Voltage Amplitude and 2) Supply frequency. Since, in the case of electric vehicles, power is drawn from a DC battery pack, we will focus our study on the use of power inverters. In power electronics, we mainly use two types of inverters: 1) Voltage source inverter (VSI) and 2) Current source inverter (CSI). In this section, we will study how we achieve AC supply from the DC battery pack with the help of an inverter so as to be suitable to feed an AC motor drive. This chapter is limited to the study of DC-AC converter-fed induction motors as the electric motor [1, 2].

DC-AC Converter-fed Induction Motor Drive

As we know, in the case of an induction motor, the rotating magnetic field rotates with synchronous speed, which can be given in Eq. (**13**).

$$N_s = \frac{120 \, f}{P} \tag{13}$$

Where N_s = Synchronous Speed, f is the supply frequency, and P is the number of field poles. The speed of the motor is given by Eq. (**14**).

$$N_r = s N_s \tag{14}$$

Where N_r is the rotor speed and s is the slip, which can be given by Eq. (**15**).

$$s = \frac{N_s - N_r}{N_s} \tag{15}$$

Hence, by observing Eqs. (**13-15**), we come to the inference that the speed of the motor can be varied by varying synchronous speed, which varies proportional to the supply frequency.

Voltage Source Inverter-fed Drives

A Voltage Source Inverter (VSI) is a DC-AC converter designed with the help of power electronic switches. By designing an appropriate switching scheme for a VSI, a variable frequency supply can be achieved from a DC supply. Fig. (**9**) shows an induction motor control fed with a voltage source inverter. The commutation circuit and protection circuits have been omitted for simplicity. It has six power electronic switches. For low-power applications, MOSFETs may be used. For medium-power applications, IGBT can be used as a switch, and for high-power applications, a thyristor may be used.

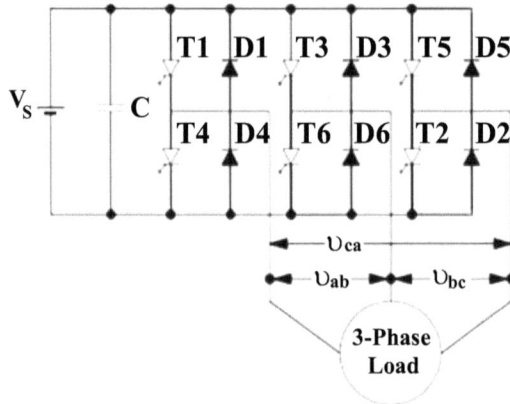

Fig. (9). Voltage Source Inverter-fed induction motor drive.

In Fig. (**9**), the power electronic switches are numbered in the sequence they are fired. By proper switching, we obtain v_a, v_b and v_c at the output terminals *a*, *b*, and *c* of the DC to AC converter. There are two patterns of switching that are followed for firing the power electronic switches: 1) 180° conduction mode, and 2) 120° conduction mode. We will briefly discuss both the patterns.

180° Conduction Mode

In 180° conduction mode shown in Fig. (**11**), each switch conducts for an interval of 180°. The switches in each leg, *i.e.*, T_1 T_4, $T_3 T_6$, and T_5 T_2 are fired one after the other in an interval of 180°. Switches in the upper position of each arm are fired at an interval of 120°. Similarly, switches in the lower position of each arm are also fired at an interval of 120°. The firing sequence varies at an interval of 60°. Thus, we get a 6-level wave with each level of 60° duration. By changing the switching patterns, one can get the desired power supply from the same dc source as per various applications.

The equivalent circuit models of steps 1 and 2 are shown in Fig. (**10**), along with the calculation of phase voltages. The phase voltages of the subsequent steps may be calculated in the same way to get the waveform shown in Fig. (**11**).

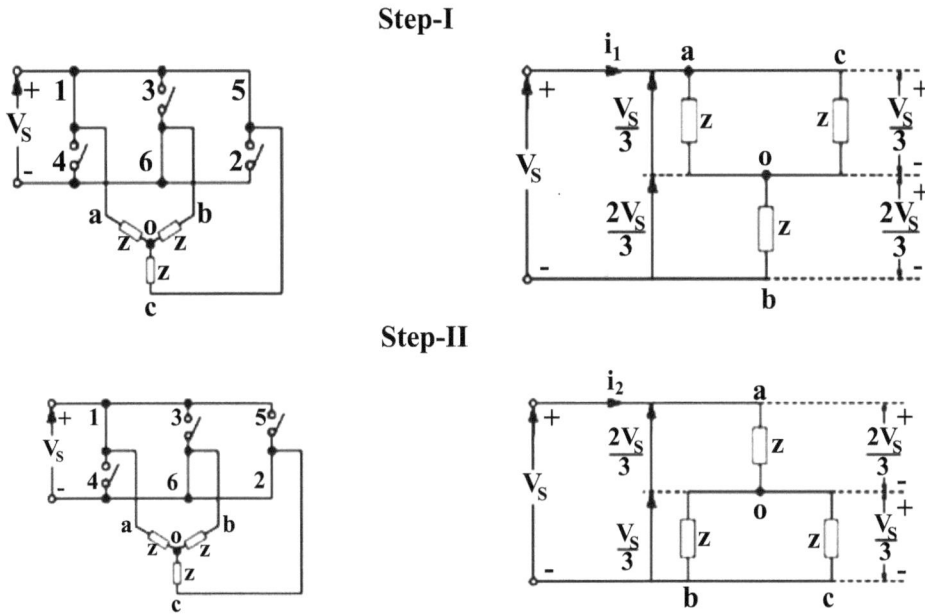

Step-I

Step-II

Fig. (10). Equivalent circuits of steps of 180° conduction mode VSI.

The line voltages v_{ab}, v_{bc} and v_{ca} may be obtained by using Eqs. (**16** and (**18**).

$$v_{ab} = v_{ao} - v_{bo} = v_{ao} + v_{ob} \qquad (16)$$

$$v_{bc} = v_{bo} - v_{co} = v_{bo} + v_{oc} \qquad (17)$$

$$v_{ca} = v_{co} - v_{ao} = v_{co} + v_{oa} \qquad (18)$$

It is evident from Fig. (**11**) that phase voltages have 6 steps per cycle, whereas line voltages have one positive and one negative half-cycle per cycle. The function is to maintain the current flow during the reactive load conditions.

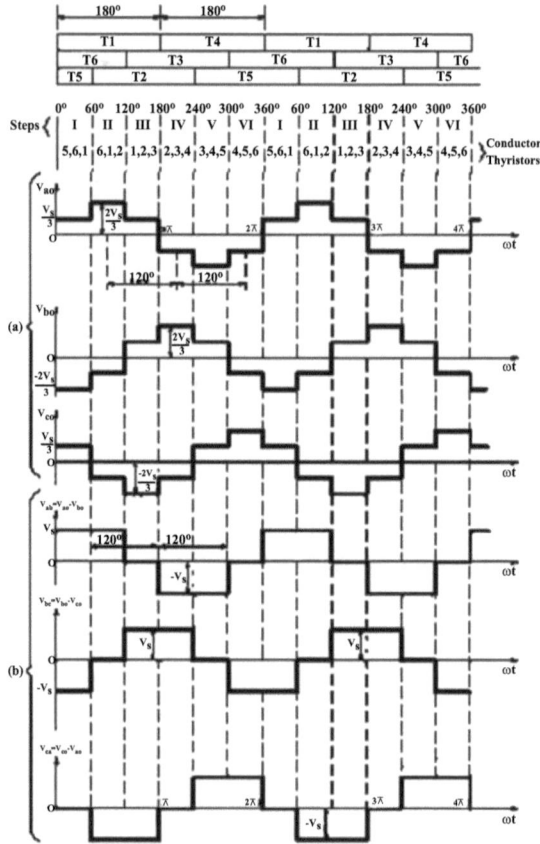

Fig. (11). Waveforms with 180° conduction mode VSI.

120° Conduction Mode

In 120° conduction mode shown in Fig. (**13**), each switch conducts for an interval of 120°. The switches in each leg, *i.e.*, $T_1 T_4$, $T_3 T_6$, and $T_5 T_2$ are fired one after the other in an interval of 180°. Since the switch in one leg conducts for 120 degrees and the other one is fired after 180 degrees, there is a duration of 60 degrees when neither of the switches of that leg is conducting. Switches in the upper position of each arm are fired at an interval of 120°. Similarly, switches in the lower position of each arm are also fired at an interval of 120°. The firing sequence varies at an interval of 60°. Thus, we get a 6-level wave with each level of 60° duration. By changing the switching patterns, one can get the desired power supply from the same DC source as per various applications.

The equivalent circuits model of step 1 is shown in Fig. (**12**), along with the calculation of phase voltage. The phase voltages of the subsequent steps may be calculated in the same way to get the waveform shown in Fig. (**13**).

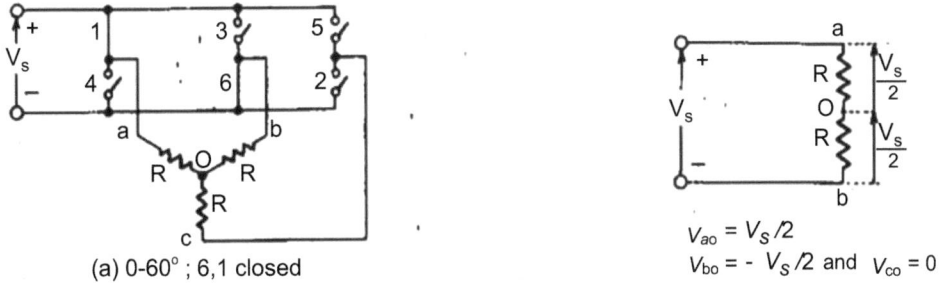

(a) 0-60° ; 6,1 closed

$V_{ao} = V_S/2$
$V_{bo} = -V_S/2$ and $V_{co} = 0$

Fig. (12). Equivalent circuit of step 1 of 120° conduction mode VSI.

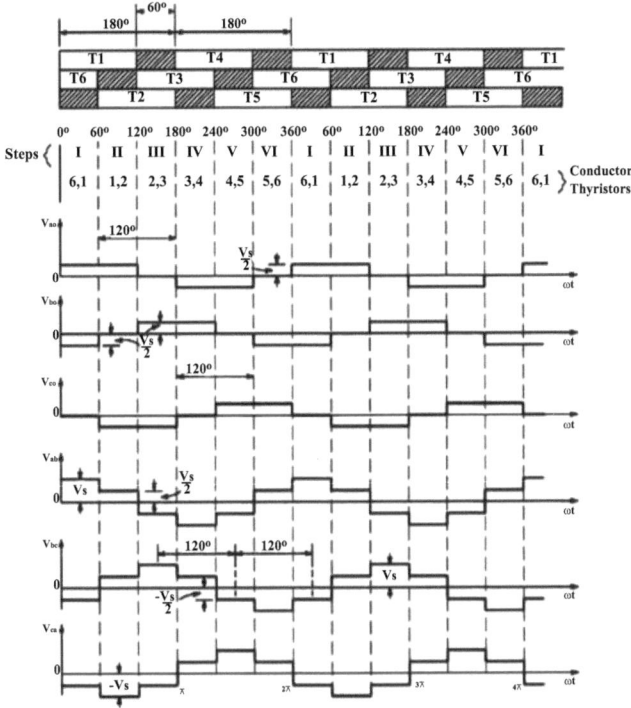

Fig. (13). Waveforms with 120° conduction mode VSI.

The line voltages v_{ab}, v_{bc} and v_{ca} may be obtained by using Eq. (**16-18**).

It is evident from Fig. (**13**) that line voltages have 6 steps per cycle, whereas phase voltages have one positive and one negative half-cycle per cycle. The function is to maintain the current flow during the reactive load conditions.

On comparing the two modes of conduction, we observe that in the 180° conduction mode, the switches on one leg are fired one after the other without any gap. Whereas a switch may take a small delay time to turn off after withdrawing the gate pulse. In such a case, the switch that has been fired comes in the forward conduction mode, but the outgoing switching has still not gone to forward blocking mode; a short circuit may be experienced by the DC source. This difficulty can be overcome by using 120° conduction mode, where there is a gap of 60° between the firing of two switches in the same leg. In 60° interval, the outgoing switch enters the forward blocking mode, and a short circuit through a DC source may be avoided.

The inverter phase voltage and line voltages may be given by Fourier series Eqs. (**19** and **20**).

$$V_{a0} = \frac{2\sqrt{3}}{\pi} V_s \left[\sin \omega t + \frac{1}{5} \sin 5\omega t + \frac{1}{7} \sin 7\omega t \right] \tag{19}$$

$$V_{ab} = \frac{2\sqrt{3}}{\pi} V_s \left[\sin \omega t - \frac{1}{5} \sin 5\omega t - \frac{1}{7} \sin 7\omega t + \frac{1}{11} \sin 11\omega t + \frac{1}{13} \sin 13\omega t \dots \right] \tag{20}$$

The root mean square value of the phase voltage may be given by Eq. (**21**).

$$V_{rms} = \frac{\sqrt{2}}{\pi} V_s \tag{21}$$

Current Source Inverter Control

The schematic diagram of the current source inverter control of the induction motor drive is shown in Fig. **14(a)**. In the given schematic diagram, the diodes and capacitors are used as a part of the commutation circuit of SCRs T_1-T_6. The SCRs are numbered in the sequence they are triggered with a phase difference of 60°. Fig. **14(b)** shows the waveform of the output current. Because of the presence of a large inductor in series with the DC source, the converter behaves like a current source. The fundamental component of the phase current may be given by Eq. (**22**).

$$I_1 = \frac{\sqrt{6}}{\pi} I_d \tag{22}$$

For torque control of an induction motor drive, we need a variable current that can be obtained by a variable power supply. If the source is DC, a variable supply may be obtained with the help of a chopper inserted between the DC supply and the inverter. If the supply is AC, variable DC is obtained by inserting a phase-controlled rectifier between the AC supply and the inverter.

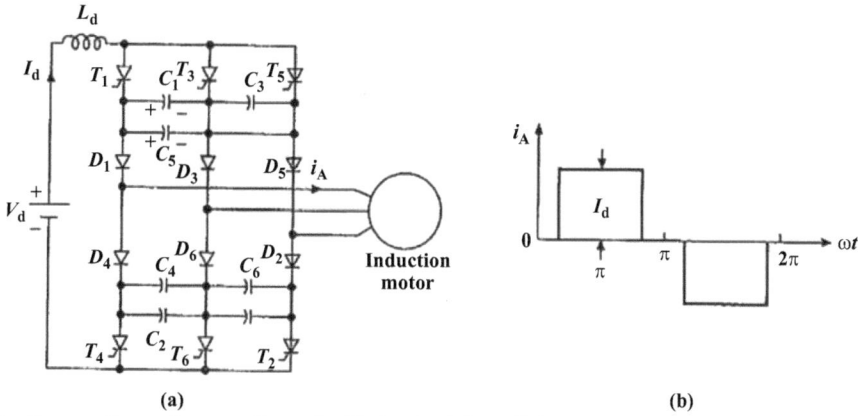

Fig. (14). Current Source Inverter Control of Induction Motor Drive.

The major drawback associated with the use of CSI is its low reliability. In VSI, if the commutation scheme fails, it will cause a short circuit of the DC supply, giving rise to the current rise to a dangerously high value. In order to protect devices against such threats, expensive high-speed semiconductor fuses are required. Whereas in the case of CSI, the presence of large inductors prevents the short circuit of the DC source due to commutation failure. Hence, less expensive HRC fuses work well with them.

It is evident from Fig. (**14b**) that the motor current rises and falls very rapidly. Such rapid change of current through the leakage inductance of the motor results in large voltage spiles. To overcome this problem, motors with low leakage inductance and commutation circuits with high capacitance are required. Hence, CSI drives are expensive, heavy, and voluminous.

Pulse Width Modulation (PWM)

Pulse Width Modulation is a technique by virtue of variable pulses with discrete timing that may be generated in accordance with the amplitude of the desired analog input signal. The PWM circuits are designed with the help of power electronic switches. These switches are switched on and off in accordance with the designed gating strategy by a desired input signal. The duration for which the signal is high is referred to as "On time". The duty cycle refers to the percentage of time the signal is "on" (active) during each period of the waveform. This on-off switching creates an average output that can be used to drive a device. Fig. (**15**) demonstrates a PWM signal whose average voltage follows the shape and frequency of the sine wave and is controlled by the switching frequency of the PWM.

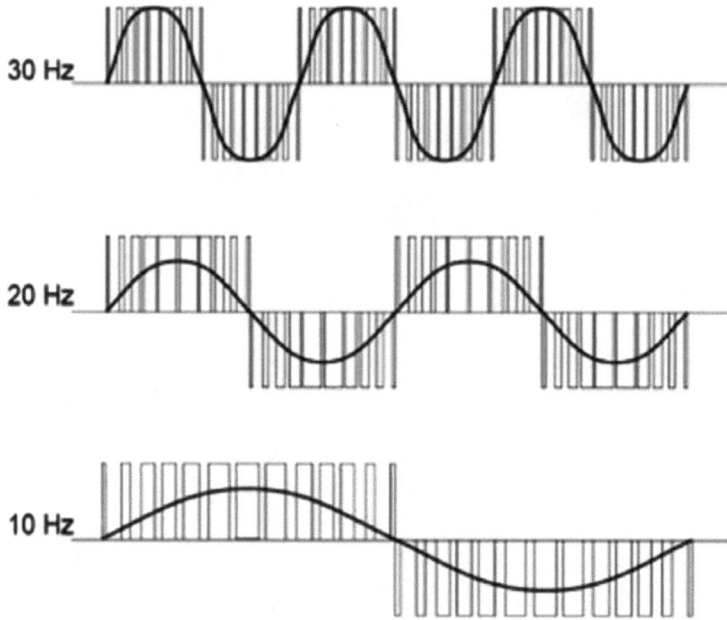

Fig. (15). A PWM signal for various frequencies.

The pulse width modulation may be achieved by three different methods: 1) Sinusoidal PWM Technique, 2) Space Vector PWM Technique, and 3) Hysteresis PWM Technique. The Space Vector PWM technique is an essential modulation strategy in modern power electronic converters, particularly for applications like electric vehicles. Its ability to produce high-quality AC output with minimal harmonic distortion and efficient use of the DC bus makes it ideal for driving the performance of inverters in EVs. As a result, SVPWM not only enhances the overall efficiency of the inverter but also improves the performance and longevity of the electric motor, making it the preferred choice in EV power electronics.

Space Vector Pulse Width Modulation (SVPWM)

The Space Vector PWM (SVPWM) technique is used to generate the gating signal (PWM signal) for the switching of IGBT or MOSFET in accordance with the desired output. The advantages of SVPWM are low switching losses and higher inverter efficiency. With the help of the SVPWM technique, distortion in the output alternating current of the inverter is reduced. To generate a PWM signal with the SVPWM technique, the armature plane is divided into 6 planes, $60°$ each. The six active vectors are represented by $(V_1\text{-}V_6)$ and correspond to the six possible active states of the inverter's three switches. These vectors represent the voltages applied to the three-phase motor. The switching sequences are generated in each sector, as shown in Fig. (**16**). These vectors are $V_1(100), V_2(110)$, $V_3(010)$, $V_4(011)$, $V_5(001)$, $V_6(101)$. The binary codes indicate which switches in the inverter are turned on or off. "1" means the switch is on, and "0" means the switch is off. The two null vectors $V_0(000)$ and $V_7(111)$ correspond to situations where no voltage is applied to the motor (all switches off or all switches on). The space vector diagram is divided into six sectors, each corresponding to a 60° region of the circle. The reference vector V_{ref} will lie within one of these sectors. To generate the switching sequence for the inverter, the angle θ of the reference vector V_ref must be determined for the sector in which it lies. The switching times T_1, T_2 and T_0 are the durations for which the active vectors V_1, V_2 and V_0, V_7 are applied to the inverter, respectively.

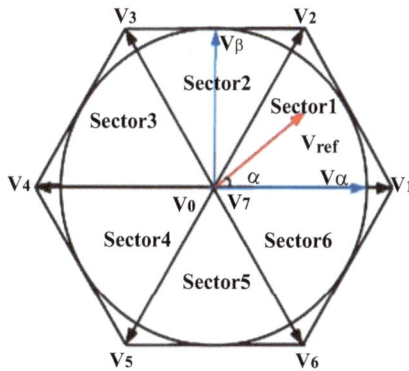

Fig. (16). SVPWM switching technique.

In Sector 1, the reference vector V_{ref} is formed using active vectors V_1, and V_2, with the time intervals for these vectors being T_1 and T_2, respectively. The null vector T_0, or T_7 is used to balance the reference voltage with the corresponding time interval T_0, as shown in Fig. (**17**). The total period T is the sum of these intervals, ensuring that the PWM period is maintained.

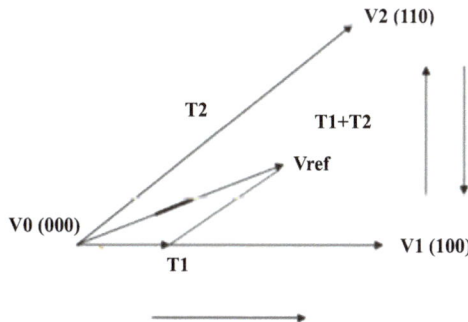

Fig. (17). Switching time scheming in SVPWM.

$$T = T_1 + T_2 + T_0 \tag{23}$$

To calculate the time intervals accurately, the angle of the reference vector within the sector must be known, and the corresponding equations for T_1, T_2 and T_0 are used. These calculations ensure the reference vector is synthesized correctly, with minimal harmonic distortion and efficient use of the DC voltage.

Review of Power Electronics Converters Used in Existing Electrical Vehicles

In the former part of this chapter, basic concepts of power electronic converters have been discussed to lay the foundation for the understanding of the working of various converters. In this section, we will review various converters that are being used in existing electric vehicles. In the subsequent part, we will discuss about existing bidirectional DC-DC converter topology with a detailed review, comparison, and applications.

The universal bidirectional DC-DC converter shown in Fig. (**18**) operates in two modes operation: 1) Boost mode and 2) Buck mode with non-inverting output. The details of various operating modes are demonstrated in Table **1**.

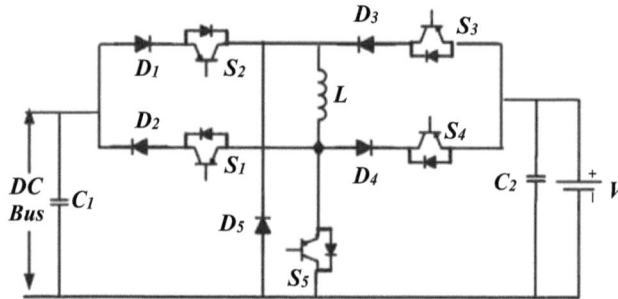

Fig. (18). Universal bidirectional DC-DC- converter [11].

Table 1. Table-I Operating Modes of Universal Bi-directional DC-DC Converter.

Direction	Mode	S_1	S_2	S_3	S_4	S_5
V_{DC} to V_1	Boost	Closed	Open	Open	Open	PWM
V_{DC} to V_1	Buck	PWM	Open	Open	Closed	Open
V_1 to V_{DC}	Boost	Open	Closed	Closed	Open	PWM
V_1 to V_{DC}	Buck	Open	Closed	PWM	Open	Open

In modern electric vehicles, various types of bidirectional converters other than universal bidirectional DC-DC converters are being used. For bidirectional power flow, electric vehicles use various single/multi-input, multistage, and multiphase isolated/non-isolated converters. A bidirectional buck-boost converter for EV applications shown in Fig. **19(a)** works in both buck and boost mode as per the switching regime. The high ripples in the current of this converter damage the battery, so a modified buck-boost converter is shown in Fig. **19(b)**, which reduces the stress across the switch and hence improves the conversion efficiency. Another topology of the buck-boost converter, which has the ability to maintain the State of Charge (Soc) of the battery and recover the energy dissipated during the braking of the electric motor, is the cascaded bidirectional buck-boost converter shown in Fig. **19(c)**. However, the number of active components in this converter makes it a bit complex and costly.

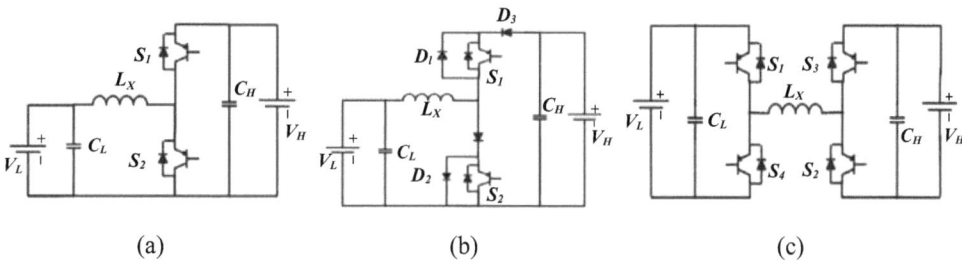

Fig. (19). Single input bidirectional DC-DC converters (**a**) Buck-Boost Converter, (**b**) Improved Buck-Boost Converter, and (**c**) Full-Bridge converter [11].

Other converters that are used in modern electric vehicles are bidirectional, CUK, and SEPIC converters with Luo converters, as shown in Fig. 20(**a and b**), respectively. These converters also operate in two modes of operation, *i.e.*, buck and boost operation. CUK converter brings in the advantage of low current ripple. The SEPIC converter operates in boost mode whereas the Luo converter operates in buck mode, but it has the drawback of discontinuous current at output.

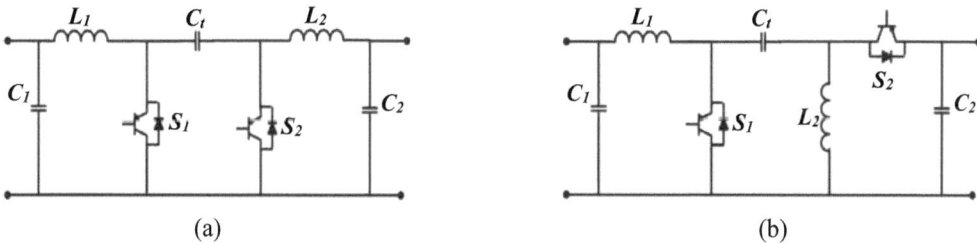

Fig. (20). Single input bidirectional DC-DC converters (**a**) Bidirectional CUK converter (**b**) Bidirectional SEPIC converter with Luo converter [11].

The converters discussed above are single-input converters. Modern electric vehicles use various sources of energy like electric batteries, fuel cells, ultracapacitors, *etc.* Each source of energy has its own dynamics. So, modern EVs use multi-input bidirectional converters also. Fig. (**21**) shows an existing non-isolated bidirectional DC-DC converter with multiple inputs. The main advantage of using a multi-input converter, especially in power electronics, lies in its ability to handle multiple input sources and convert them into a usable output voltage without a transformer.

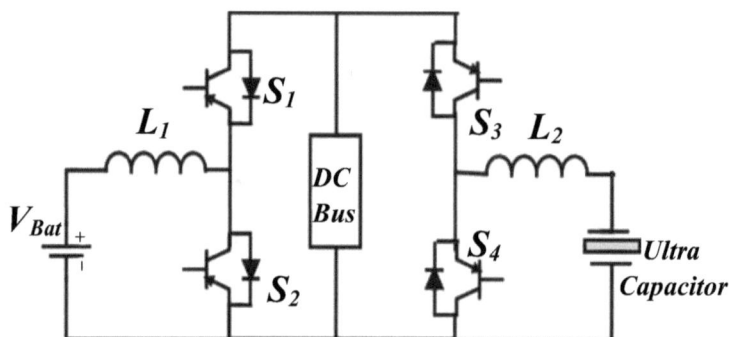

Fig. (21). Multi-input non-isolated Buck-Boost converter [11].

In a multi-input converter, if multiple sources are being combined to feed into the same DC link, the sum of the input voltages from these sources must be lower than the DC link voltage. This is because the converter is designed to manage and regulate the voltage in such a way that it does not exceed the DC link's voltage capacity. If the input voltages exceed this limit, it can lead to inefficiencies or even damage to the system.

The efficiency of the converter is optimized when the power from all input sources flows in the same direction. If one or more sources are producing power in the opposite direction (*e.g.*, one source is discharging while another is charging), the converter's efficiency will decrease due to the additional complexity in managing bi-directional power flow and potential losses in the power conversion stages.

CASE STUDY

Design and Development of Bidirectional Charger for Electric Vehicle

The design and development of bidirectional chargers stand at the forefront of innovations in Electric Vehicle (EV) technology, offering a transformative solution for efficient energy management and grid integration. This abstract presents a comprehensive overview of the design considerations, technological advancements, and potential applications of bidirectional chargers, highlighting their pivotal role in shaping the future of sustainable transportation and energy systems.

The on-board system charging utilizes a DC-DC step-down converter, commonly known as a buck converter, to provide the necessary power to charge the battery. This converter regulates the power output. Sensor current measures the true current output from the buck inverter and sends this information back to the processor. The controller works by calculating the subtracting, or error, between the true current and the desired (reference) current. It then generates a suitable signal for the Pulse Width Modulator (PWM). This PWM signal controls the switching mechanism of the buck converter, determining how much power is supplied to the battery. The PID (Proportional-Integral-Derivative) controller parameters are manually fine-tuned using a trial-and-error method to optimize the system's performance [2 - 10].

PID controllers are commonly used in charger design, especially in applications where precise and stable control of charging parameters is required.

MATLAB Simulation and Results:

SYSTEM PARAMETERS FOR THE THREE-PHASE BIDIRECTIONAL EV CHARGER

Parameter Value:

Phase voltage, Vs - **230Vrms**

Line frequency, fline - **50Hz**

Line inductance, Lg - **10mH**

Line internal resistance, Rg - **0.5Ω**

Converter side filter inductance, Li -**1.6mH**

Grid side filter inductance, Lgrid - **1mH**

Filter capacitance, Cf - **300mF**

Filter damping resistance, Rd - **0.5Ω**

DC link capacitance, C0 - **2mF**

DC link voltage, Vdc - **500V**

Switching frequency for AC/DC PWM converter, fsw, ac - **5 kHz**

Inductance of DC/DC converter, L - **250µH**

Internal resistance of inductance in DC/DC converter, RL - **10mΩ**

On state resistance of transistors in DC/DC converter, Rds - **8mΩ**

Rated power, Pout - **5kW**

Output battery voltage, V- **248 V**

Current I- **23.1 A**

Switching frequency for DC/DC converter, fsw, dc - **100 kHz**

AC-DC / DC-AC Converter

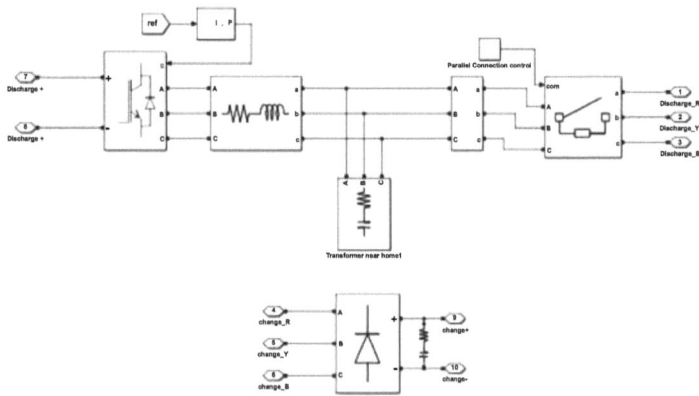

AC-DC / DC-AC Converter:

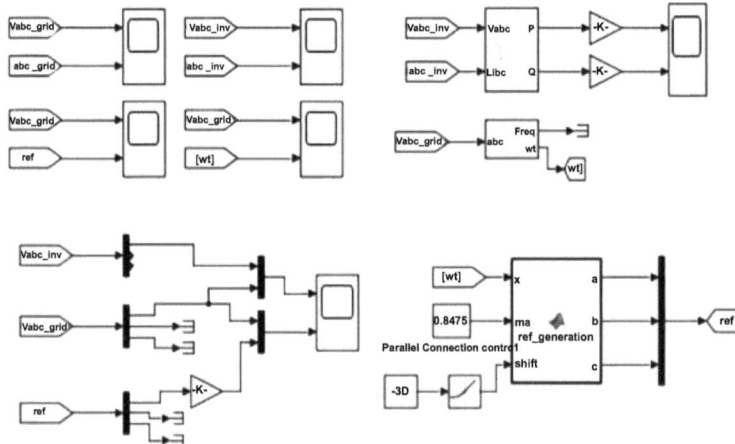

Bidirectional Charger for Electric Vehicle

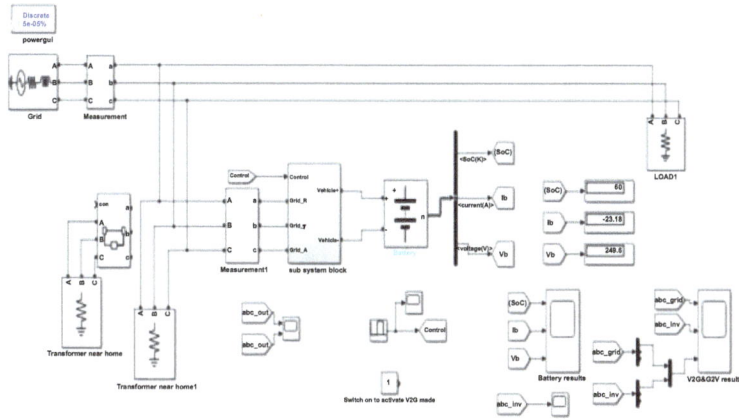

Simulation Results

Vabc grid and Iabc grid

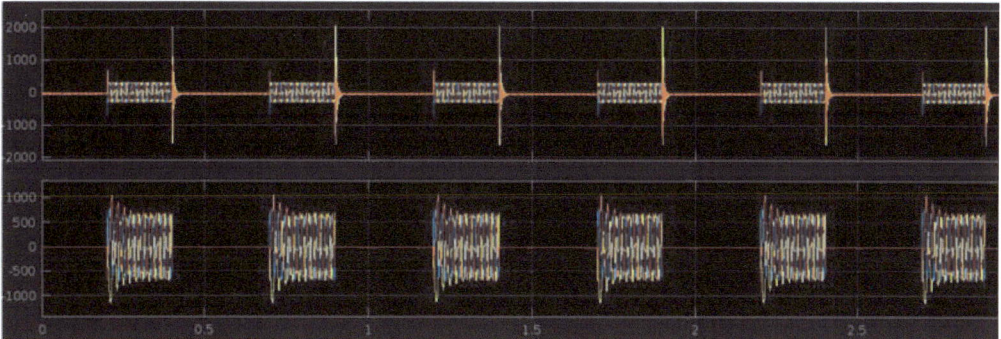

Vabc inv and Iabc inv

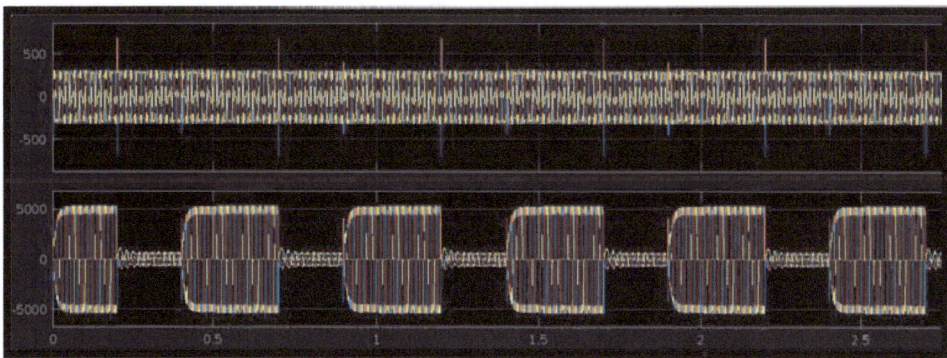

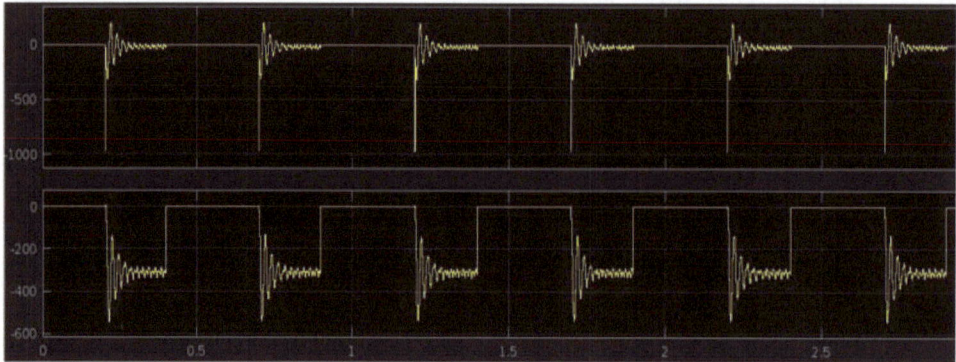

V2G and G2V Result

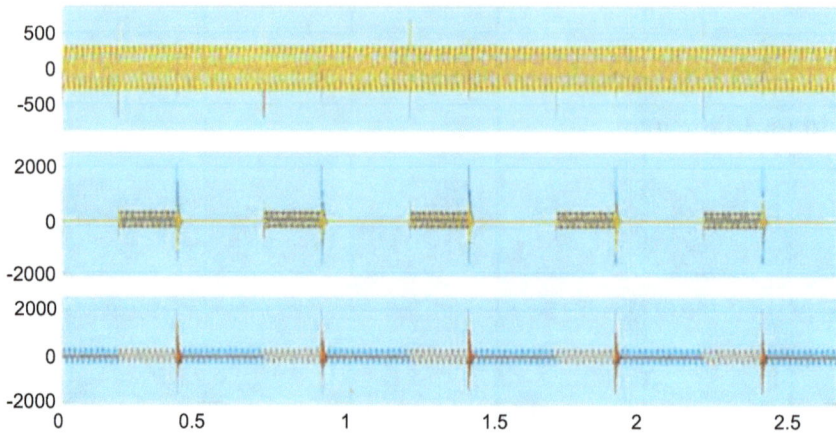

In this study, a three-phase grid-connected bidirectional EV charger model is proposed, designed, and simulated to facilitate vehicle battery charging in G2V mode and provide reactive power support or reverse power to the grid in V2G mode. The system comprises two stages: an AC/DC PWM converter for converting AC grid voltage to DC link voltage and a synchronous DC/DC converter capable of operating as a buck or boost converter. An LCL filter is included on the grid side to suppress unwanted harmonics generated by switching operations. Design considerations for both the AC/DC and DC/DC stages are discussed, focusing on component selection and the development of control algorithms to form two-loop control systems. The proposed bidirectional EV charger system is then implemented with these control algorithms in MATLAB/Simulink. The model is designed to operate in inverter mode as well as the traditional G2V mode. Simulations are conducted to evaluate the closed-loop performance and harmonic distortion of the entire system. The results show that while the bidirectional charger model operates stably under various conditions, it may exhibit a line current THD value not exceeding 5% in inverter mode, which complies with grid connection standards.

CONCLUSION

The chapter deals with the fundamentals of various semiconductor devices that are employed in power electronic converters used for electric vehicles. The semiconductor devices have been compared to give the reader an insight into the suitability of a particular semiconductor device for a specific application. There is adequate coverage of various DC-DC and DC-AC converters, along with their mathematical modeling and waveforms for turning the electrical energy received from the EV battery suitable for the electric drive.

A case study of the design and development of bidirectional chargers for electric vehicles has been presented. This study presents a model of a three-phase grid-connected bidirectional EV charger, designed and simulated to facilitate vehicle battery charging in G2V mode and provide reactive or reverse power support to the grid in V2G mode. The system comprises two stages: an AC/DC PWM converter for converting AC grid voltage to DC link voltage and a synchronous DC/DC converter capable of operating as a buck or boost converter. An LCL filter on the grid side is integrated to suppress harmonics generated during switching operations. For a better understanding of the reader, design considerations for both AC/DC and DC/DC stages are discussed, focusing on component selection and the development of control algorithms for forming two-loop control systems.

AUTHOR'S CONTRIBUTION

The author herself was involved in the study conception and design, data collection, analysis and interpretation of results, and chapter preparation.

REFERENCES

[1]   G. K. Dubey, *Fundamentals of Electrical Drives*, 2nd ed. New Delhi, India: Narosa Publishing House, 2001.

[2]   P. S. Bimbhra, *Power Electronics*, 3rd ed. Delhi, India: Khanna Publishers, 1999.

[3]   A. Emadi, *Advanced Electric Drive Vehicles*. Boca Raton, FL, USA: Taylor & Francis, an imprint of CRC Press, 2015.

[4]   A. Khaligh and M. D'Antonio, "Global trends in high-power on-board chargers for electric vehicles," *IEEE Transactions on Vehicular Technology*, vol. 68, no. 4, pp. 3306–3324, Apr. 201910.1109/TVT.2019.2897050

[5]   "*BRUSA NLG513 Water*," Available from: http://www.brusa.biz/en/ products /charger /charger -400 - v/nlg513-water. html

[6] *"Chevy Volt Lear 3.3kW High Voltage Charger,"* Available from: http://media3.ev-tv. me/ Chevy Volt Lear Charger Operations. pdf

[7] H. Xiucheng, L. Zhengyang, L. Quango *et al.*, "Evaluation and Application of 600 V GaN HEMT in Cascade Structure," *Power Electronics*, IEEE Transactions on, vol. 29, no. 5, pp. 2453-2461, 2014..

[8] E. H. E. Bayoumi, "Design of three-phase LCL-filter for grid-connected PWM voltage source inverter using bacteria foraging optimization," in *Energy Systems*, Mar. 2016, pp. 192–1910.10.1007/978---662-49434-9_8

[9] A. Arancibia and K. Strunz, "Modeling of an electric vehicle charging station for fast DC charging," *IEEE International Electric Vehicle Conference, Greenville*, SC, USA, Mar. 4-8, 2012.10.1109/IEVC.2012.6183232

[10] G. B. Sahinler and G. Poyrazoglu, "V2G Applicable Electric Vehicle Chargers, Power Converters & Their Controllers: A Review," *2nd Global Power, Energy and Communication Conference (GPECOM)*, Ephesus, Izmir, Turkey, 20-23, 2020.. 10.1109/GPECOM49333.2020.9247870

[11] Pandav Kiran Maroti, Sanjeevikumar Padmanaban, Mahajan Sagar Bhaskar, Vigna K. Ramachandaramurthy, Frede Blaabjerg, "The state-of-the-art of power electronics converters configurations in electric vehicle technologies", *Power Electronic Devices and Components*, Vol 1, 2022.. 10.1016/j.pedc.2021.100001

CHAPTER 4

Field-Oriented Speed Control of BLDC Motor for Practical Drive Cycle

S. Karmakar[1] and **T.K. Saha**[1,*]

[1] *Department of Electrical Engineering, National Institute of Technology Durgapur, Durgapur, India*

Abstract: The widespread adoption of Electric Vehicles (EVs) relies on achieving high efficiency and precise motor control. Although Brushless DC (BLDC) motors offer advantages for EVs, traditional control methods struggle to deliver the desired performance. This chapter discusses the operation of BLDC and investigates the development and evaluation of a Field-Oriented Control (FOC) system that enables precise speed control of BLDC motors in an electric vehicle application. The developed FOC with necessary coding is provided for a clear understanding of the control. FOC offers superior control over more straightforward methods, allowing for independent torque and flux control, improving efficiency and dynamic response.

This research implemented a novel angle-based strategy within the FOC system. This approach controls the flux position of the motor using a constant 48V supply, significantly reducing switching losses compared to traditional PWM or PID control methods. Consequently, the system achieves a peak-to-peak speed ripple of less than 0.3 rpm and demonstrates improved efficiency. The machine dynamics, with the help of currents, fluxes, and changes in rotor position, are explained in this work.

A practical urban cycle is developed to test the proposed control topology. The successful operation of the vehicle with produced results highlights the effectiveness of the developed FOC system with the novel angle-based strategy in achieving precise speed control and improved efficiency for BLDC motors in EVs, contributing to the development of EVs with extended range and reduced environmental impact, paving the way for more sustainable transportation solutions.

Keywords: BLDC model, Back EMF, Developed torque, DC-AC inverter, Flux position estimation, Flux estimation, Hall effect sensing, Load variation, Position-based speed control, Practical drive cycle, Practical wheel RPM, Position sensor, Switching scheme of inverter, Speed tracking, Torque ripple.

---

* **Corresponding author T.K. Saha:** Department of Electrical Engineering, National Institute of Technology Durgapur, Durgapur, India; E-mail: tksaha.ee@nitdgp.ac.in

Nitesh Tiwari, Shekhar Yadav and Sabha Raj Arya (Eds.)

INTRODUCTION

Electric Vehicles (EVs) have emerged as a better alternative for a cleaner and more sustainable transportation future with a proper energy management policy. However, the widespread adoption of EVs hinges on their ability to deliver a compelling driving experience and achieve exceptional levels of efficiency. At the heart of this challenge lies the electric motor, the workhorse responsible for propelling the vehicle. Brushless DC (BLDC) motors have garnered significant attention for their unique blend of desirable characteristics among various electric motor technologies. BLDC motors boast high efficiency, compact size, robust construction, and excellent torque-to-weight ratios – all crucial attributes for powering EVs effectively [1 - 13].

Motors Used in EVs

The design currently, electric vehicles primarily rely on three main types of electric motors.

- AC Induction Motors: These motors offer a simple and robust design, making them a cost-effective choice for many EVs. The rotating magnetic field, produced by stator current in the stator windings, produces induced EMF to allow current in the rotor cage, generating torque. While AC induction motors are reliable and efficient, they typically offer less precise control than BLDC motors.
- Permanent Magnet Synchronous Motors (PMSMs): This category encompasses BLDC motors as a specific type. PMSMs utilize permanent magnet rotors and three-phase stationary windings on the stator. Like BLDC motors, PMSMs employ electronic control to regulate the current in the windings, creating a rotating magnetic field that interacts with the permanent magnets and generates torque. PMSMs, including BLDC motors, generally offer higher efficiency and superior controllability than AC induction motors. However, the presence of rare earth elements in the permanent magnets of some PMSMs can raise cost and sustainability concerns.
- DC Motors: These motors offer a simple design and high starting torque, making them suitable for low-speed electric vehicles such as neighborhood electric cars, golf carts, or industrial utility vehicles. However, DC motors generally have lower efficiency than AC induction motors and PMSMs, and brush wear can be a maintenance concern. Electric vehicle Charging facilities fall into two categories: slow and fast. Slow-charging systems, including Level-1 and Level-2 onboard charging configurations, are one of its types. Level-1 onboard systems typically charge one fully discharged battery for 8-10 hours. These systems are usually installed in residential areas and use power in the

range of 10 kW. On the other hand, Level-2 charging stations charge faster than Level-1 systems and are commonly found in public places, rated up to 20 kW.

Unlike brushed DC motors that utilize physical brushes for current commutation, BLDC motors employ permanent magnet rotors and stationary windings on the stator. The electronic controller orchestrates the switching sequence of these windings, generating a rotating magnetic field in the stator [14 - 16]. This rotating magnetic field interacts with the permanent magnets on the rotor, creating a force according to the Lorentz force principle. This force causes the rotor to spin, and by precisely controlling the sequence and timing of the current in the windings, the electronic controller dictates the speed and direction of the BLDC motor. This electronic control mechanism eliminates the friction and wear associated with brushes, leading to higher efficiency, longer lifespan, and smoother operation than traditional brushed DC motors.

Unleashing the full potential of BLDC motors in EVs necessitates implementing sophisticated control strategies. Traditional control methods, while functional, often need help to deliver the precise and efficient operation demanded by high-performance electric vehicles [17 - 25]. This is where Field-Oriented Control (FOC) steps in, revolutionizing the field of BLDC motor control.

BLDC Motors is considered very promising in modern drive technology. Their rapid gain in popularity increased different applications [26 - 30]. Some are automotive industry, consumer appliances, aerospace, industrial automation, and instrumentation.

Brushed DC Motors support the sub-kilowatt range drives and power generation for a long time. However, these applications were limited because of some control and material technology disadvantages. The recent development in integrating power electronics and digital control has allowed the small BLDC Motors to compete in price and performance.

A Brushless DC Motor is not similar to a Brushed DC Motor. The main difference is that the BLDC does not use brushes for commutation. Instead, the commutation is made unnecessary. In conventional Brushed DC Motors, the brushes make the rotor field almost fixed while the currents in the rotor windings change the direction. In contrast, the BLDC motor uses equivalent electronic commutation by shifting the relative position of the stator field concerning the rotor and thus eliminates the mechanically torn brushes.

CONSTRUCTION

The BLDC Motor operates as a synchronous motor, where the magnetic field generated by the stator revolves at the same frequency as the rotor. The mechanical commutator of the brushed DC motor is not required in this motor.

Three types of windings are there in BLDC Motors. Single-phase, two-phase, and three-phase stator windings are available. The three-phase stator winding is mainly used in the BLDC motors.

The cross-section of a BLDC Motor is presented in Fig. (**1**).

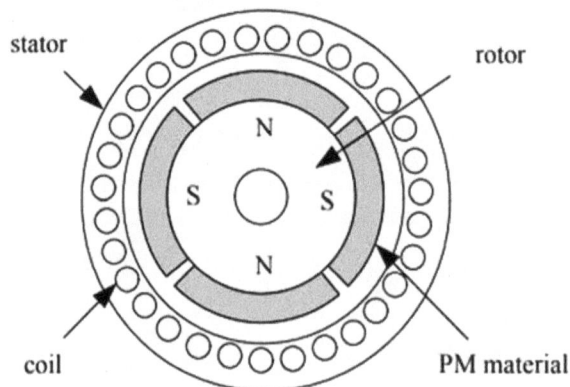

Fig. (1). Cross-sectional view of BLDC motor.

Stator

The design of the stator winding and the stator core of a BLDC Motor is similar to that of a squirrel cage induction motor. However, the winding in BLDC is slightly different from that of the traditional induction motor. It comprises stacked steel laminations with axially cut slots for winding.

Most BLDC motor stator windings are connected in a star or 'Y' fashion (without a neutral point). The stator windings are interconnected in trapezoidal and sinusoidal modes.

The back EMF is in the shape of a trapezoid (sinusoidal shape in the case of sinusoidal motors) in a trapezoidal motor. The natures of back emf developed in the BLDC motors are presented in Fig. (**2**).

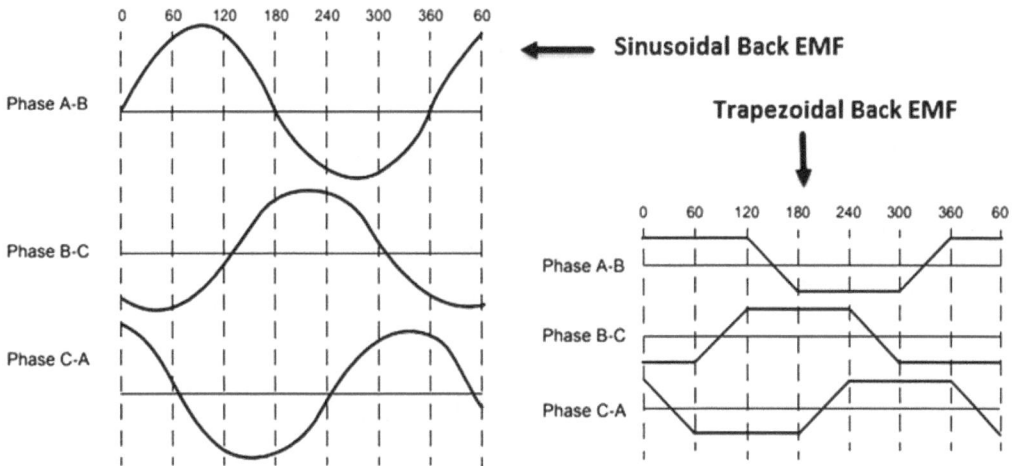

Fig. (2). Type of back emf in BLDC motor.

Rotor

The permanent magnet rotor of the BLDC Motor is usually made of rare earth alloy magnets like Samarium Cobalt (SmCo), Neodymium (Nd), and alloy of Neodymium, Ferrite, and Boron (NdFeB).

Position Sensors

Commutation is not required for BLDC motors. The windings of the stator are energized, following the position (*i.e.*, the North and South poles of the rotor) in a sequence. Accordingly, the position of the rotor is necessary for the controllers to generate gate pulses for the inverter, which are connected to the stator windings.

A position sensor is necessary to convert the position information to an electrical signal. Usually, a Hall sensor is embedded into the stator to sense the rotor's position. Presently, the exact requirements are also fulfilled by incremental encoders.

The output of the Hall sensor or the incremental encoder is decoded through proper programming. In the case of Hall sensors, there are three signals. In the case of incremental encoders, six signals are generated to produce precise information on the position of the rotor concerning one fixed point of the stator.

Rotary Encoders

For applications demanding exact speed control, rotary encoders can be employed as an alternative to Hall effect sensors for rotor position sensing in BLDC motors. Unlike Hall effect sensors, which provide a simple on/off signal indicating the presence of a magnetic field, encoders offer a more detailed digital output that encodes the angular position of the rotor. This digital output can be high resolution, allowing for meticulous determination of the rotor's position at any given time.

In the context of our BLDC motor speed control system, using an encoder with a high output frequency (2500 outputs per second in this case) translates to a significant advantage. The increased resolution of the position information enables the FOC algorithm to react to even the most minute changes in rotor position. This fine-grained control over rotor position ultimately contributes to superior speed control accuracy and dynamic response, crucial for electric vehicle applications where precise motor operation translates to efficient and smooth performance.

GENERAL CONTROL TECHNIQUES OF BLDC

Some commonly used control techniques of BLDC motors are as follows:

- Six-Step Commutation: This is a simple and widely used method for controlling BLDC motors. It relies on the sequence of the stator windings being switched based on the position of the rotor, typically determined by Hall effect sensors. Six-step commutation offers ease of implementation but can lead to lower efficiency and torque ripple than FOC due to its more straightforward approach.
- Block Commutation: This method builds upon the six-step commutation by incorporating information about the motor's back EMF (electromotive force) to improve torque control and reduce torque ripple. Block commutation balances simplicity and performance, making it suitable for applications where cost and complexity are considerations.
- Indirect Torque Control: This technique directly controls the motor's torque by manipulating the stator currents. It does not require precise rotor position information but may exhibit slower response times than FOC. Indirect torque control is often used in applications prioritizing simplicity and robustness.

The selection of the most suitable control technique depends on several factors, including:

- Desired performance: FOC offers the highest level of control and efficiency, but more straightforward techniques may be sufficient for applications with less stringent requirements.
- Cost and complexity: FOC typically requires more complex hardware and software than straightforward control methods.
- Sensor availability: Some techniques, like FOC, rely on position sensors (*e.g.*, Hall effect sensors) for accurate control, while others may not.

FOC CONTROL TECHNIQUE

FOC operates on a principle that fundamentally redefines how the motor is commanded. Unlike traditional methods that directly manipulate voltage and current, FOC adopts a more sophisticated approach. It leverages the concept of the motor's magnetic field orientation to achieve independent control of torque and flux. This nuanced control translates to a multitude of benefits for EV applications:

- Enhanced Efficiency: By enabling independent control of torque and flux, FOC optimizes the motor's operation in real time, minimizing energy losses and maximizing the utilization of electrical energy. This translates to a significant improvement in the vehicle's range and overall efficiency.
- Superior Speed Regulation: FOC offers unparalleled precision in controlling the BLDC motor's speed. This translates to smoother and more stable vehicle operation, ensuring a comfortable and predictable driving experience. Additionally, precise speed control is crucial in optimizing energy recovery during regenerative braking, enhancing the vehicle's efficiency.
- Improved Dynamic Response: The real-time control offered by FOC allows for a faster and more precise response to changes in torque demands. This translates to quicker acceleration, smoother gear changes (in multi-motor configurations), and enhanced handling characteristics, contributing to a more dynamic and responsive driving experience.

The general form of FOC demands the modeling of the machine in a rotating reference frame.

Normally, the stator voltage and flux equations are written in the stator axis, and rotor variables are in the rotor axis reference frames, respectively.

Now, let us introduce two more axes. Stator flux and rotor flux axes are presented in Fig. (**3**).

The stator and rotor fluxes are rotating at the speed of $\omega_{ms} = \dfrac{d\rho_{ms}}{dt}$ and $\omega_{mr} = \dfrac{d\rho_{mr}}{dt}$ with respect to stator and rotor axes, respectively.

Moreover, we can write the fluxes in polar form as:

$$\overline{\Psi_s} = \Psi_s e^{j\rho_{ms}} \quad \text{and}$$

$$\overline{\Psi_R} = \Psi_R e^{j\rho_{mr}}$$

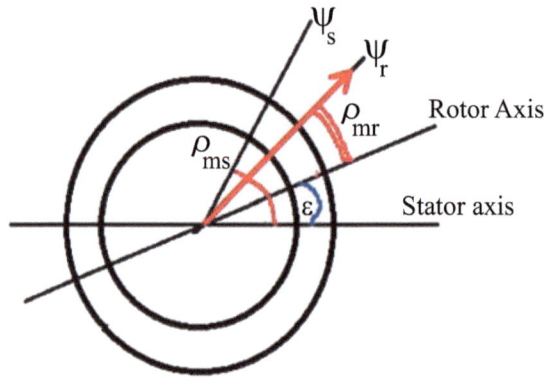

Fig. (3). Field-oriented reference axis.

A general control scheme in rotor flux-oriented control involves the transformation of the variables in the reference frame. The angle information is obtained with the help of the position encoder. One basic field-oriented control strategy is presented in Fig. (**4**).

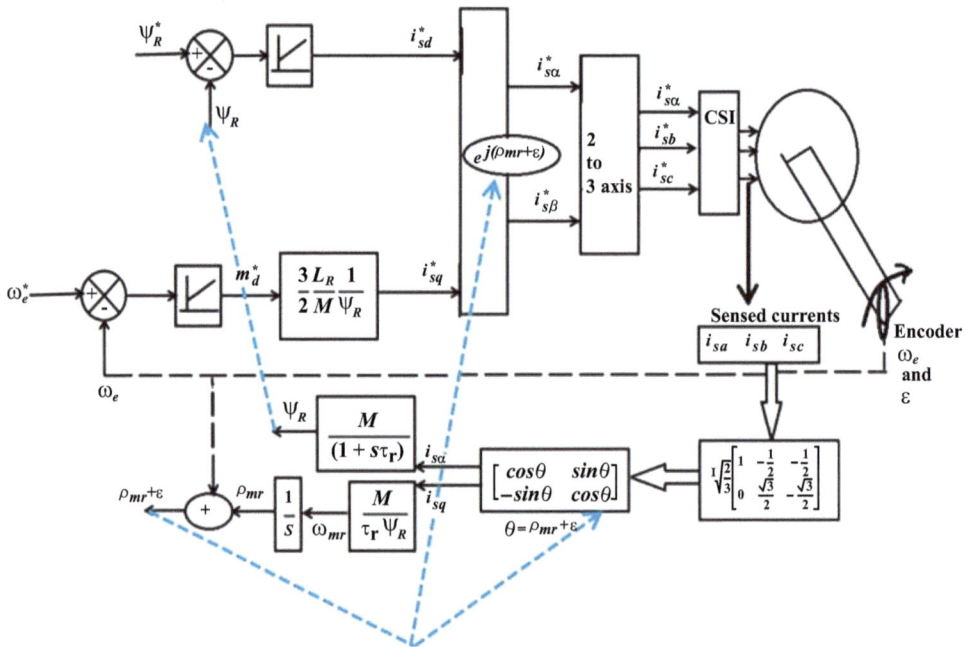

Fig. (4). Speed Control scheme utilizing the field-oriented reference axis.

This chapter delves into developing and evaluating an FOC system specifically designed for precise speed control of a BLDC motor intended for electric vehicle applications.

DRIVING BLDC MOTORS

The drive circuitry is the Electronic Speed Controller System (ESC). The complete circuit consists of a three-phase inverter. Another essential part is the central control unit (MCU) or the microprocessor-based digital control platform with PWM outputs. The PWM signals are buffered and isolated for the six switches of the three-phase inverter—the position feedback from the Hall sensors and some power supply-related components. The scheme is displayed in Fig. (5).

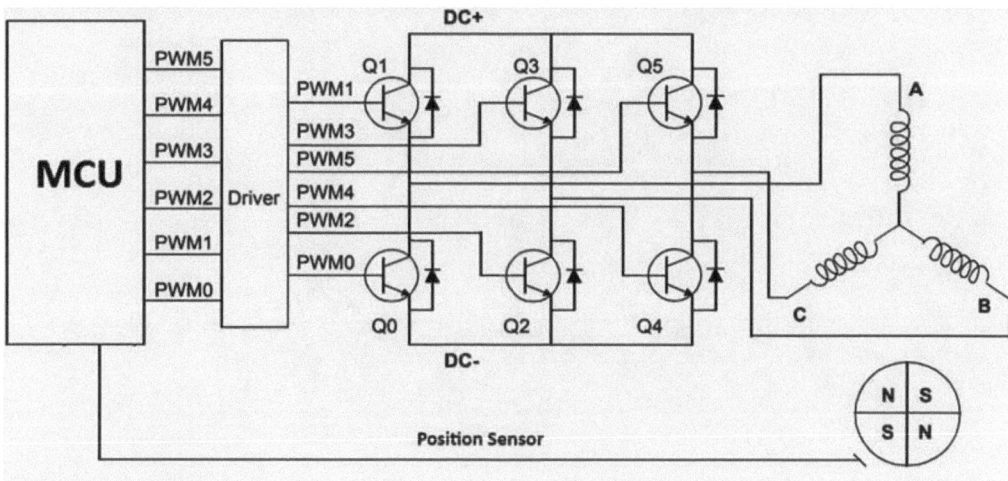

Fig. (5). Full Bridge Drive Circuit.

The 3-phase inverter is a critical component within the Field-Oriented Control (FOC) system for driving Brushless DC (BLDC) motors in electric vehicle applications. Its primary function is to convert a DC voltage source (typically the battery pack in an EV) into a three-phase AC voltage waveform that powers the BLDC motor. This AC voltage waveform is generated based on the control signals provided by the FOC algorithm, enabling precise control of the motor's speed and torque.

ANGLE-BASED CONTROL FOR A 3-PHASE 2-POLE BLDC MOTOR: A DETAILED EXPLANATION

This section delves into the design and operation of the Angle Based Control system implemented for a 3-phase, 2-pole Brushless DC (BLDC) motor in an electric vehicle application. This system is based on controlling the position of the stator magnetic field to produce a torque on the rotor, hence controlling the speed. We will use a constant DC voltage source for operation in this system. Therefore, we cannot control the magnitude of the voltage across the stator phases. This system is similar to field-oriented control systems. FOC is a powerful control strategy that enables precise speed and torque control in BLDC motors, improving efficiency and dynamic performance.

The electrical connection of your 3-phase BLDC motor plays a vital role in understanding the FOC strategy. The BLDC motor and its connections with the 3-phase inverter are shown in Figs. (6 and 7).

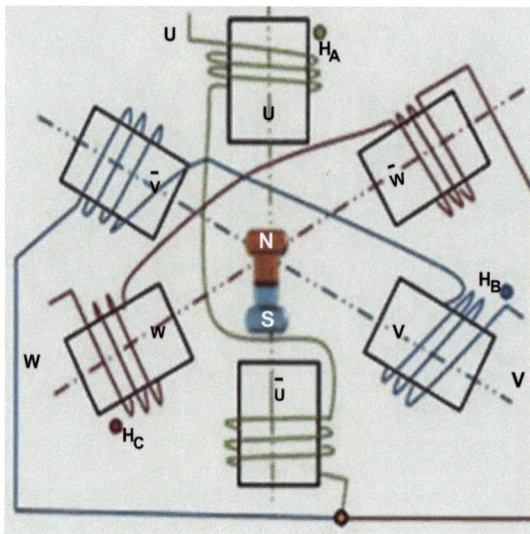

Fig. (6). Electrical connections of a BLDC motor.

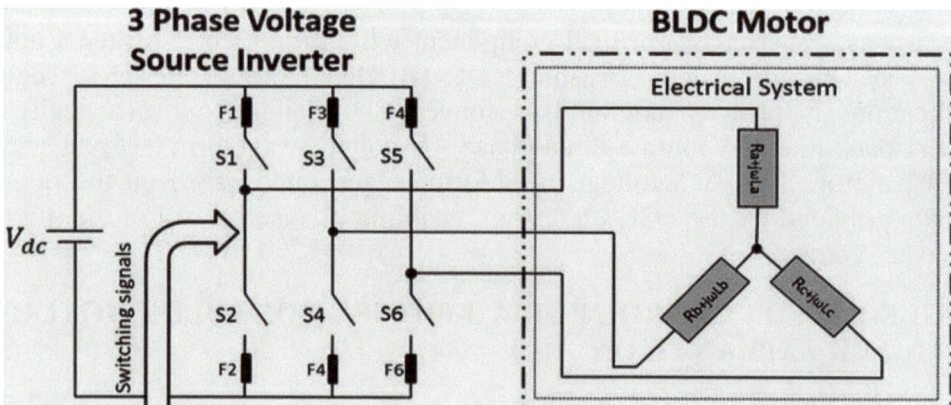

Fig. (7). BLDC with inverter.

Table **1** presents the available types and levels of charging as reported by K. Zhou *et al.* [6].

Table 1. Electric vehicle charging types and levels.

Charging Type	Charging Location	Specifications			Charging time (Battery Capacity)	Criterion
		Voltage/V	Current/A	Power/kW		
Level 1	On-board	120/230	12-16	1.44-1.92	11-36 h (16-50 kWh)	International Electrotechnical Commission (IEC)
Level 2	On-board	208/240	15-80	3.1-19.2	2-6 h (16-30 kWh)	
Level 3 (Fast)	Off-board	300-600	≤ 400	50-350	≤ 30 min (20-50 kWh)	
Ultra-Fast	Off-board	> 800	> 400	≥ 400	≈ 10 min (20-50 kWh)	

Since we are using a DC voltage source, the possible combinations of positive and negative voltage applied to each phase create six distinct magnetic field vectors in the stator. These vectors are spaced 60 electrical degrees apart, effectively dividing the 360-degree rotation of the motor into six sectors. Now, positioning these field vectors in their desired position can result in force in a positive direction, *i.e.*, acceleration, or in a negative direction, *i.e.*, deceleration. By using this concept accurately, we can control the speed of the BLDC motor. Different angles and switching of the inverters are portrayed in Fig. (**8**).

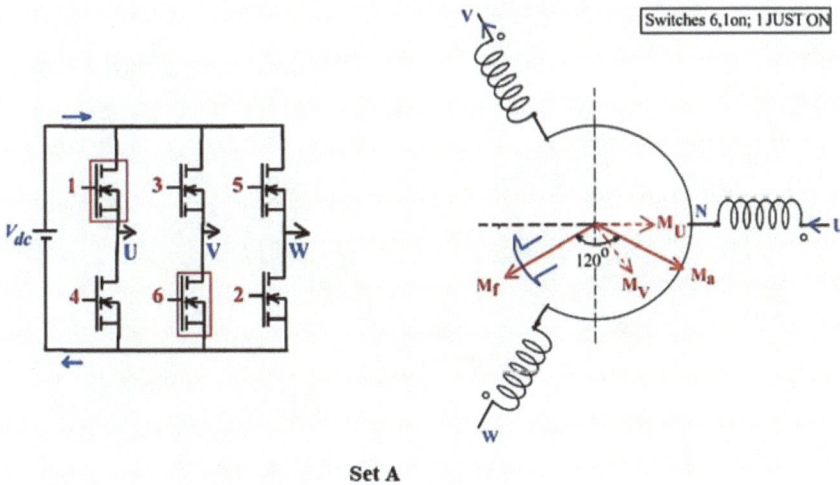

Set A

(Fig. 8) contd.....

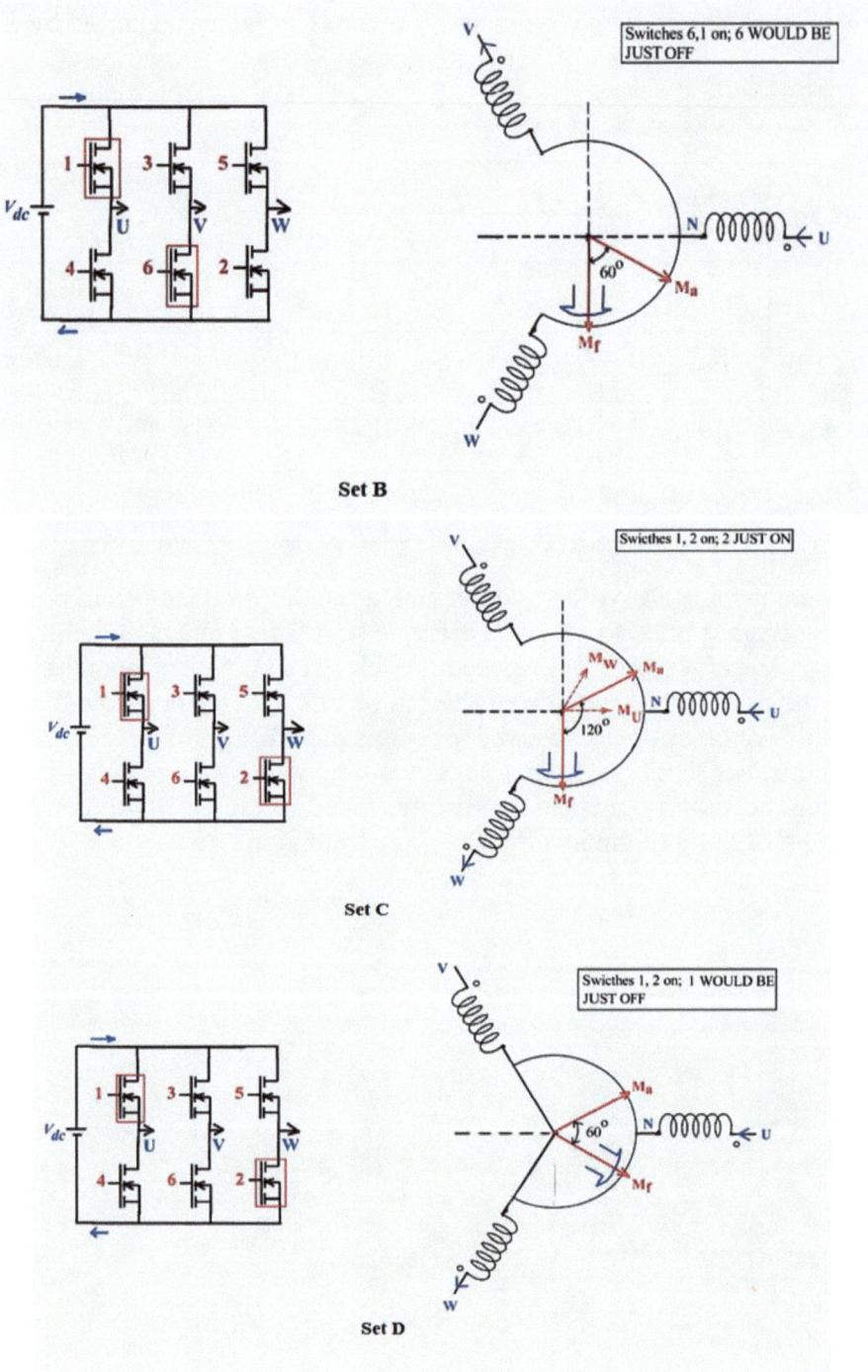

Switches 6,1 on; 6 WOULD BE JUST OFF

Set B

Swicthes 1, 2 on; 2 JUST ON

Set C

Swicthes 1, 2 on; 1 WOULD BE JUST OFF

Set D

(Fig. 8) contd.....

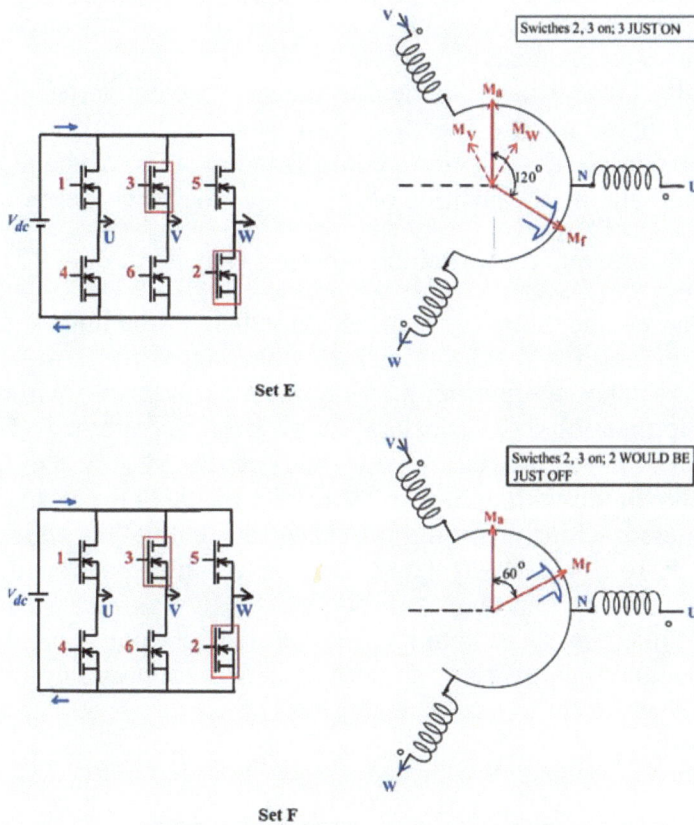

Fig. (8). Set A-F for different switching related to the position of Rotor.

ANGLE-BASED CONTROL: CORE REQUIREMENTS

This angle-based control system employs a mathematical approach to control the BLDC motor. Here is a breakdown of the key steps involved:

- Position Estimation: We aim to compare and check the speed error; concerning this speed error, we place the motor in accelerating mode and deaccelerating mode. These modes are accomplished by placing the stator magnetic field and the rotor magnetic field phase difference within a specific range, which is decided with the help of torque-angle characteristics. To accomplish this angle-based positioning, a rotary encoder is a must. The rotary encoder can provide the exact position of the rotor since the rotor magnetic field position is fixed concerning the rotor; we can tell the rotor magnetic field position.
- Control Signal Generation: The BLDC motor is split into six equal sectors. Once the angle concerning which the phases will be excited is decided, this angle is

checked to determine which sector of the BLDC motor this angle lies on; the respective phases are excited.

- Switching Pulse Generation: The decided sectors are converted into switching signals (gate pulses) for the inverter's transistors. By adjusting the timing of these pulses, the angle-based system controls the position of the magnetic field, ultimately manipulating the position of the stator's magnetic field vectors.

A sample code to generate the switching pulses is provided in Fig. (**21**).

In this ABS strategy, the motor is controlled to remain in the highest torque region so that the acceleration is maximum till it catches up with the reference speed. The controller switches to open-loop mode once it catches up with the required speed. In EV applications, the acceleration is generally gradual. To efficiently maintain the desired speed during regular rotation, the ABS system transitions to an open-loop-like mode with a 30-rpm hysteresis band. This selection minimizes computational load while ensuring proper phase excitation through periodic updates. The 30-rpm hysteresis band acts as a safe speed gap, chosen by considering the motor's parameters through extensive simulations. This buffer zone prevents unnecessary switching between acceleration and braking due to minor speed fluctuations, resulting in smoother operation and optimized energy consumption.

The strategy can be implemented through a code provided in Fig. (**22**).

DIFFERENT MODES IN ANGLE-BASED STRATEGY

This angle-based control system employs a mathematical approach to control the BLDC motor. Here is a breakdown of the key steps involved:

Accelerating Mode

In accelerating mode, the torque must lie in the positive region so that the motor's speed keeps increasing continuously. The process is as follows:

- Continuous Position Calculation: The ABS system continuously estimates the angular position of the rotor concerning the reference speed command. This estimation can be achieved using the feedback signal from the rotary encoder (in a natural system) or through an estimator in our simulation.
- Positive Torque Region Control: The ABS system compares the reference and measured speeds; if the speed is too low, the motor operates in acceleration mode. This is done by maintaining the phase difference between the stator and rotor magnetic fields within the positive torque region (180 degrees to 0 degrees); the controller ensures that the motor experiences positive torque for

acceleration.

- Optimizing Torque Range: While the maximum torque occurs at an 80-degree phase difference, our ABS system targets a range between 120 and 60 degrees for acceleration. This selection offers a balance between achieving good torque and minimizing current consumption. Operating at the peak torque point (80 degrees) requires higher currents, which can lead to increased motor losses and heating. By targeting the 120-60 degree range for acceleration, the ABS system achieves sufficient torque for adequate acceleration while maintaining good efficiency.

The code for the above scenario is shown below:

```
elseif(Ref_Speed3>actual_speed)
    y = Actual_angle + 120;
```

Braking Mode

The ABS system utilizes a similar principle for braking applications but operates in the negative torque region. The basic concept remains the same: the ABS system maintains the phase difference between the stator and rotor fields within a specific range to induce a braking torque. However, in this case, the targeted range would be between 240 and 300 degrees in the negative torque region of the torque-angle characteristic curve.

The torque-angle curve for the range 180-360 degrees is the mirror image of the curve from 0-180 degrees about the X-axis.

- Negative Torque Region Control: The ABS system adjusts the switching sequence of the inverter to create a stator magnetic field vector that opposes the rotor's permanent magnet field. This creates a force that acts to slow down the motor shaft.
- Regenerative Braking: The motor acts as a generator during braking. The kinetic energy of the rotating shaft is converted into electrical energy, which can be fed back to the battery pack (in a natural system) or dissipated through resistors in our simulation setup.

The code for the same is shown:

```
if(actual_speed> Ref_Speed2)
    y = Actual_angle-120;
```

Reaching Steady State: Transition from Acceleration

Once the FOC system successfully accelerates the BLDC motor to the desired reference speed, a smooth transition occurs to maintain that speed efficiently. This reduces the overshoot. In this steady-state operation, the control strategy deviates from the ABS used for acceleration.

During regular rotation, the ABS system can operate in a manner akin to an open-loop system. Here is the critical difference: while an accurate open-loop system will not consider the actual motor position, your ABS system still receives feedback on motor current. However, it primarily focuses on maintaining a constant voltage pattern to the motor phases based on the reference speed. This simplifies the control logic and reduces the computational burden.

However, this open-loop-like operation does not imply a complete disregard for the motor's position. Using the angle-based strategy, the ABS system still ensures proper phase excitation by periodically updating the stator field based on the reference speed. This update refreshes the alignment between the stator and rotor fields, preventing the motor from entering the negative torque region and experiencing unwanted deceleration.

The code is shown below:

```
elseif(actual_speed>Ref_Speed)
    y = ref_angle;
```

Angle-Based Strategy Benefits

By maintaining this buffer, smoother operation and optimized energy consumption are achieved, enhancing overall system performance.

- Precise Speed Control: FOC allows for independent control of the motor's torque and speed, enabling precise regulation of the motor's behavior based on the desired operating conditions.
- Improved Efficiency: ABS optimizes the motor's efficiency since it only requires 12 switching to complete one revolution.
- Enhanced Dynamic Performance: The ability to rapidly adjust the torque and speed allows for improved acceleration and deceleration characteristics, leading to a more responsive driving experience (in the case of an electric vehicle application).

IMPLEMENTATION OF FOC IN SIMULATION ENVIRONMENT

Having established the theoretical underpinnings of the FOC system, let's delve into the practical realm by examining the results obtained from the designed BLDC model.

The scheme of the BLDC drive is presented in Fig. (**9**).

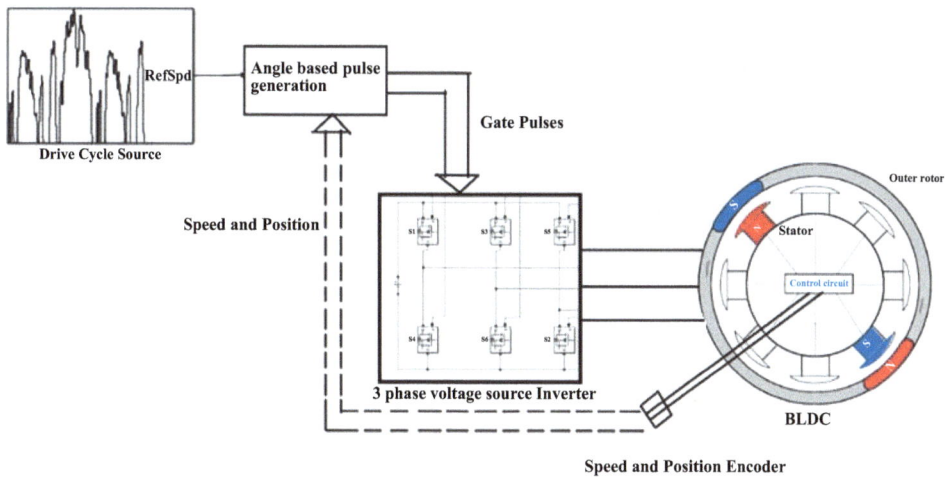

Fig. (9). The scheme of the BLDC drive system.

The simulation model is run with a drive cycle obtained from a practical Indian automobile company.

The complete model consists of:

- Reference Speed Input: This block represents the source of the desired speed profile for the motor, such as the UDC.
- FOC Algorithm Blocks: These blocks encapsulate the core functionalities of the FOC system, including reference frame transformations, control signal generation, and PWM generation.
- BLDC Motor Model: This block represents the mathematical model of the BLDC motor within your simulation environment.
- Feedback Signal Blocks: These blocks represent sensors (like a rotary encoder in a real system) or estimators (used in your simulation) that provide feedback on motor current and position.
- Output Display Blocks: These blocks allow you to visualize the simulation results, such as motor speed and torque.

THE URBAN DRIVE CYCLE

The first step in evaluating the performance of your FOC system is to establish the desired speed profile for the BLDC motor. The reference speed profile, the Urban Drive Cycle (UDC), is adopted from the available data of Indian automobile companies. The UDC is a standardized driving pattern that simulates common stop-and-go traffic conditions in urban environments. This choice of reference speed is particularly relevant if the ultimate application for the BLDC motor is in an electric vehicle. The UDC's dynamic nature, with frequent speed variations and accelerations, provides a comprehensive test for your FOC system's ability to effectively regulate the motor's speed.

The controlled speed and the reference speed for the considered system are provided in Fig. (**10**). The full driving cycle is used for this presentation.

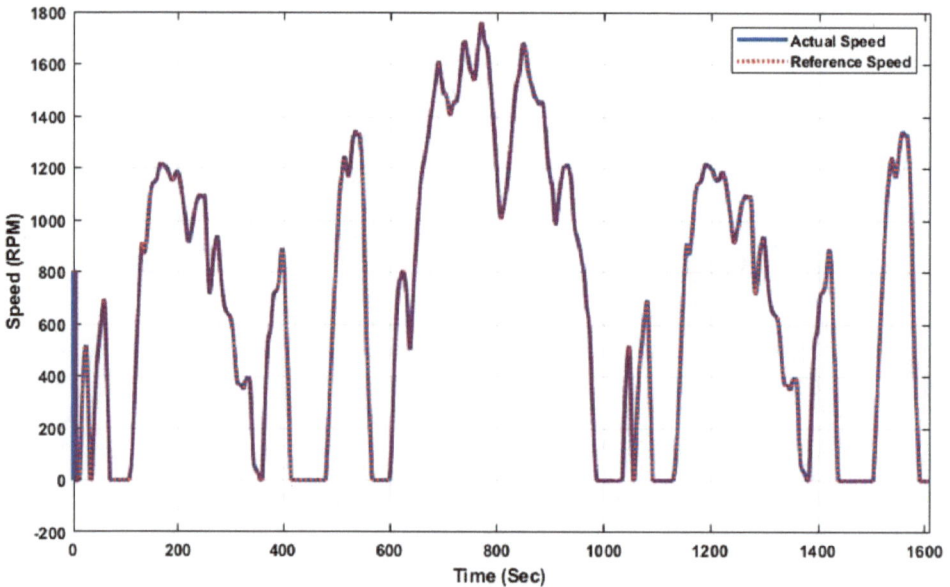

Fig. (10). Reference and actual speed of the FOC-Controlled BLDC.

The actual speed closely follows the reference speed throughout the driving cycle range. Different rates of change in speed and zero-speed operations are portrayed here.

A part of Fig. (**10**) is presented in Fig. (**11**), where the different natures of change in speed are provided for better understanding.

One area where the speed increases and decreases quickly is chosen from Fig. (**11**), and the zoomed version is presented in Fig. (**12**).

A further zoomed version of Fig. (**12**) is presented to portray the speed ripple within this area.

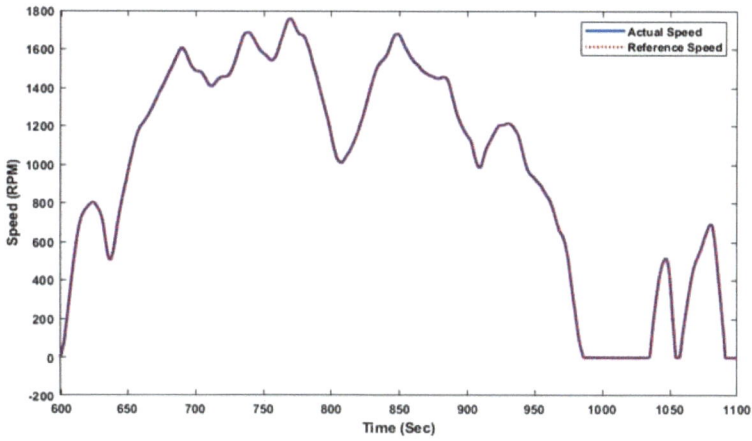

Fig. (11). Partial driving cycle with all types of speed changes.

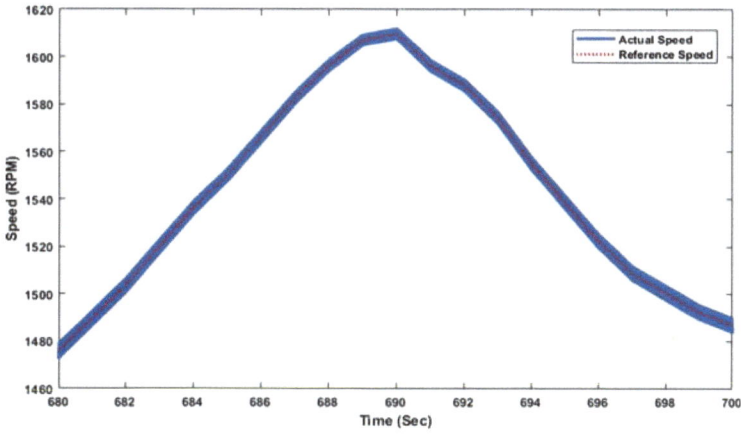

Fig. (12). Sharp speed increment and decrement.

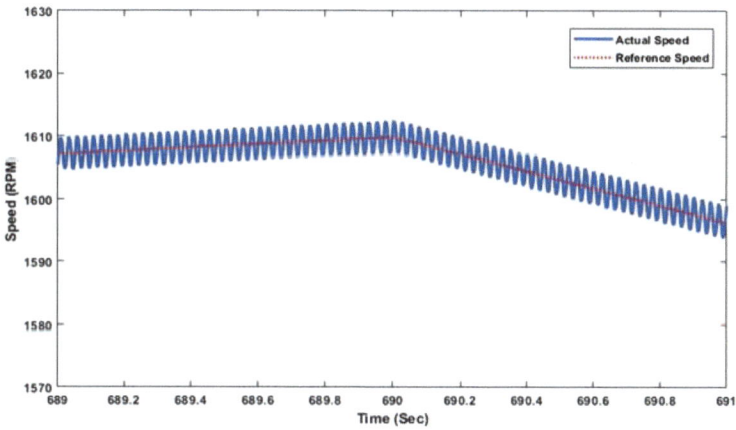

Fig. (13). Speed ripple of the BLDC.

The peak-to-peak speed ripple presented for the BLDC is found to be 5 rpm only, which is around 0.25% of the reference speed. This proves the efficacy of the control successfully.

Additionally, the critical zero speed operation, with rated load and without power off the drive, is obtained in this control, and the result is portrayed in Fig. (**14**).

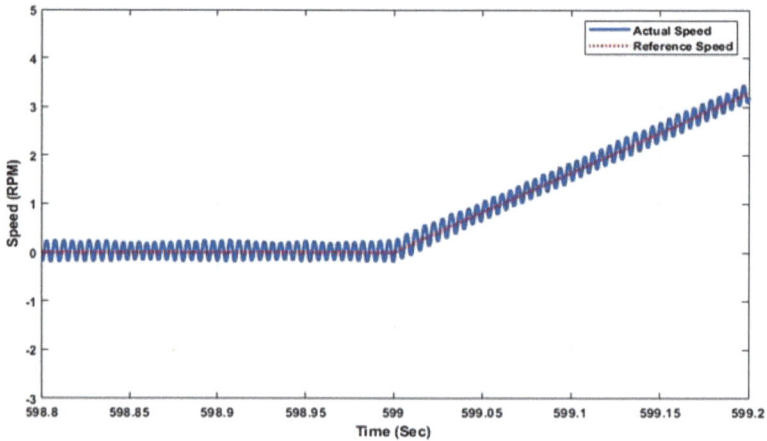

Fig. (14). Zero speed operation of the BLDC drive.

In this case, the developed torque is sufficient to keep the speed ripple within the shown range. The deficient speed ripple is achieved with a high instantaneous change in torques. The considered BLDC operates with fixed load, T_L, 10 Nm. The variation in load during the whole drive cycle is presented in Fig. (**15**).

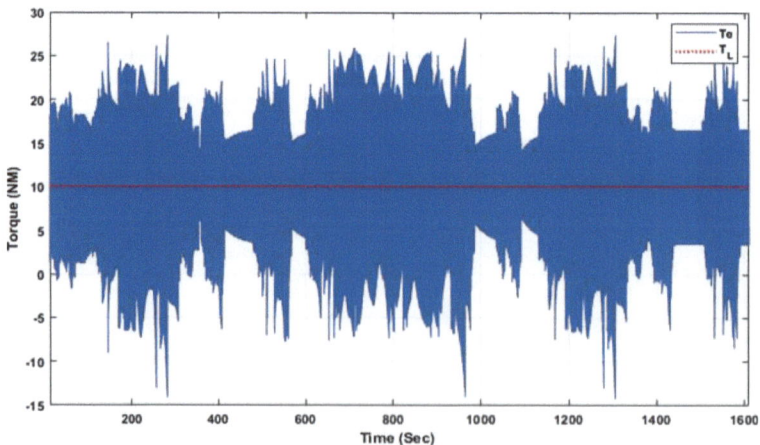

Fig. (15). Developed torque and load torque of the BLDC.

Two different speed conditions, shown in Fig. (**10**), are at 1091 sec and 1416 sec. These two conditions are achieved with two different magnitude torque ripples, as shown in Fig. (**16**).

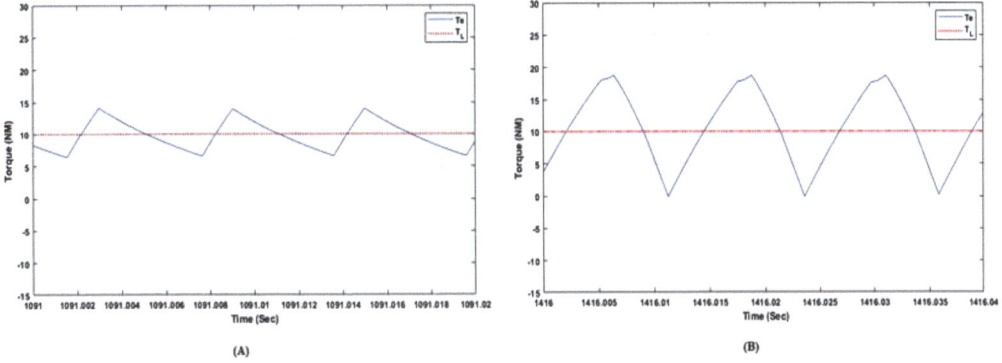

(A)   (B)

Fig. (16). Torque ripple at two different operating speeds.

The stator's phase currents with the low switching frequency for the full operating range are observed in Fig. (**17**).

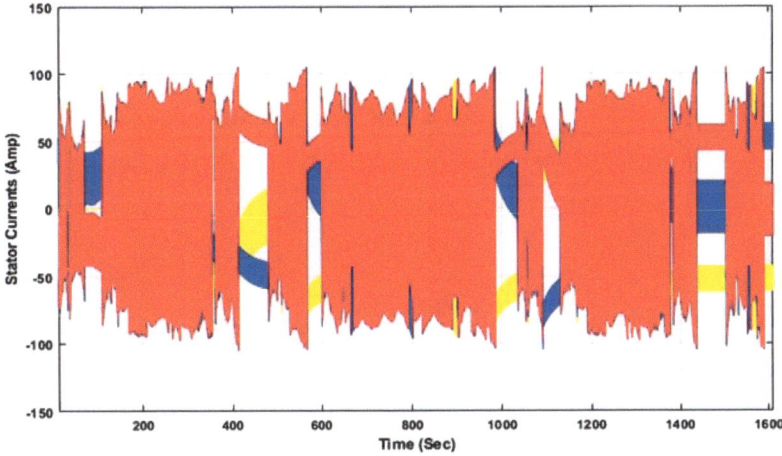

Fig. (17). BLDC stator currents for full driving cycle.

The frequency and waveform of the stator currents change according to the motor's rotational speed. For example, around 700 rpm is achieved by stator currents with a low-frequency waveform, as shown in Fig. (**18**).

The developed trapezoidal fluxes for the three phases during these operations are shown in Fig. (**19**). The time of the flux generation is considered the same as the time of current waveforms, shown in Fig. (**18**).

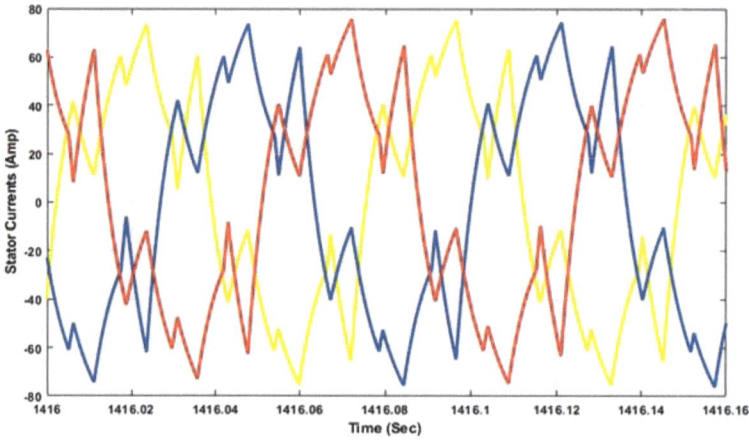

Fig. (18). Low-frequency stator current waveforms.

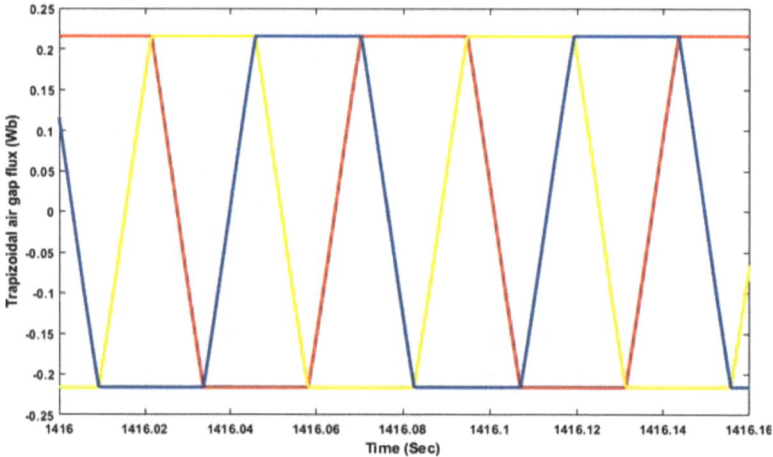

Fig. (19). The trapezoidal three-phase fluxes for the BLDC.

As described earlier, the Hall sensor successfully sensed the rotor angle. The angle information necessary for this control is updated for each 60-degree rotation. Accordingly, six possible angular positions, starting from 30^0 to 60^0, are observed in this scheme. The complete 360^0 rotational time varied with the speed and is shown for two different speeds in Fig. (**20**).

The time taken in Fig. **20(a)** to complete the entire period is 50% higher than in Fig. **20(b)**.

The operation of the BLDC for the considered urban drive cycle is successfully presented with the FOC control technique.

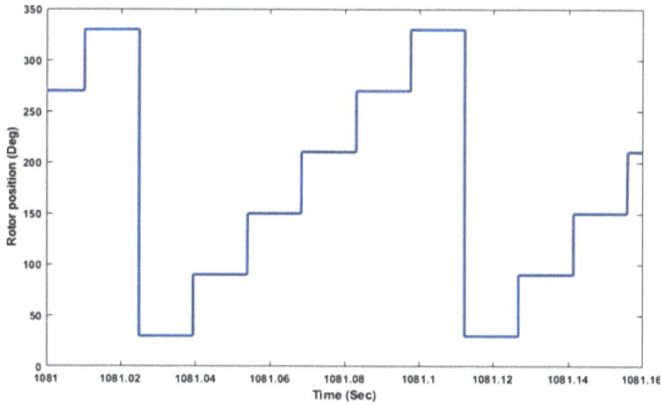

(a)

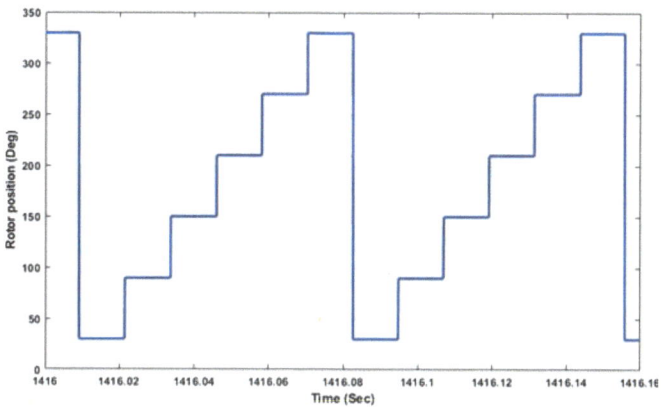

(b)

Fig. (20). The rotor's angular position during two different rotation speeds.

CONCLUSION

This chapter has explored the application of Field-Oriented Control (FOC) for BLDC motors in Electric Vehicles (EVs). While FOC offers significant advantages over traditional control methods, challenges remain in fully addressing:

- Initial Rotor Position Detection: Despite advancements, accurately determining the initial rotor position at startup, especially after manual rotation when the controller loses track, remains an ongoing area of research. Future efforts may focus on sensorless techniques or more efficient sensor-based methods.
- Torque Ripple Reduction: FOC helps mitigate torque ripple but is not entirely eliminated. Future research can explore advanced control algorithms, motor design optimizations, and other techniques to reduce ripple further and achieve

even smoother operation.

Future Research Directions:

Building upon the knowledge gained from this thesis, the following areas offer significant potential for further research in overcoming these challenges and further refining FOC for BLDC motors in EVs:

• Advanced Control Techniques:

o Model Predictive Control (MPC): It investigates the implementation of MPC within the FOC framework. This approach offers a more predictive control strategy, potentially surpassing traditional FOC in efficiency optimization, torque ripple mitigation, and achieving superior transient response.

Sensorless Control Strategies: These explore and develop sensorless control techniques that eliminate the dependence on a position sensor. This can significantly reduce system cost and complexity.

Adaptive Control: It is the development of FOC systems that dynamically adapt to changing motor parameters and operating conditions. This might involve online estimation of motor parameters or real-time adjustments to control gains for optimal performance across various scenarios.

SAMPLE CODES

Two sample codes, generated by the authors, are provided for the reader to implement the control in simulation.

AUTHOR'S CONTRIBUTION

This chapter is presented to explain a Field-Oriented Control (FOC) of BLDC with the contributions from the authors:

(a) Souham Karmakar: Development of the concept, development of the model, implementation of the scheme, result analysis, writing draft.

(b) Tapas Kumar Saha: Supervising the work, visualizing the application with necessary extensions, final writing, editing, and reviewing.

```
1
2    function [a,b,c]= fcn(u)
3    if u<=60
4        a=1;
5        b=-1;
6        c=0;
7    elseif (u>60)&&(u<=120)
8        a=1;
9        b=0;
10       c=-1;
11   elseif (u>120)&&(u<=180)
12       a=0;
13       b=1;
14       c=-1;
15   elseif (u>180)&&(u<=240)
16       a=-1;
17       b=1;
18       c=0;
19   elseif (u>240)&&(u<=300)
20       a=-1;
21       b=0;
22       c=1;
23   else
24       a=0;
25       b=-1;
26       c=1;
27   end
28   end
29
30
```

Fig. (21). Code for Switching pulse generation.

```
1    function y= fcn(ref_angle, actual_speed, Ref_Speed, Actual_angle)
2
3        Ref_Speed2 = Ref_Speed + 30;
4        Ref_Speed3 = Ref_Speed + 30;
5
6        if(actual_speed> Ref_Speed2)
7            y = Actual_angle-120;
8        elseif(actual_speed>Ref_Speed)
9            y = ref_angle;
10       elseif(Ref_Speed3>actual_speed)
11           y = Actual_angle + 120;
12       else
13           y= ref_angle;
14       end
15   end
```

Fig. (22). Code for Angle-based strategy implementation.

REFERENCES

[1] Y. Yasa, "A system efficiency improvement of DC fast-chargers in electric vehicle applications: Bypassing second-stage full-bridge DC-DC converter in high-voltage charging levels", *Ain Shams Eng. J.,* vol. 14, no. 9, p. 102391, 2023.
[http://dx.doi.org/10.1016/j.asej.2023.102391]

[2] B. Nallamothu, B. S. Krishnan and R. Janga, "Performance Evolution of Small Signal Model based Peak Current Mode Controller for Off-board Fast Charging DC-DC Converter," *IEEE 17th India Council International Conference (INDICON)*, New Delhi, India, 2020.
[http://dx.doi.org/10.1109/INDICON49873.2020.9342288]

[3] Nasir, Abdulkarim. "Design and Development of a Constant Current Constant Voltage Fast Battery Charger for Electric Vehicles." *4th International Conference on Modern Research in Science, Engineering and Technology*, 2021.
[http://dx.doi.org/10.33422/4th.msetconf.2021.03.02]

[4] Venkat Jakka, Anshuman Shukla & S.V Kulkarni. "A novel dq-vector based control for the three-phase active rectifier in a power electronic transformer." *INDICON Annual*, 2013.

[5] AryaP, S and R. Chithra. "Phase Shifted Full Bridge DC-DC Converter." *International Research Journal of Engineering and Technology (IRJET)*, vol. 02, no. 04, 2015.

[6] K. Zhou, Y. Wu, X. Wu, and Y. Sun, "Da Teng, and Yang Liu". 2023. "F" *Electronics (Basel)*, vol. 12, no. 7, 1581.

[7] Shih, L.C.; Liu, Y.H.; Chiu, H.J, "A Novel Hybrid Mode Control for Phase-shift Full Bridge Converter Featuring High Efficiency over Full Load Range." *IEEE Trans. Power Electron*, 2019.

[8] Kanamarlapudi, V.R.K.; Wang, B.F.; Kandasamy, N.K.; So, P.L "A New ZVS Full-Bridge DC-DC Converter for Battery Charging with Reduced Losses Over Full-Load Range." *IEEE Trans. Ind. Appl.,* 2018

[9] Yang, Y.Z.; Li, H.J.; Wu, C.; Xu, J.Z.; Bi, Y.X.; Zhao, Y, "An Improved Control Scheme for Reducing Circulating Current and Reverse Power of Bidirectional Phase-Shifted Full-Bridge Converter" *IEEE Trans. Power Electron*, 2022.

[10] Covic, G. A., & Boys, J. T. "Fast charging systems for electric vehicles. IET Electric Power Applications" *SAE International. Electric Vehicle and Plug in Hybrid Electric Vehicle Conductive Charge Coupler*, SAE International: Warrendale, PA, USA, 2017.

[11] Y. Wei, Q. Luo, and A. Mantooth, "Hybrid Control Strategy for LLC Converter With Reduced Switching Frequency Range and Circulating Current for Hold-Up Time Operation", *IEEE Trans. Power Electron.,* vol. 36, no. 8, pp. 8600-8606, 2021.
[http://dx.doi.org/10.1109/TPEL.2021.3054850]

[12] L. Zhao, Y. Pei, L. Wang, L. Pei, W. Cao, and Y. Gan, "Design Methodology of Bidirectional Resonant CLLC Charger for Wide Voltage Range Based on Parameter Equivalent and Time Domain Model", *IEEE Trans. Power Electron.,* vol. 37, no. 10, pp. 12041-12064, 2022.
[http://dx.doi.org/10.1109/TPEL.2022.3170101]

[13] N. Vazquez, and M. Liserre, "Peak Current Control and Feed-Forward Compensation of a DAB Converter", *IEEE Trans. Ind. Electron.,* vol. 67, no. 10, pp. 8381-8391, 2020.
[http://dx.doi.org/10.1109/TIE.2019.2949523]

[14] E. Monmasson, and M.N. Cirstea, "FPGA design methodology for industrial control systems—a review", *IEEE Trans. Ind. Electron.,* vol. 54, no. 4, pp. 1824-1842, 2007.
[http://dx.doi.org/10.1109/TIE.2007.898281]

[15] A. Monti, E. Santi, R.A. Dougal, and M. Riva, "Rapid prototyping of digital controls for power electronics", *IEEE Trans. Power Electron.,* vol. 18, no. 3, pp. 915-923, 2003.
[http://dx.doi.org/10.1109/TPEL.2003.810864]

[16]   O. Moseler, and R. Isermann, "Application of model-based fault detection to a brushless DC motor", *IEEE Trans. Ind. Electron.*, vol. 47, no. 5, pp. 1015-1020, 2000.
[http://dx.doi.org/10.1109/41.873209]

[17]   L. Pan, H. Sun, B. Wang, G. Su, X. Wang, and G. Peng, "Torque ripple suppression method for BLDCM drive based on four-switch three-phase inverter", *Journal of Power Electronics*, vol. 15, no. 4, pp. 974-986, 2015.
[http://dx.doi.org/10.6113/JPE.2015.15.4.974]

[18]   P. Pillay, and R. Krishnan, "Modeling of permanent magnet motor drives", *IEEE Trans. Ind. Electron.*, vol. 35, no. 4, pp. 537-541, 1988.
[http://dx.doi.org/10.1109/41.9176]

[19]   P. Pillay, and R. Krishnan, "Modeling, simulation, and analysis of permanent-magnet motor drives. II. The brushless DC motor drive", *IEEE Trans. Ind. Appl.*, vol. 25, no. 2, pp. 274-279, 1989.
[http://dx.doi.org/10.1109/28.25542]

[20]   P. Pillay, and R. Krishnan, "Application characteristics of permanent magnet synchronous and brushless DC motors for servo drives", *IEEE Trans. Ind. Appl.*, vol. 27, no. 5, pp. 986-996, 1991.
[http://dx.doi.org/10.1109/28.90357]

[21]   D. Potnuru, K.P. Bharani Chandra, I. Arasaratnam, D-W. Gu, K. Alice Mary, S.B. Ch, and S.B. Ch, "Derivative-free square-root cubature Kalman filter for non-inear brushless DC motors", *IET Electr. Power Appl.*, vol. 10, no. 5, pp. 419-429, 2016.
[http://dx.doi.org/10.1049/iet-epa.2015.0414]

[22]   Quijano, N., Passino, K., Jogi, S., A Tutorial Introduction to Control Systems Development and Implementation with dSPACE. Tutorial, Ohio State Univ. Rubaai, A., Ofoli, A., Castro, M., 2006. dSPACE DSP-based rapid prototyping of fuzzy PID controls for high performance brushless servo drives. *IEEE Ind. Appl. Soc. 3*, 1360– 1364, 2022.
[http://dx.doi.org/10.1109/IAS.2006.256707]

[23]   A. Rubaai, M.J. Castro-Sitiriche, and A.R. Ofoli, "Design and implementation of parallel fuzzy PID controller for high-performance brushless motor drives: an integrated environment for rapid control prototyping", *IEEE Trans. Ind. Appl.*, vol. 44, no. 4, pp. 1090-1098, 2008.
[http://dx.doi.org/10.1109/TIA.2008.926059]

[24]   Jianwen Shao, D. Nolan, M. Teissier, and D. Swanson, "A novel microcontroller-based sensorless brushless DC (BLDC) motor drive for automotive fuel pumps", *IEEE Trans. Ind. Appl.*, vol. 39, no. 6, pp. 1734-1740, 2003.
[http://dx.doi.org/10.1109/TIA.2003.818973]

[25]   E.G. Shehata, "Speed sensorless torque control of an IPMSM drive with online stator resistance estimation using reduced order EKF", *Int. J. Electr. Power Energy Syst.*, vol. 47, pp. 378-386, 2013.
[http://dx.doi.org/10.1016/j.ijepes.2012.10.068]

[26]   B. Singh, and V. Bist, "A reduced sensor power factor corrected bridgeless flyback converter fed brushless DC motor drive", *Electr. Power Compon. Syst.*, vol. 41, no. 11, pp. 1114-1128, 2013.
[http://dx.doi.org/10.1080/15325008.2013.809821]

[27]   F. Vasca and L. Iannelli, *Dynamics and Control of Switched Electronic Systems*, vol. 53, 2013.

[28]   C. Xie, J.M. Ogden, S. Quan, and Q. Chen, "Optimal power management for fuel cell–battery full hybrid powertrain on a test station", *Int. J. Electr. Power Energy Syst.*, vol. 53, pp. 307-320, 2013.
[http://dx.doi.org/10.1016/j.ijepes.2013.05.016]

[29]   A.B. Yildiz, "Electrical equivalent circuit based modeling and analysis of direct current motors", *Int. J. Electr. Power Energy Syst.*, vol. 43, no. 1, pp. 1043-1047, 2012.
[http://dx.doi.org/10.1016/j.ijepes.2012.06.063]

[30]   M. Escudero, D. Meneses, N. Rodriguez, and D.P. Morales, "Modulation Scheme for the Bidirectional Operation of the Phase-Shift Full-Bridge Power Converter", *IEEE Trans. Power Electron.,* vol. 35, no. 2, pp. 1377-1391, 2020.
[http://dx.doi.org/10.1109/TPEL.2019.2923804]

Phase Shifted Full Bridge Converter-Based Battery Charger for Fast Charging of Electric Vehicles

S. Sen[1] and **T.K. Saha**[1,*]

[1] *Department of Electrical Engineering, National Institute of Technology Durgapur, Durgapur, India*

Abstract: The challenge of emission-free transportation is currently a much-discussed issue that has led to the development of innovative charging solutions. A major technical challenge for the potential market is the significant charging time involved, especially for long-range EVs. This chapter develops two design solutions: Phase-Shifted Full-Bridge (PSFB) Converter-based battery charger and grid-connected bidirectional charging schemes for a plug-in EV. A Constant-Current and Constant-Voltage (CC-CV) charging scheme is developed using industrial standards. The mathematical model of the EV Chargers has also been developed using the above control scheme to demonstrate Vehicle-to-Grid (V2G) and Grid-to-Vehicle (G2V) operations. The introductory part discusses the relevance of this topic, emphasizing the need for fast-charging technologies. After that, we discuss the available options for DC-DC converters and justify the choice of the PSFB converter, concluding with its design parameters. The following section compares two different control strategies for the DC-DC converter, leading to the choice of the CC-CV scheme and its implementation. Next comes the implementation of the 3-phase Controlled Rectifier, employing the d-q Current Control approach to regulate the rectifier through advanced direct-quadrature-coordinate controllers. The schemes are successfully implemented in the simulation environment for the considered operation mode. The results successfully present the charge controller performances with CC-CV charging for different batteries.

Keywords: Bi-directional converter, Battery SOC, Close loop current control, Control in d-q frame, CC-CV scheme, DC-DC converter, DC-AC Inverter, Grid connected operation, Grid to vehicle, Practical charging limit, Switching Scheme of Inverter, Voltage control, Vehicle to grid.

INTRODUCTION

The world has to shift toward a sustainable future, pushed back by the inefficient use of fossil fuel-based energy. The adoption of Electric Vehicles (EVs) has

---

* **Corresponding author T.K. Saha:** Department of Electrical Engineering, National Institute of Technology Durgapur, Durgapur, India; E-mail: tksaha.ee@nitdgp.ac.in

Nitesh Tiwari, Shekhar Yadav and Sabha Raj Arya (Eds.)

surged in this context, with one primary challenge being the inconvenience and time-consuming nature of recharging compared to traditional refueling [1].

Under these circumstances, the fast charging of batteries offers the promise of significantly reducing the time required to recharge electric vehicles. This chapter deals with the intricacies of fast charging for electric vehicles, including its technological advancements, benefits, and challenges [2].

Electric vehicles are automobiles powered by rechargeable batteries or other energy storage systems storing electricity as fuel. Other than average Battery Electric Vehicles (BEVs) that run only on stored electrical power, another popular choice is Hybrid Electric Vehicles (HEVs), which use both an electric motor and a traditional IC engine [3].

Even with an excellent future for EVs, some barriers still need to be overcome, such as limited range between charges, long charging times, and inadequate infrastructure for charging points. However, with advances in battery technology and increasing concerns about environmental protection, the future looks bright for these vehicles, which can reduce the global carbon footprint [4].

Charging Level of Electric Vehicles

The EV battery must float. Electric vehicle charging facilities fall into two categories: slow and fast. Slow-charging systems, including Level-1 and Level-2 onboard charging configurations, are one of its types. Level-1 onboard systems typically charge one fully discharged battery for 8-10 hours of charging time. These systems are usually installed in residential areas and use power in the range of 10 kW. On the other hand, Level-2 charging stations charge faster than Level-1 systems and are commonly found in public places, rated up to 20 kW [5].

As the EV market grows, faster charging options will also rise. The quick charging devices, categorized as Level-3, provide high currents capable of a complete battery replenishment in 30-40 minutes, normally operating up to 350 kW. Ultra-fast charging schemes of 400kW or above fully charge the battery in 20 minutes. The temperature limit of a battery is going to be the only constraint in this path of decreasing charging time. Table **1** presents the available types and levels of charging as reported by K. Zhou *et al.* [6].

STATE-OF-THE-ART PRACTICES

The accelerated adoption of Electric Vehicles (EVs) has stimulated extensive research into fast charging technologies, which are pivotal for alleviating range anxiety and enhancing user convenience. This comprehensive literature review scrutinizes the evolutionary trajectory of fast-charging technologies for EVs, highlighting significant advancements, current obstacles, and prospects, explicitly focusing on DC-DC converters and battery controller design [7].

Table 1. Electric vehicle charging types and levels.

Charging Type	Charging Location	Specifications			Charging Time	(Battery Capacity)	Criterion
		Input/ Output Voltage (V)	Current (A)	Power (kW)			
Level 1	On-board	120/230	12–16	1.44–1.92	11–36 h	16–50 kWh	International Electrotechnical Commission (IEC)
Level 2		208/240	15–80	3.1–19.2	2–6 h	16–30 kWh	
Level 3 (Fast)	Off-board	300–600	≤400	50–350	≤30 min	20–50 kWh	
Ultra-fast		>800	>400	≥400	≈10 min	20–50 kWh	

In the nascent stages of research, efforts primarily concentrated on augmenting charging efficiency and curtailing charging durations. Seminal works such as "Fast Charging Systems for Electric Vehicles" by Covic and Boys (2010) and "Development of a Fast Charger for Electric Vehicles" by Ueda *et al.* (2012) laid the foundational groundwork, emphasizing the critical role of DC-DC converters and battery controller design in enabling rapid charging [8].

Establishing uniform charging networks, epitomized by standards like CHAdeMO and Combined Charging System (CCS), facilitated market expansion by ensuring universal access to fast charging stations. Noteworthy studies such as Kato *et al.* (2014) on "Highly efficient, fast charging system for electric vehicles" and Liu *et al.* (2016) on "Development of high-power, fast charging station for electric vehicles" significantly contributed to the robust development of charging infrastructure, underscoring the importance of optimized DC-DC converters and advanced battery controllers.

Advancements in power electronics, particularly in DC-DC converters, have played a pivotal role in enhancing rapid charging capabilities. Research by Wang *et al.* (2018) on "Ultra-fast charging stations for electric vehicles: International development and China's experience" elucidated the significance of efficient DC-DC conversion in achieving ultra-fast charging speeds, while Zhang *et al.* explored factors influencing fast/rapid charging capacity for lithium-ion battery electric vehicles [9].

Furthermore, battery controller design has become a crucial determinant of charging efficiency and battery health. Studies such as "Enhanced Battery Controller Design for Fast Charging of Electric Vehicles" by Park *et al.* (2020) and "Optimized Battery Management Systems for high-power EV Charging" by Chen *et al.* (2019) have underscored the importance of intelligent battery control algorithms in maximizing charging performance while mitigating battery degradation risks.

Despite notable progress, challenges persist, including grid integration, thermal management, and battery degradation. Ongoing research endeavors aim to address these barriers, focusing on developing advanced DC-DC converters and intelligent battery management systems. Early investigations such as "Challenges and Prospects of Fast Charging Technologies for Electric Vehicles" by Lin *et al.* (2021) offer valuable insights into potential solutions for overcoming these challenges, emphasizing the pivotal role of optimized DC-DC converters and battery controllers in driving the future of fast charging for EVs [10].

The evolution of fast charging technologies for EVs epitomizes interdisciplinary collaboration and technological innovation. Continued efforts in research and development, particularly in the domains of DC-DC converters and battery controller design, are indispensable for surmounting remaining obstacles and unlocking the full potential of fast charging, propelling widespread EV adoption, and fostering sustainable transportation solutions.

DIFFERENT TYPES OF DC-DC CONVERTERS

In Electric Vehicle (EV) charger systems, the DC/DC converter performs the function of the interface between the AC/DC front-end that provides power to the automobile's battery. The primary function is to provide the device with the necessary tools to record and manipulate the power flow from and to the grid, focusing on optimal charging performance. Having the functions of an EV battery required to float continuously for safety and avoiding physical contact between the grid and the battery galvanic isolation is a necessary tool. These mechanisms are intended to guarantee that charging will not adversely affect the protection system of the battery. The converter of DC/DC, especially its isolated form, is critical for the EV's charging process to be a safe concern.

Isolated DC-DC Converter

The EV battery must float at a potential equal to the ground for safety purposes. Accordingly, the galvanic isolation becomes mandatory. The battery and the grid are kept separate to keep the battery's overcharge protection mechanism intact. An isolated DC/DC converter will help to achieve this isolation requirement.

Different researchers demonstrate separate DC/DC converter topologies suitable for EV chargers. Y.Q. discusses the high efficiency and high power density of the LLC resonant converter. According to Wei *et al.* [11], the bidirectional power flow has become a leading technical indicator of fast-charging systems. The efficiency of the system is also essential. The bidirectional CLLC resonant converter, on the other hand, is favored for EV charging systems because of its soft-switching topology. Afterward, a CLLC design method was proposed by L Zhao *et al.,* which considers parameter equivalence and a model in the time domain [12]. In a study [13], a current control (dual-band) method was proposed by N. Vazquez *et al.* for DAB converters to avoid the risk of transformer saturation. The PSFB converter has a lower root-mean-square current than DAB and CLLC converters. This minimizes the current stress and conduction loss.

The said converters are presented in Fig. (**1**).

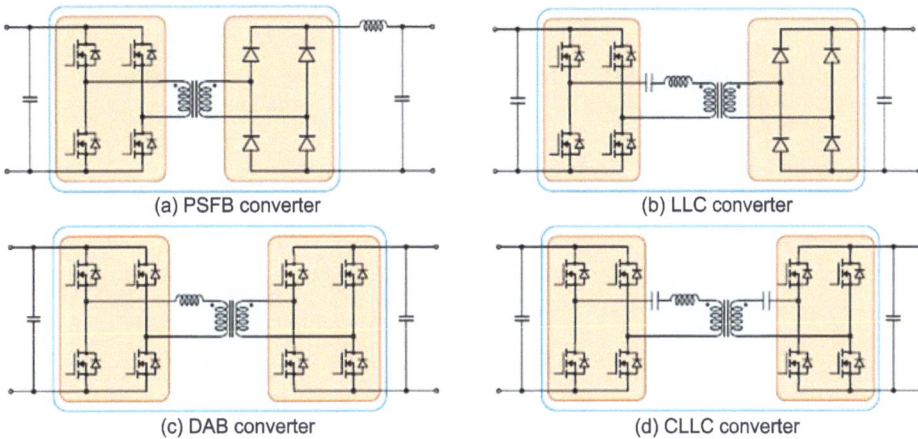

(a) PSFB converter

(b) LLC converter

(c) DAB converter

(d) CLLC converter

Fig. (1). Isolated DC-DC converters for fast charging.

Non-isolated DC-DC Converter

The non-isolated DC/DC converters are an additional option for supplying power to EV batteries in cases where isolation has already been provided by a preceding power conversion station, like a line-frequency transformer followed by an AC/DC front end. Under such a scenario, the charging system takes over the given isolation and utilizes a non-isolated DC/DC converter. From the standpoint of not being intrinsic galvanic isolation, a non-isolated converter may also provide a floating power supply to the car battery. This approach optimizes efficiency and simplicity and achieves those goals without extra isolation components. In addition, non-isolated DC/DC converters provide a valuable and inexpensive solution for EV chargers that rely on the supply of existing isolation mechanisms.

Non-isolated DC/DC converter topologies for EV chargers are presented in Fig. (2).

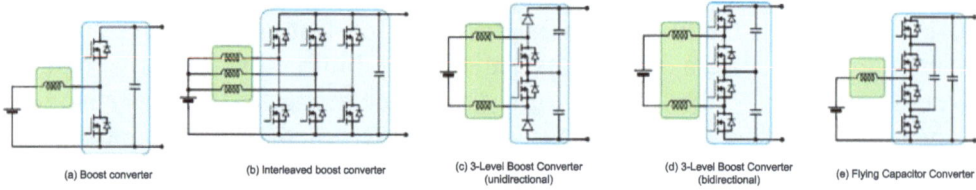

(a) Boost converter   (b) Interleaved boost converter   (c) 3-Level Boost Converter (unidirectional)   (d) 3-Level Boost Converter (bidirectional)   (e) Flying Capacitor Converter

Fig. (2). Non-isolated DC-DC converters used for fast charging.

JUSTIFICATION FOR PSFB CONVERTER

The PSFB converter has a number of key advantages over a conventional full bridge converter, including high efficiency, high power density, high reliability, and low Electromagnetic Interference (EMI) due to Zero Voltage Switching (ZVS) operation [12]. The impacts of the two charging strategies on the battery have been investigated by the simulation of a Phase Shift Full Bridge (PSFB) DC-DC converter in a study [13]. The PSFB advantages are established from these points of view here.

The reason why the PSFB converter is chosen for EV battery chargers can be explained by comparing it with other converter topologies such as LLC, DAB, and Cuk Converter with LLC Resonant Tank (Cuk Converter).

PSFB Converter *vs.* LLC Converter

- Advantages of PSFB: The PSFB has easy control and a broad output voltage range. It is efficient in transferring power and precise regulation, hence becoming a suitable choice for EV battery charging where charging voltage might differ.
- Disadvantages of LLC: On the contrary, the range of the variables is narrow, which does not give flexibility as opposed to a Closed-loop Load-dependent converter. Keeping high efficiency and achieving Zero-Voltage Switching (ZVS) in LLC converters over the whole input and output range can be a complex task.

PSFB Converter *vs.* DAB Converter

- Advantages of PSFB: The PSFB converter is renowned for its vast output voltage range, which makes it ideal for different EV battery voltages. It is easy to control and has very efficient power transfer.
- Advantages of DAB: However, the DAB converter provides a two-way power flow capability that can benefit a V2G setup. In certain EV charging scenarios,

the control complexity and higher component count may outweigh these advantages.

PSFB Converter *vs.* CLLC Converter

- Advantages of PSFB: Similar to the DAB converter, the PSFB converter also has simple control and high power efficiency. This one is the most versatile because of the wide range of output voltage.
- Advantages of CLLC: Another critical feature of the CLLC converter is its low reactive current and wide ZVS operating range. It can be beneficial in certain types of applications. However, it is still subject to output controllability errors over a wide range that would make it inappropriate for EV charging.

The PSFB converter stands out for EV battery chargers due to its simple control, wide output voltage range, and efficient power transfer. While other converter topologies offer unique advantages, such as bi-directional power flow or low reactive current, the PSFB converter balances simplicity, efficiency, and adaptability to varying EV battery charging requirements.

WORKING AND FILTER DESIGN OF PHASE SHIFTED FULL BRIDGE DC-DC CONVERTER

Operating Principle

The Phase-Shifted Full Bridge (PSFB) DC-DC converter is a complete power circuit with an H-bridge inverter feeding a high-frequency transformer. The output of the transformer is rectified through a full bridge uncontrolled rectifier. An output low-pass filter is necessary in this scheme. The principle of shifts in phases governs different switches to make Zero Voltage Switching (ZVS) possible [14]. The circuit is portrayed in Fig. (**3**).

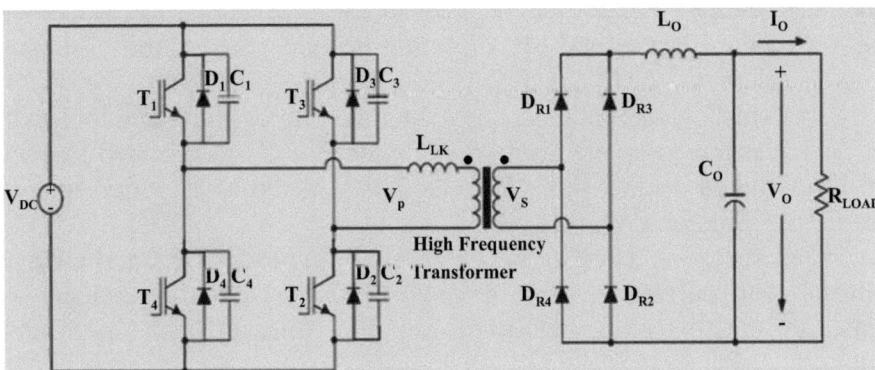

Fig. (3). Phase shifted full bridge DC-DC converter.

It is a complete inverter consisting of four semiconductor switches with antiparallel diodes. The phase-shifted control is represented by moving specific device signals ahead of others. The high-frequency transformer matches the lower battery end voltage with a higher supply end voltage in the working power range of the PSFB converter. A full-wave rectifier filters the secondary side AC output to attain a smooth DC output voltage. The parasitic capacitances of the switches (C1, C2, C3, C4) and an inductor in the series with the primary winding of a transformer define its leakage inductance. Other inductors can be added if needed.

In the phase-shifted converter, a part of the transformer's switch-output capacitance and leakage inductance is used to achieve Zero Voltage Switching (ZVS). This approach reduces the switching losses, and this DC-DC converter topology based on the PSFB is highly beneficial for medium- and high-power applications.

Modes of Operations

The operation of the Phase-Shifted Full Bridge (PSFB) DC-DC converter involves six circuit modes during the first half cycle, which repeat in the second half cycle.

The modes are considered as follows:

- Mode 1: Both switches, T1 and T2, are on, transferring power from input to output.
- Mode 2: The switch T1 is deactivated, directing primary current through capacitors C1 and C4. During this phase, C1 charges to VDC while C4 discharges to zero. The inductor supplies the energy during this charging.
- Mode 3: Capacitor C4 is completely discharged, and freewheeling diode DR4 associated with switch T4 conducts, initiating zero voltage switching turn on for T4.
- Mode 4: Switch T2 is turned off, directing primary current through capacitors C2 and C3. Here, C2 charges while C3 discharges, with energy for this process sourced from the leakage inductance of the transformer and the output inductor.
- Mode 5: It sees the complete discharge of capacitor C3 to zero and freewheeling diode DR3 linked with switch T3 conducts. T3 turns on under zero voltage across it, fulfilling the ZVS criteria.
- Mode 6: It witnesses a decrease in current through diodes DR1 and DR2 to zero, permitting load current to flow through DR2 and DR4. Secondary voltage escalates during this phase, facilitating energy transfer from the input to the output.

The voltage and currents during these modes follow the natures presented by S P Arya *et al.* [5] in Fig. (**4**).

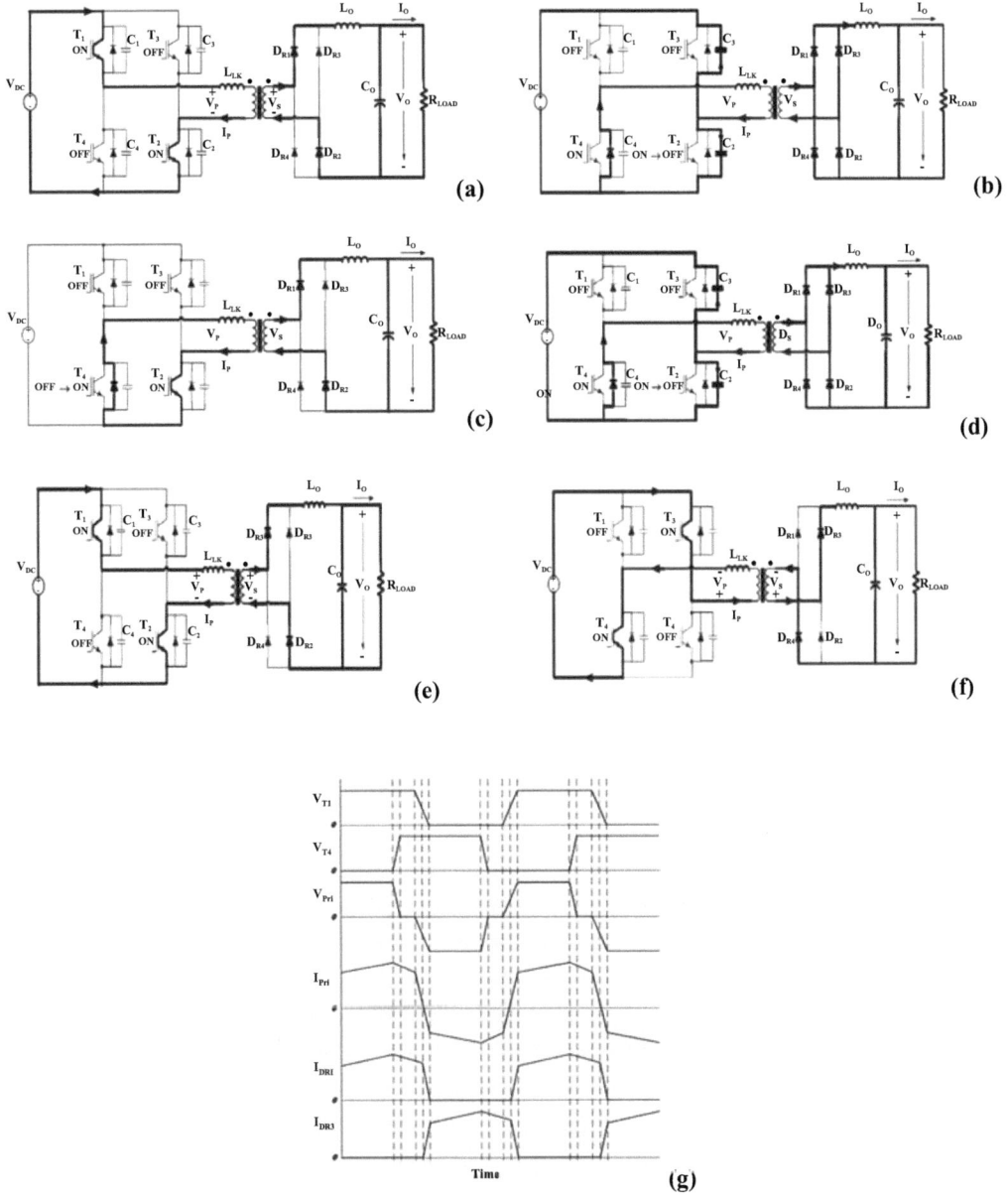

Fig. (4). The operation for all modes and voltage and current of the PSFB converter.

A sample PSFB converter may be taken for design and implementation to demonstrate the fast charging through constant current-constant voltage (CC-CV) charging modes [15].

Sample Design Specification

Input Voltage = 200 V

Output Voltage = 26 V

Rated Power = 1100 W

Output Current = 22A

Switching Frequency = 50 kHz

Current Ripple = 20%

Voltage Ripple = 1%

The LC filter in Fig. (**3**) can now be designed using the following steps:

- Required max output voltage= 50 V

- Turn ratio of the transformer(Ns/Np)= 0.25

- $V_L = V_i \left(\frac{Ns}{Np}\right) - V_0 = 200*0.25 - 26 = 24$ V

- $D = 0.5 * \frac{26}{50} = 0.26$

- $I_r = 2\% \; 22A = 0.44$ A

- $V_L = L\frac{di}{dt}$

- $L = V_L \; (DT_S/I_r) = \dfrac{24 \times 0.26 \times \left(\frac{1}{50^3}\right)}{0.44} = 283 \; \mu H$

- $C = I_r \; (DT_S/V_r) = \dfrac{0.44 \times 0.26 \times \left(\frac{1}{50^3}\right)}{24} = 8.8 \; \mu F$

Implementation of the Battery Charge Controller with the Designed Filter

This section mainly deals with designing and implementing the CC-CV Controller Scheme on the PSFB Converter, discussed earlier, to charge a Li-Ion Battery of considered specification for one standard electric vehicle.

The control methods in the PSFB converter are similar to those applied in the DAB converter. SPS modulation, which is predominantly used in PSFB control, gave the possibility of adjusting the output power and the voltage by varying the phase-shift angle. However, light-load soft switching is also a complicated issue. In a study [9], a new hybrid-mode controller was proposed for the PSFB converter to improve efficiency over light and heavy loads. This method accomplishes this by reducing the transformer turns ratio so the circulating current vanishes, reducing the circulating losses. In another study [10], an asymmetric pulse-width modulation technique was employed to overcome the issue of circulating currents, allowing the converter to sustain high efficiency under all output voltage conditions.

Besides, in a paper [11], an adaptive-burst-mode control strategy was suggested, causing the effective switching frequency to be more minor and the switching losses to be reduced. We have a new control schema to overcome technical problems in PSFB converters for EV applications, such as large circulation currents and reverse power [12]. Here, the method changes the phase-shifting angle and the duty cycle to prolong the pre-charging and expected charging times. This technique can address voltage overshoot during pre-charging and lower circulating and transformer root mean squared currents by optimizing pre-charging time and applying a cold compensator with a PI controller.

Constant Current – Constant Voltage (CC-CV) Control

The main task of a DC-DC converter within a charging station is ensuring that the charging of EV batteries is possible over different voltages. Batteries of electric vehicles with various voltage levels show different features when their SOC is within a specific range. Fig. (5) describes the primary circuit and control diagram illustrating the CC-CV charging methodology.

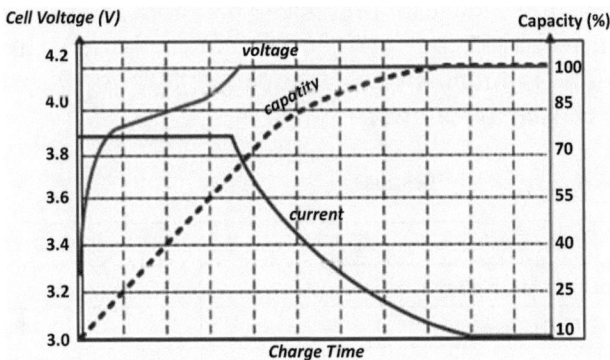

Fig. (5). Typical CC-CV charging directive for batteries.

In the CC charging mode, the charge current, defined by the BMS, is compared with the actual battery current. The PI controller provides the phase shift reference angle next. On the other hand, the other PI controller is responsible for the battery reference voltage during the battery charging mode. In the case of both circuits, the shift of a power semiconductor gate signals gates either output voltage or current. Therefore, the DC-DC converter is designed to function in either constant current or constant voltage mode.

The EV battery master control board dialogs with the charger, instructing the requested charging output current level. The charger sets the constant charge current at the start, where the battery cell achieves a designated voltage threshold. Next, the charger keeps the voltage at this level and slowly reduces the output current for the charging duration. This approach accelerates the charging process and reduces the risk of overcharging.

Advanced charging methods may add functionality to the output current and voltage levels, adjusting to the battery cell temperatures. The figure below demonstrates a typical CC-CV charging process for a single Li-Ion battery cell. Charging usually starts in constant current mode and will stay in this mode until the 80% SOC mark. Therefore, the charger then switches to the constant voltage mode for the safety of the battery based on its operation specifications. When the charge continues, the battery management system may engage cell balancing to maximize the battery's performance and duration.

Implementation of the Control in the Simulation Environment

The PSFB converter is implemented for a Li-Ion battery in a MATLAB-Simulink environment. The complete scheme is presented in Fig. (**6**).

The battery's initial SOC is considered here to be 60%. The other variables used in the model are following industrial practice. This model transitions from constant current to constant voltage mode at 70% SOC of the battery. In some cases, this CC to CV transition is found to be practiced at 80% or 90% SOC. The other specifications are chosen as follows:

Table 2. The battery and charger specifications.

Parameter	Considered Values with Units
Input DC Voltage	200 V
DC-DC Topology	PSFB

(Table 2) cont.....

Parameter	Considered Values with Units
Transformer Specs	2866 H, 1.08 μΩ, 4:1 1100W
Magnetization Inductance L_m, Magnetization Resistance R_m Turns Ratio	-
Output Power	1100W
Switching Frequency of the Converter	50 KHz
Nominal Voltage of the Battery	24 V
Capacity of the Battery	12KWh

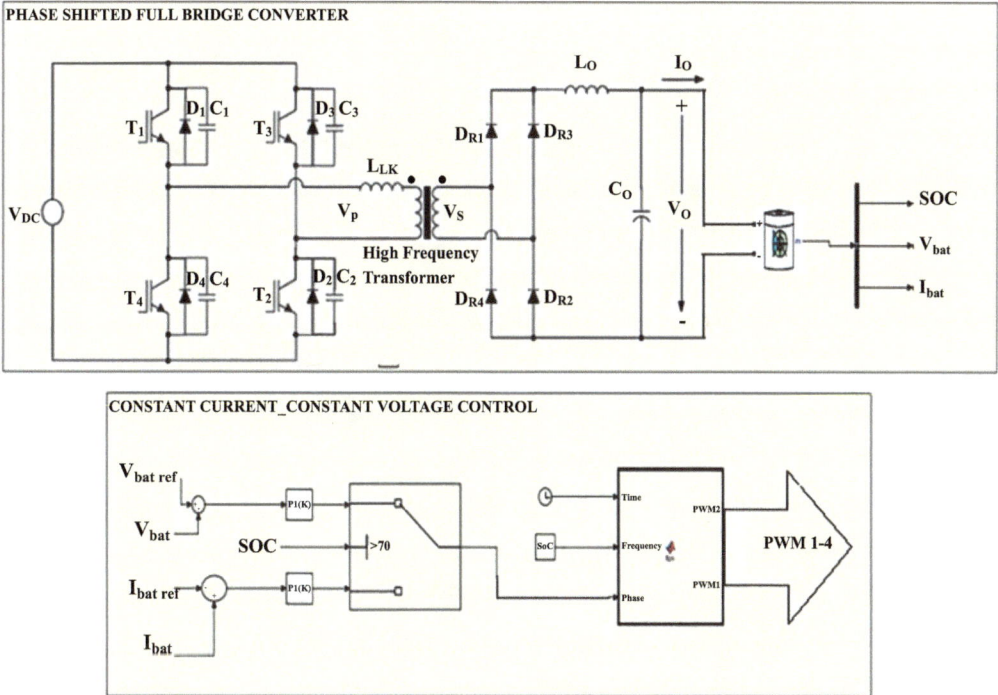

Fig. (6). Complete scheme of CC-CV control for fast charging.

The SOC of the battery is found to be increasing through the controlled PSFB and is portrayed in Fig. (7).

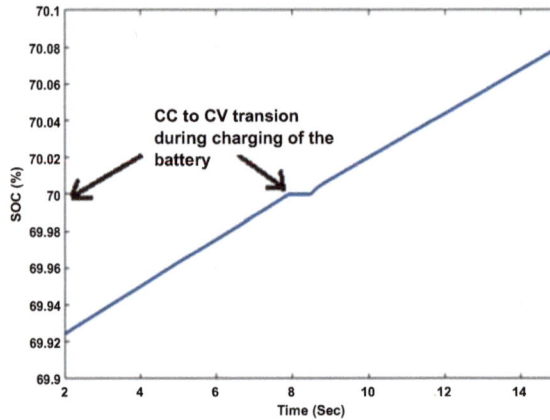

Fig. (7). Change in SOC during CC-CV charging through PSFB.

The battery is initially charged with a fixed current reference of 23 Amp. The constant current is observed in Fig. (**8**). However, after the SOC reaches 70% point, as shown in Fig. (**7**), the current is not controlled through PSFB. The nature of the current is found to be gradually decreasing with transient change because of the battery voltage controller. The zoomed view of the current during this CC-CV transition is portrayed in Fig. **8(b)**.

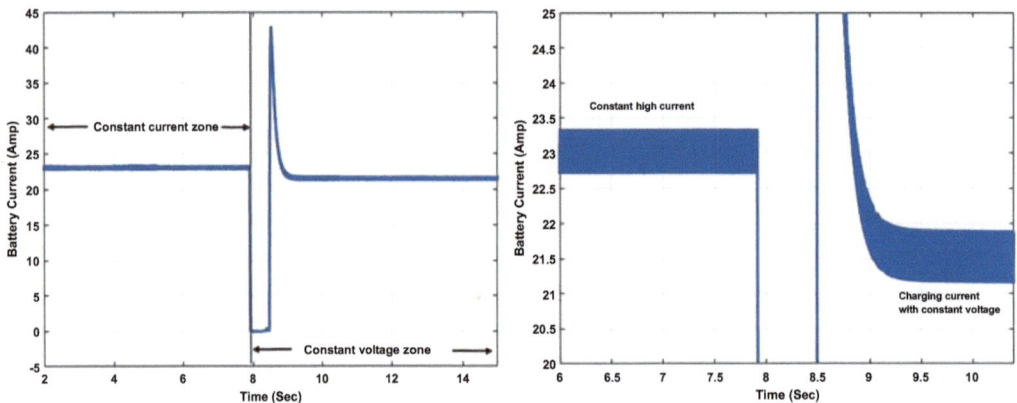

Fig. (8). (**a**) The battery current during CC-CV transition, (**b**) Zoomed view.

Similar transients are observed with battery voltage also. The nature of the change in the battery voltage is shown in Fig. (**9**).

The charger initially kept the voltage level at the required value to keep the current constant at 23 Amp. The voltage is controlled to 26.25 Volt by transition from CC to CV mode after the SOC is increased to 70%. The transient change in the voltage is presented in a zoomed view of it in Fig. **9(b)**.

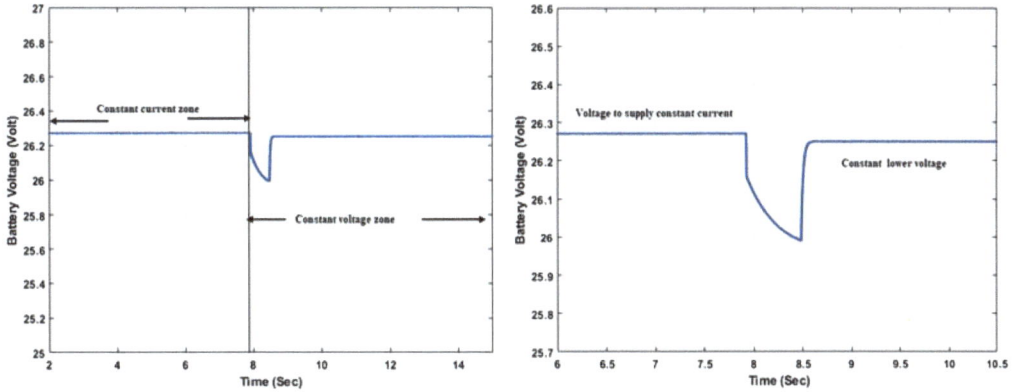

Fig. (9). (**a**) The battery voltage during CC-CV transition, (**b**) Zoomed view.

The PSFB converter operates through the switching pulses produced through the developed MATLAB program. The 50 kHz switching pulses for the four switches are portrayed for both CC and CV operations in Fig. (**10**).

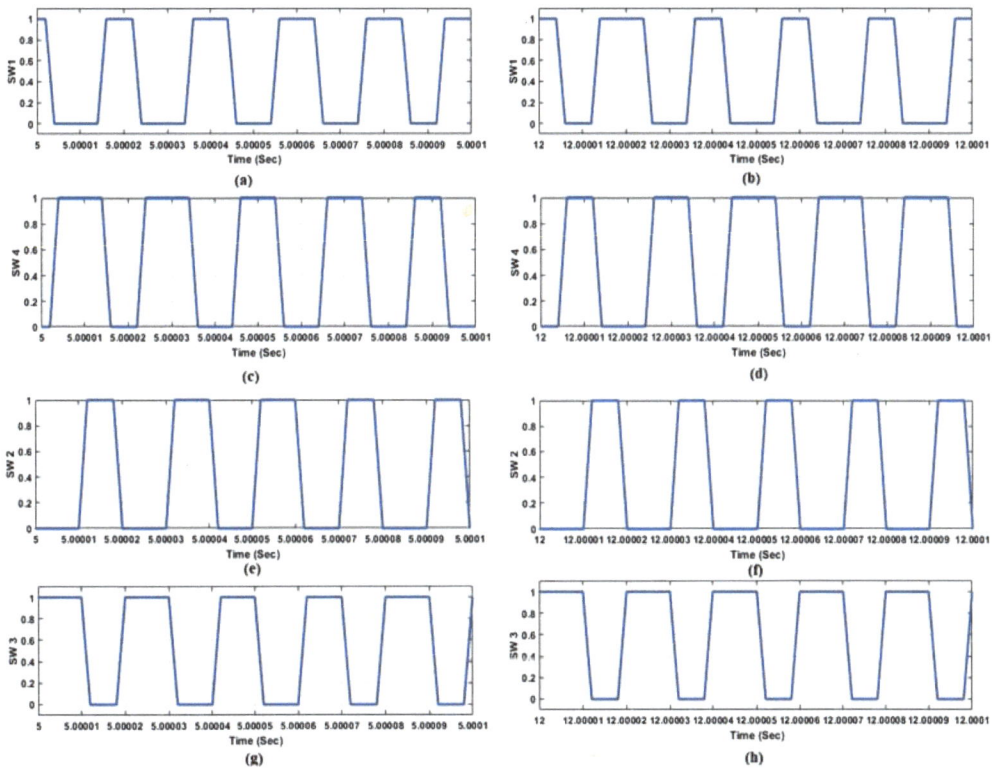

Fig. (10). Duty ratio of switches during CC and CV operations.

Switch-1 and 4 are complimentary, as expected from the power circuit in Fig. (**3**). switch-3 and 2 are also complimentary, as shown in Fig. (**10**). The phase shift between SW 1 and SW 3 is generated to produce the required voltage at the input of the high-frequency transformer. The input voltage is sufficient to maintain the output current at a constant level and maintain the output voltage at a steady level after SOC reaches 70%. The secondary voltage from the transformer is rectified through the diode bridge rectifier. The primary and rectified secondary voltages associated with the diode currents are portrayed in Fig. (**11**).

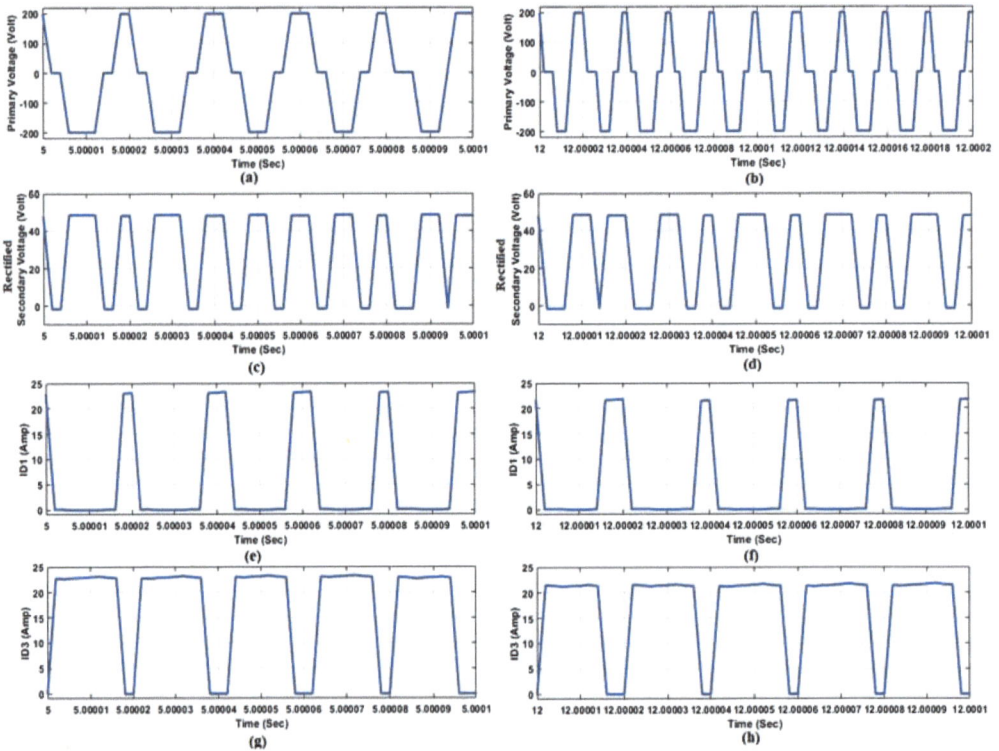

Fig. (11). Output variables during CC and CV operations (**a**) primary voltage, (**b**) rectified secondary voltage, (**c**) one phase top diode current, (**d**) other phase top diode current.

WORKING DESIGN OF ANOTHER EV FAST CHARGER

This section discusses another type of EV Charger consisting of an input filter, a 3-phase inverter, a bidirectional DC-DC converter, an output filter, and the battery. This scheme of the EV Charger, presented in Fig. (**12**), demonstrates both Grid-to-Vehicle (G2V) and Vehicle-to-Grid (V2G) operations.

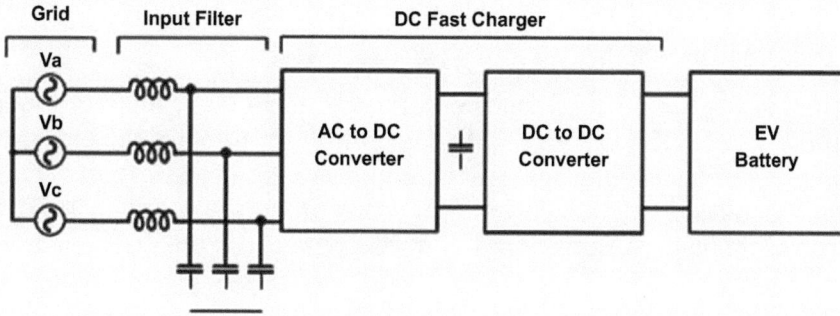

Fig. (12). Grid connected bidirectional EV fast charger.

The basic philosophy of fast charging through the efficient transition of CC-CV operation is also ensured in this scheme. Moreover, in extreme cases, the front-end 3-phase converter can supply power to the grid if available at the battery end.

This scheme has two different controllers, which are designed independently to support the essential charging and discharging phenomena of the EV.

Three-phase Inverter Control

The 3-phase inverter is controlled to maintain the DC link voltage across the capacitor, placed within the inverter and DC-DC converter, shown in the scheme of Fig. (**12**). The power input and output across the capacitor are to be equal to have constant DC link voltage. Accordingly, the DC link voltage is controlled by controlling the active power component of the grid side current, as shown in Fig. (**13**).

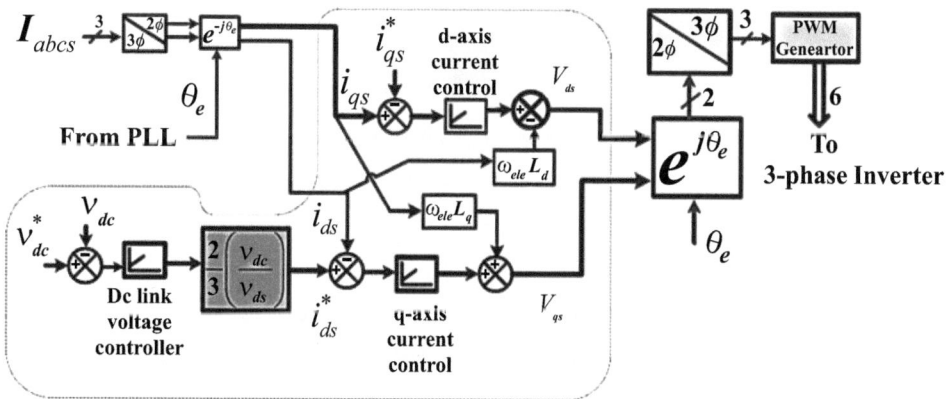

Fig. (13). DC link voltage control scheme.

The Phase-Locked Loop (PLL) structure is a prevalent structure to estimate the grid-voltage vector position.

The DC link voltage control scheme comprises an inner current control loop in the d-q reference frame. The design of current controllers assumes the current control response is much faster than that of the outer voltage control loop. The voltage controller generates the d-axis current reference, as shown in Fig. (**13**). The q-axis current reference can be considered zero to operate the charging system at the unity power factor.

The inner control loop is shown in the Fig. (**14**).

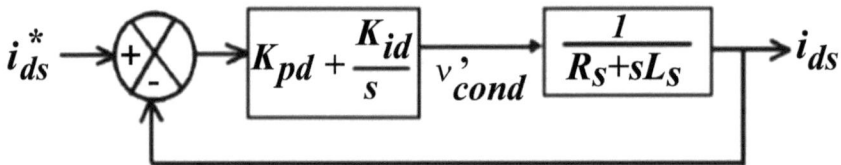

Fig. (14). Inner current control loop.

Input Filter Description

Implementing LCL filters is crucial in grid-connected inverters to mitigate harmonics and address power quality concerns. The LCL filters enhance system stability, reduce voltage distortions, and prevent grid resonance by attenuating high-frequency components. The transfer function is derived as $IgVi=1sL1+s2CLP$ for the filter, shown in Fig. (**15**).

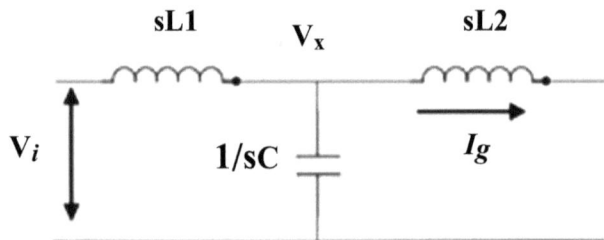

Fig. (15). LCL Filter.

With 0.3% current ripple, the inductor and capacitor values came as 1.645 mH and 30 μF, respectively.

Implementation of the Control in the Simulation Environment

The complete charger scheme for implementation in the Simulink environment is presented in Fig. (**16**).

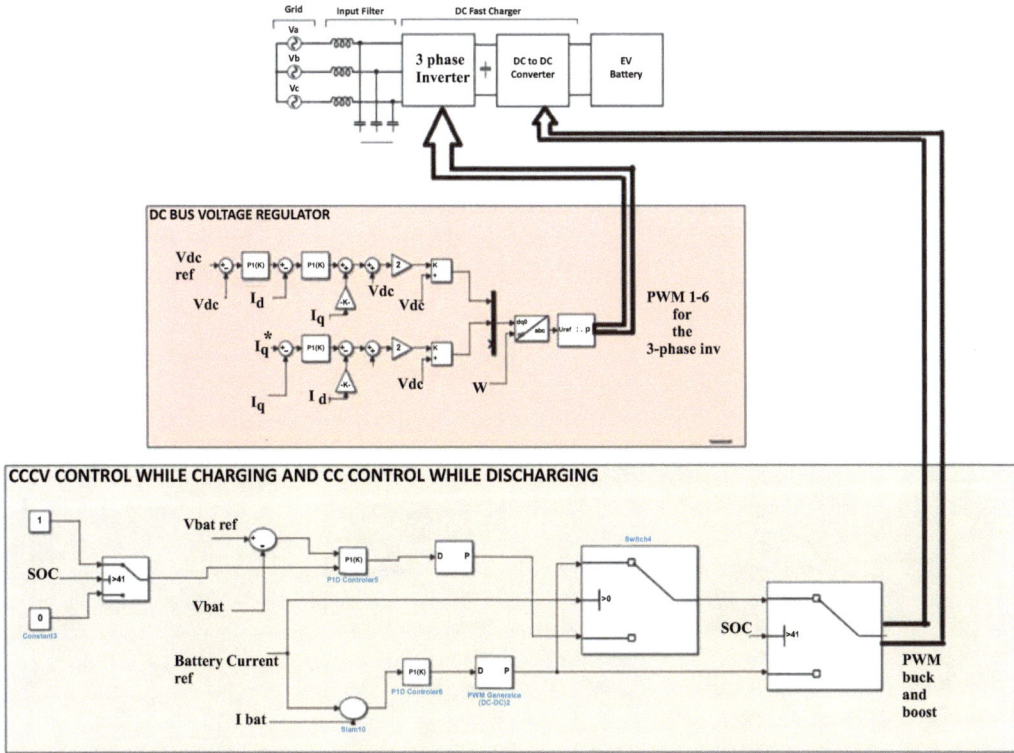

Fig. (16). Scheme of grid-connected bidirectional EV fast charger.

The different operating specifications taken for this model operation are tabulated and presented in Table **3**.

Table 3. Electric vehicle charging types and levels.

Parameters	Grid Voltage	DC Bus voltage	Battery Voltage	Battery Capacity	Switching Frequency	Input Filter	Output Filter
Values with Units	415 V (line to line)	800V	360 V	300 AH	10 kHz	1.645 mH, 30 µF	30 mH, 225 µF

Grid to Vehicle Operation

The SOC level of the battery is considered to be 70%, and it is expected to go through the transition from CC to CV mode of charging. We can also set any other SOC level to check the efficacy of the controllers.

The CC to CV transition is initiated at SOC 41% in this part of the work. The simulation environment for the presented scheme shows the transition from CC to CV mode of charging and maintenance of power flow through DC link voltage control performance.

The change in SOC during this transition is shown in Fig. (**17**). The change in the positive slope of SOC clearly depicts the two different charging conditions in Fig. **17(b)**. The battery undergoes fast charging through the CC mode operation. The change in slope can also be initiated afterward. This result presents the efficacy of the control at any desired point.

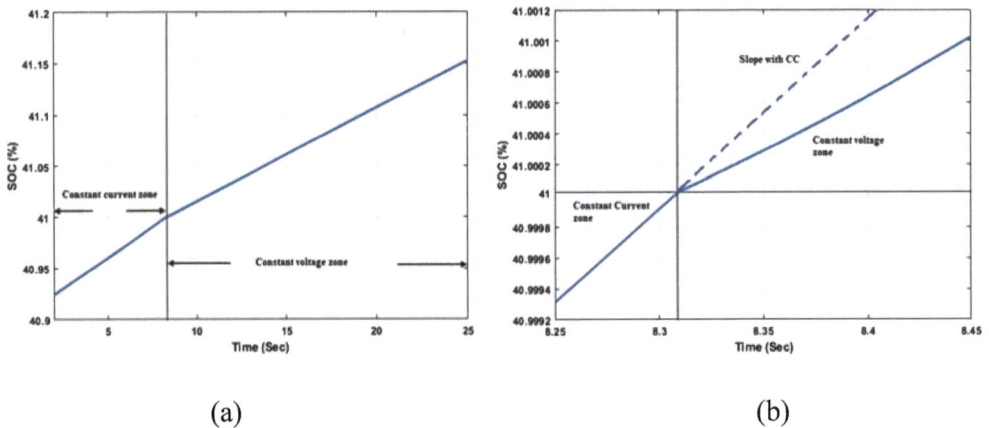

| (a) | (b) |

Fig. (17). (**a**) Change in SOC during CC-CV charging (**b**) Zoomed view depicting reduction in the positive slope in CV mode of charging.

The constant current reference is kept at 130 Amp for the chosen battery. The usual practice is to keep the constant current reference at the nominal discharging current level of the battery. The PI controller decides the voltage required to charge this current, presented in the control scheme, (Fig. **16**). Afterwards, the constant voltage reference is taken as the battery voltage at the 70% SOC level, which is 389.2 V, for the chosen battery in this case. The current drawn by the battery in this mode is dependent upon the battery's character.

The battery current during this CC-CV transition is shown in Fig. (**18**).

The battery current seems to be reduced during the CV mode of charging, resulting in a lower rate of rise in CC, as shown earlier in Fig. (**17**).

The battery voltage during this transition is portrayed in Fig. (**19**).

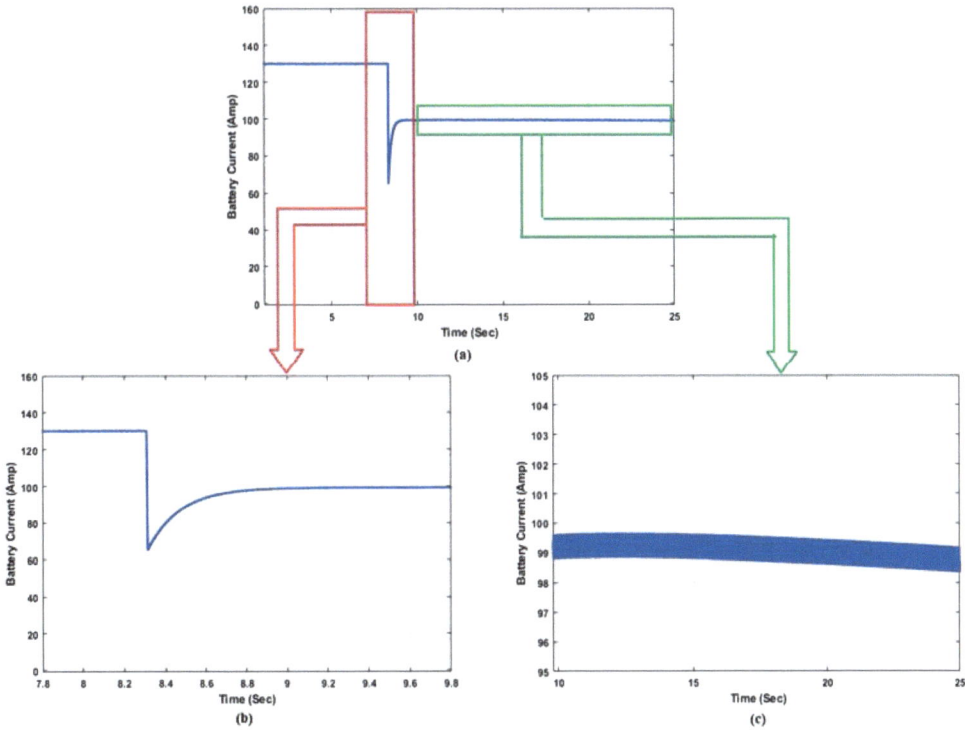

Fig. (18). (a) Battery current during CC-CV transition, **(b)** Constant current reference to variable current, **(c)** reduction in current during CV mode of charging.

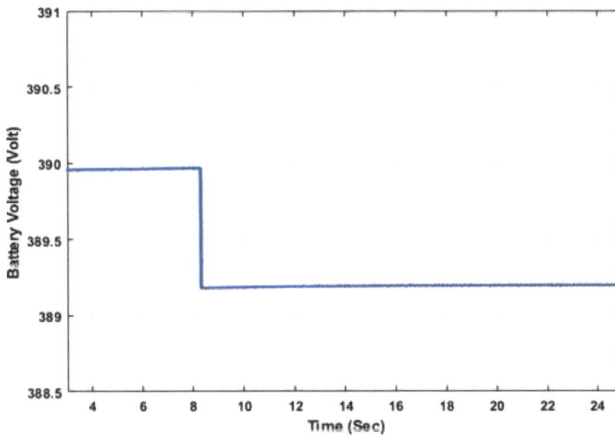

Fig. (19). Battery voltage during CC-CV transition.

The control of the three-phase inverter maintains the DC link voltage. The power supply from the grid changes due to a lower charging rate at CV mode. This transition results in a transient increase in the DC link voltage. The nature of the DC link voltage is presented in Fig. (**20**).

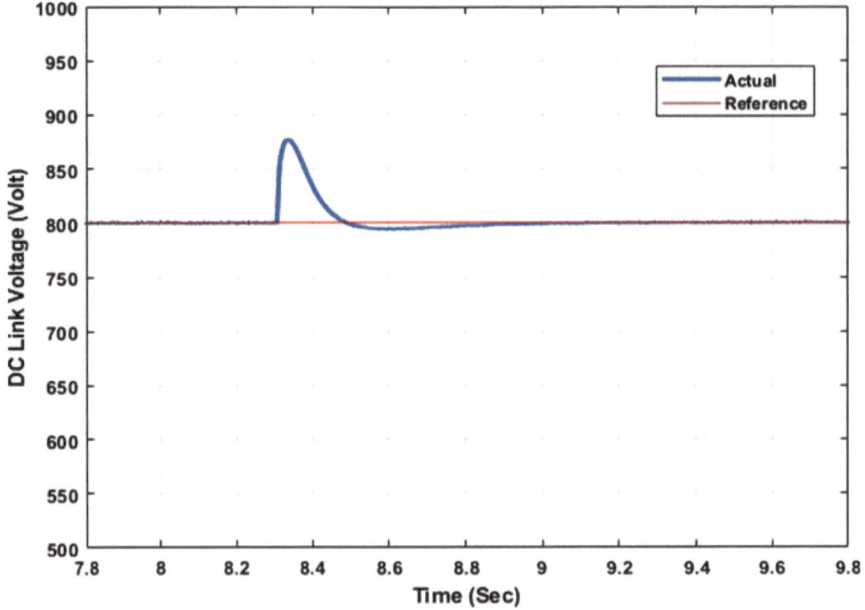

Fig. (20). The DC link voltage during CC-CV charging of EV.

The transient rise in the DC voltage dies within 0.2 sec, and the voltage returns within the 2% band.

The reduction in power drawn from the grid is reflected in the magnitude of the inverter input current from the grid. This grid current variation is presented in Fig. (**21**).

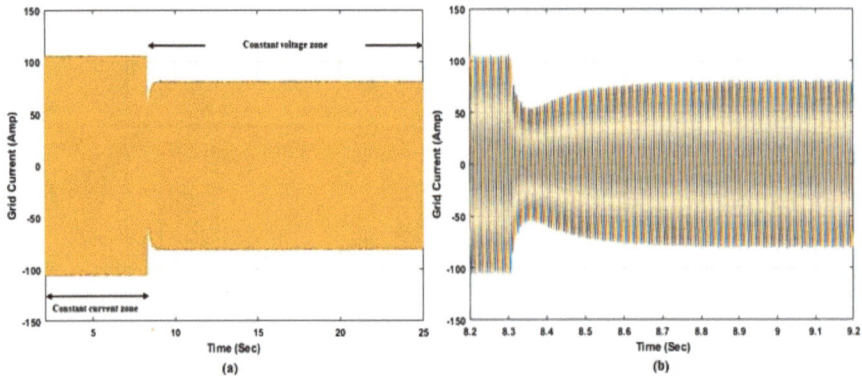

Fig. (21). (**a**) Grid current during CC-CV transition, (**b**) zoomed view of three-phase grid current during CC-CV transition.

All of these results ensure the successful fast charging of the charging scheme of the EV.

Now, the scheme is tested with extreme conditions to supply power from the vehicle to the grid.

Vehicle-to-Grid Operation

This particular operation mode discharges the battery in constant current mode. The battery current and the SOC are portrayed in Fig. **22(a)** and Fig. **22(b)**, respectively.

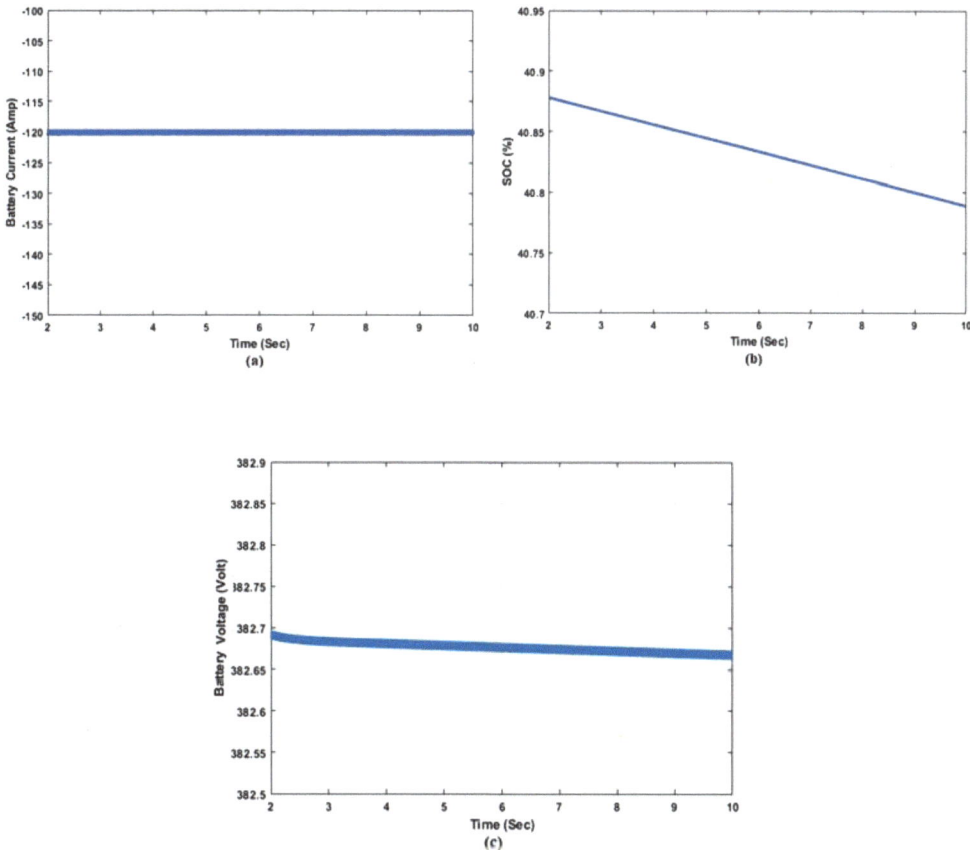

Fig. (22). (**a**) Battery current, (**b**) SOC of battery, and (**c**) Battery voltage during discharging mode of operation.

The SOC of the battery gets reduced during this mode of operation. The battery voltage also gets reduced because of this fall in the SOC. The nature of battery voltage is shown in Fig. **22(c)**.

The control of the 3-phase inverter maintains the DC link voltage in this case. The nature of the DC link voltage is portrayed in Fig. (**23**).

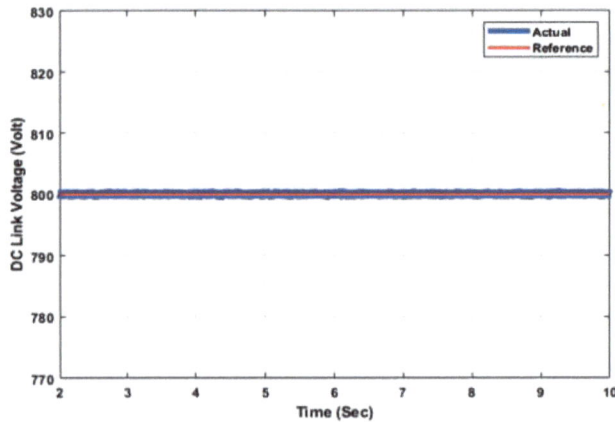

Fig. (23). DC link voltage during discharging mode of operation.

DEVELOPMENT AND IMPLEMENTATION OF CC CV OPERATION IN REAL TIME

A hardware setup has been built in the laboratory to verify the claims made during the simulation. The converter's CC and CV control is implemented through the dSAPCE control board. The generated output of the converter feeds the standalone load and can be synchronized with the grid.

DC-DC Converter

The setup is prepared with power electronic components like IGBT and DIODE, with the part numbers SKM150GAL12T4 and MUR1020CT, respectively. The control scheme is developed and implemented with the dSPACE 1104 digital control board. The controlled variables are sensed through the sensors. The sensed signals are fed through the available ADC to the controller. The output gate pulses are buffered and isolated through external circuits.

Sensing Circuits

Various feedback signals are required to implement the control algorithm in the digital controller. These are obtained through current and voltage sensors.

Hall effect sensors with a conversion ratio of 1000:1 are used to sense current. Average current sensing refers to the processing circuit of two filters and two line currents. These Hall effect sensors (LA55-p) are used to sense three-phase currents. The output of the filters is given to the respective ADC channels of DSP. The voltage sensor circuits refer to the DC link voltage processing circuit. The isolation amplifier (AD202) is used to sense the desired voltage signals. The voltage signals are filtered and buffered by the digital controller.

The controller board, dSPACE DS1104, is installed in the PCI slot. The board comprises two processors. The central processor is MPC8240, which has a clock speed of 250 MHz, and the internal cache memory is 32 kB. This processor works as the master processor on this board. The TMS320F240 DSP acts as the slave one, containing 4k words of dual port RAM. (Fig. **24**) shows functional units and the internal architecture of the DS1104.

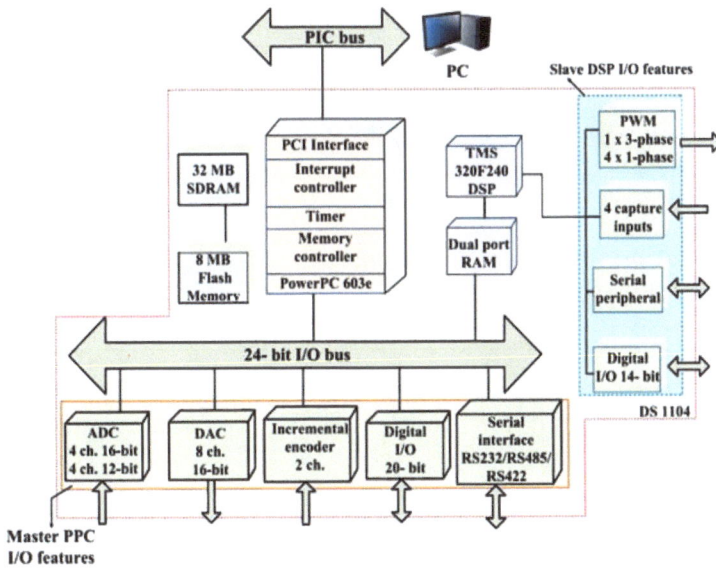

Fig. (24). Block diagram of dSPACE1104.

The master power PC consists of a synchronous DRAM controller, an interrupt controller, six timer devices, and a PCI interface (5 V, 32-bit, 33 MHz). The board has standard I/O features, *i.e.*, ADCs, DACs, bit I/Os, and serial interfaces. The ADC unit consists of two different types of A/D converters. Four ADC channels are multiplexed, and the other four are parallel A/D converters. The multiplexed A/D converters have a 16-bit resolution +10 V input voltage range. The other parallel A/D converters have a 32-bit resolution +10 V input voltage range. The converters provide an interrupt at the end of the A/D conversion.

The complete setup is presented in Fig. (**25**).

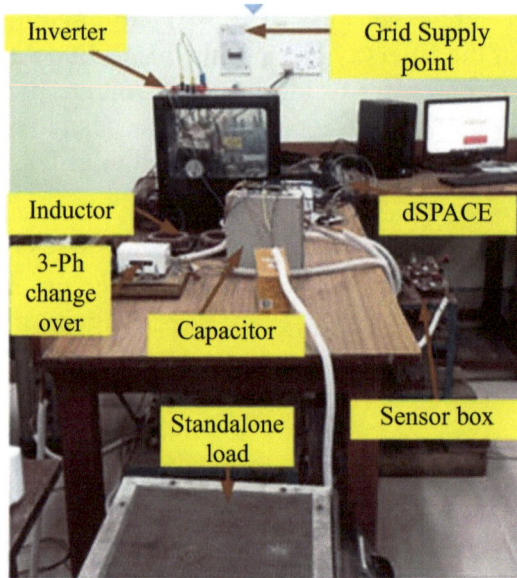

Fig. (25). Experimental setup.

The constant current and constant voltage tracking performances are verified in this mentioned platform.

The variation of current reference and tracking of the actual currents are portrayed in Fig. (**26**). The change in the output DC voltage to accommodate the change in the exact current is shown in Fig. **26(b)**. It is observed that the current controller is working satisfactorily.

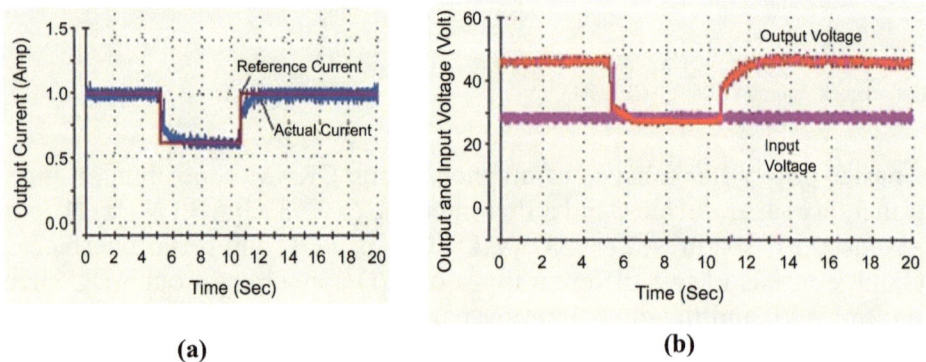

(a)   (b)

Fig. (26). (**a**) Tracking of output current, (**b**) Output and Input voltage of the DC-DC converter.

The zoomed version of the increment in this current and voltage is presented in Fig. (**27**).

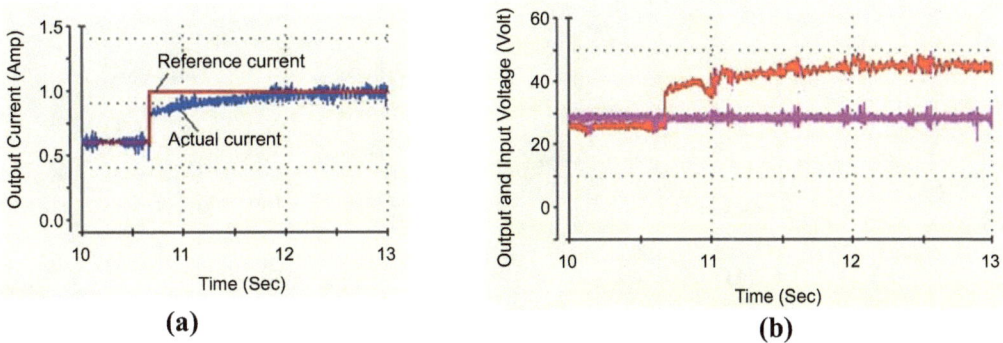

(a)   **(b)**

Fig. (27). (**a**) Increment in the reference and actual output current of the converter, (**b**) Change in the Output and Input voltage of the DC-DC Converter.

The zoomed version of the decrement in this current and voltage are presented in Fig. (**28**).

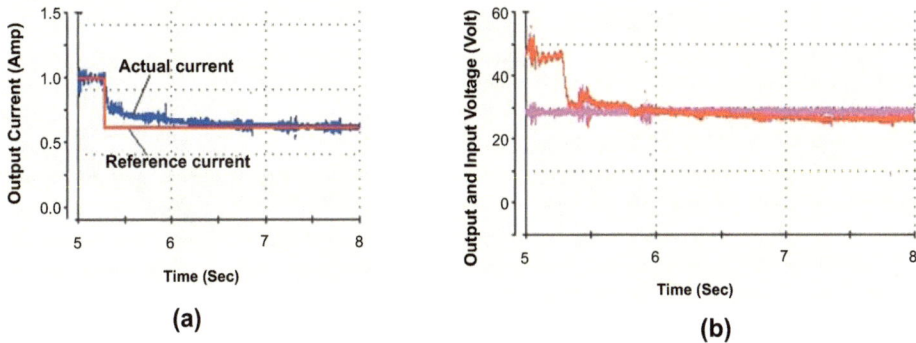

(a)   **(b)**

Fig. (28). (**a**) Decrement in the reference and actual output current of the converter, (**b**) Change in the Output and Input voltage of the DC-DC Converter.

The variation of the output voltage reference and tracking of the actual voltage are portrayed in Fig. (**29**). The change in associated output current with this voltage change is shown in Fig. **29(b)**. It is observed that the current controller is working satisfactorily.

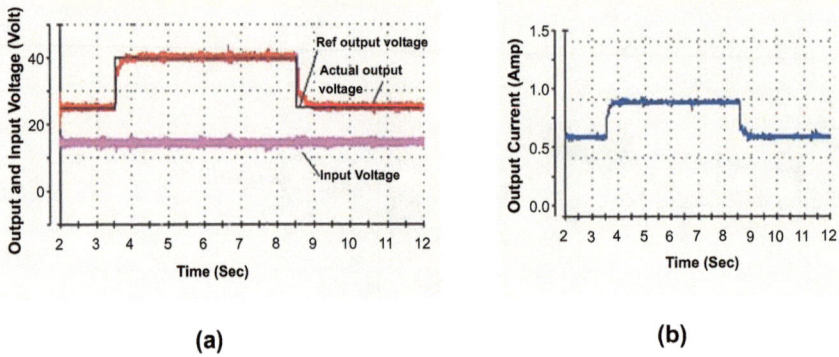

Fig. (29). (**a**) Tracking of output DC voltage and the Input voltage, (**b**) Output current of the DC-DC converter.

The zoomed version of the increment and decrement in this current and voltage are presented in Fig. (**30**). The voltage successfully tracks the reference within 250 ms in both cases.

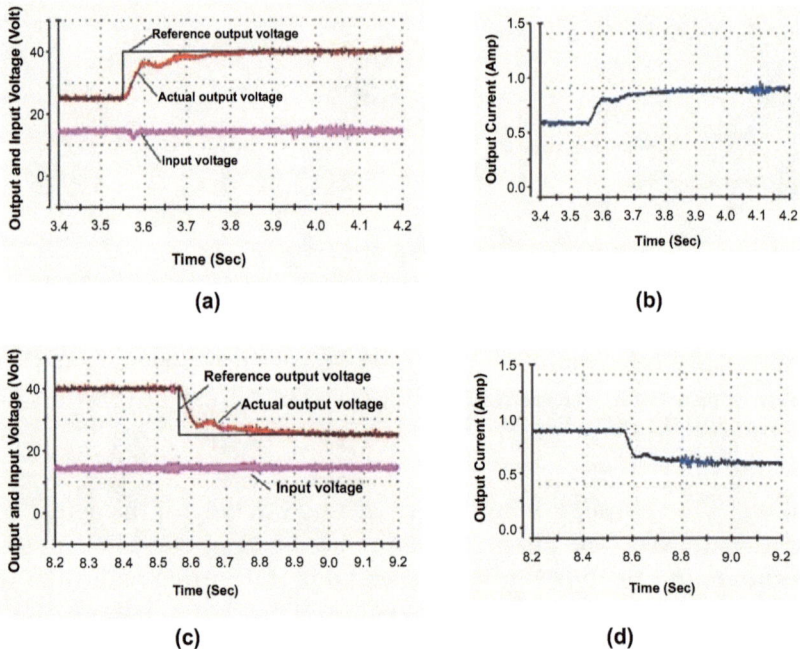

Fig. (30). (**a**) Increment in the output DC voltage and the Input voltage, (**b**) Increment in the output current of the DC-DC converter, (**b**) Decrement in the output DC voltage and the Input voltage, (**b**) Decrement in the output current of the DC-DC converter.

CONCLUSION

The study and implementation of a CC-CV Controller scheme was the main theme of this chapter for EV Fast Charging. The charging system is presented for a general understanding. As an example, the control is developed for one specific converter, a phase-shifted full bridge DC-DC converter with a Lithium-ion battery system. The battery was charged from its initial volumetric energy content (SOC) of a low value. The transition from CC to CV mode is scheduled at 70% SOC. The performance of the developed scheme is found satisfactory.

The described control can improve the performance of the power electronic converters of the EV chargers. The charging current rate increment results in the space of improvement for the charging cycle efficiency and utilization rate of the installed power. The time of operating at partial power increases the charging cycle efficiency.

Finally, the design of the EV charger is proposed, which employs the Three Phase PWM VSR as the front-end converter, and the DC-DC stage utilizes the Bidirectional Buck-Boost Converter, and still, the CC-CV controller scheme is used. The LCL filter, PLL, DQ current controller, and output filter are designed for the charger. The Grid-to-Vehicle (G2V) and Vehicle-to-Grid (V2G) modes of operation of the charger are tested successfully.

The current waveforms, which were constant at steady state and (CC mode) and then decreased close to the Open Circuit Voltage at the set SOC (CV mode), were recorded, verifying both fast and safe charging.

A laboratory prototype is prepared to present the results in real time. The results are found to be satisfactory and prove the efficacy of the developed control.

Accordingly, the reader can gain a comprehensive idea of the fast charging system and its implementation.

AUTHOR'S CONTRIBUTION

The battery charger with two different power circuits and controls is presented in this chapter with the contributions from the authors:

a) Subhra Sen: Development of the concept, development of the model, implementation of the scheme in simulation and in real-time, result analysis, writing draft.

b) Tapas Kumar Saha: Supervising the work, visualizing the application with necessary extensions, final writing, editing, and reviewing.

REFERENCES

[1]   Y. Yasa, "A system efficiency improvement of DC fast-chargers in electric vehicle applications: Bypassing second-stage full-bridge DC-DC converter in high-voltage charging levels", *Ain Shams Engineering Journal,* vol. 14, no. 9, p. 102391, 2023.

[2]   K. Zhou, Y. Wu, X. Wu, Y. Sun, D. Teng, and Y. Liu, "Research and Development Review of Power Converter Topologies and Control Technology for Electric Vehicle Fast-Charging Systems", *Electronics (Basel),* vol. 12, no. 7, p. 1581, 2023.
[http://dx.doi.org/10.3390/electronics12071581]

[3]   S.A.E-N. Khaled, M. Abdelrahem, and M. Nayel, "Phase-Shifted Full-Bridge Converter Used for Fast Simultaneous Charging of EV Batteries", *24th International Middle East Power System Conference (MEPCON),* pp. 19-21, 2023.

[4]   Yang, Y.Z.; Li, H.J.; Wu, C.; Xu, J.Z.; Bi, Y.X.; Zhao, Y, "An Improved Control Scheme for Reducing Circulating Current and Reverse Power of Bidirectional Phase-Shifted Full-Bridge Converter" *IEEE Trans. Power Electron,* 2022.

[5]   L. Zhao, Y. Pei, L. Wang, L. Pei, W. Cao, and Y. Gan, "Design Methodology of Bidirectional Resonant CLLC Charger for Wide Voltage Range Based on Parameter Equivalent and Time Domain Model", *IEEE Trans. Power Electron.,* vol. 37, no. 10, pp. 12041-12064, 2022.
[http://dx.doi.org/10.1109/TPEL.2022.3170101]

[6]   A. Nasir, "Design and Development of a Constant Current Constant Voltage Fast Battery Charger for Electric Vehicles", *4th International Conference on Modern Research in Science, Engineering and Technology,* 2021.
[http://dx.doi.org/10.33422/4th.msetconf.2021.03.02]

[7]   D. Lyu, T.B. Soeiro, and P. Bauer, "Impacts of Different Charging Strategies on the Electric Vehicle Battery Charger Circuit Using Phase-Shift Full-Bridge Converter", *19th IEEE International Power Electronic and Motion Control Conference (PEMC),* pp. 25-29, 2021.
[http://dx.doi.org/10.1109/PEMC48073.2021.9432497]

[8]   Y. Wei, Q. Luo, and A. Mantooth, "Hybrid Control Strategy for LLC Converter With Reduced Switching Frequency Range and Circulating Current for Hold-Up Time Operation", *IEEE Trans. Power Electron.,* vol. 36, no. 8, pp. 8600-8606, 2021.
[http://dx.doi.org/10.1109/TPEL.2021.3054850]

[9]   N. Vazquez, and M. Liserre, "Peak Current Control and Feed-Forward Compensation of a DAB Converter", *IEEE Trans. Ind. Electron.,* vol. 67, no. 10, pp. 8381-8391, 2020.
[http://dx.doi.org/10.1109/TIE.2019.2949523]

[10]   B. Nallamothu, B.S. Krishnan, and R. Janga, "Performance Evolution of Small Signal Model based Peak Current Mode Controller for Off-board Fast Charging DC-DC Converter", *IEEE 17th India Council International Conference (INDICON),* 2020.
[http://dx.doi.org/10.1109/INDICON49873.2020.9342288]

[11]   M. Escudero, D. Meneses, N. Rodriguez, and D.P. Morales, "Modulation Scheme for the Bidirectional Operation of the Phase-Shift Full-Bridge Power Converter", *IEEE Trans. Power Electron.,* vol. 35, no. 2, pp. 1377-1391, 2020.
[http://dx.doi.org/10.1109/TPEL.2019.2923804]

[12]   L.C. Shih, Y.H. Liu, and H.J Chiu, "A Novel Hybrid Mode Control for Phase-shift Full Bridge Converter Featuring High Efficiency over Full Load Range", *IEEE Trans. Power Electron,* 2019.
[http://dx.doi.org/10.1109/TPEL.2018.2838572]

[13]   V.R.K. Kanamarlapudi, B.F. Wang, N.K. Kandasamy, and P.L So, "A New ZVS Full-Bridge DC-DC Converter for Battery Charging with Reduced Losses Over Full-Load Range", *IEEE Trans. Ind. Appl.,* 2018.
[http://dx.doi.org/10.1109/TIA.2017.2756031]

[14]   Arya P, S and R. Chithra. "Phase Shifted Full Bridge DC-DC Converter." *International Research Journal of Engineering and Technology (IRJET)* Vol. 02, no. 04, 2015.

[15]   Venkat Jakka, Anshuman Shukla & S.V Kulkarni. "A novel dq-vector based control for the three-phase active rectifier in a power electronic transformer." *INDICON Annual*, 2013.

CHAPTER 6

An Adaptive Passivity-based Controller for Battery Charging Application: The Lagrangian Framework

Kumari Shipra[1] and **Rakesh Maurya**[2,*]

[1] *Department of Electrical Engineering, Noida International University, Greater Noida-201312, India*

[2] *Department of Electrical Engineering, Sardar Vallabhbhai National Institute of Technology, Surat-395007, Gujarat, India*

Abstract: This chapter reveals the design and application of an adaptive passivity-based controller in the Lagrangian framework for the three-level (TL) boost converter as an EV battery charger. The proposed control technique is based upon the dynamic model of the proposed system along with the idea of energy shaping and damping injection. First, the state-space equations are developed using the EL formulation. Furthermore, the adaptive PBC on the average dynamics of the TL boost converters is designed along with the stability analysis. To reduce the steady-state errors and to obtain a robust controller against dynamics and external disturbances, a PI controller is added parallel to the proposed controller. The performances of the proposed controller are studied for two different loads (resistive and battery) under several operating conditions through MATLAB/ Simulink and tested through the OPAL-RT simulator. The power quality feature of the TL boost PFC converter is also assessed through total harmonic distortion of input source current under different operating conditions. Less than 5% total harmonic distortion is observed in the source current under various loading conditions, which lies in the range of international harmonic standard IEC 61000-3-2 Class C. Further, the comparative discussion of the proposed adaptive PBC with the PI controller is included in terms of peak overshoot, rise time, peak time and settling time.

Keywords: Adaptive passivity-based control, Euler-lagrange equation, Mathematical modeling, Three-level boost converter.

INTRODUCTION

In recent years, Electric Vehicles (EVs) have been getting more attention due to their low transportation cost, low maintenance, high efficiency, and reduction in CO_2 emission as compared to internal combustion engines [1, 2]. For successful

* **Corresponding author Rakesh Maurya:** Department of Electrical Engineering, Sardar Vallabhbhai National Institute of Technology, Surat-395007, Gujarat, India ; E-mail:kumarishipra2005@gmail.com

Nitesh Tiwari, Shekhar Yadav and Sabha Raj Arya (Eds.)

implementation of EVs, the battery chargers play a key role that must have a well-regulated DC power supply along with improved power qualities quality features like low THD and nearly unity power factor. The switched mode power converters are very popular for EV battery charging due to reduced losses, high efficiency, compact size, and lighter weight [3, 4]. The boost converter-based power factor correction is the most common for the design of general-purpose power supply because of its simple circuit that draws low-distorted input current from the supply main along with unity power factor [5, 6]. However, its switch experienced large switching stresses and switching losses that yielded low efficiency. Hence, a TL boost PFC converter topology is reported that reduces stresses on the switch as well as filter size by adding an additional capacitor, diode, and switch in the existing circuit [7, 8].

Several linear and non-linear controllers have been devised in the literature to achieve the desired output of the switched-mode power supply [9 - 15]. Conventionally, the switched power converters have been controlled with the help of fast controllers (P, PI, PID) [9]. Various non-linear control techniques have been reported [10-12] to improve the system's performance. In a study [10], an SMC approach is studied, which has robust features but suffers from chattering problems. In order to charge EV batteries, various control methodologies have been reported [11, 12]. The PI controller is employed for designing the EV battery charger [11]. It has the complex problem of tuning the controller parameters. In a study [12], the Fuzzy Logic Controller (FLC) is examined, and there is no need for either mathematical modelling or complex calculations, but there is no systematic and proper approach to designing the controller.

Recently, Passivity-Based Controllers (PBCs) have been extensively used to alter system energy by incorporating a virtual damping term that helps to achieve asymptotic stability, and the system becomes passive [13, 14]. The PBC in the Lagrangian framework for a conventional switched electrical system like a buck, boost, and buck-boost has been addressed [15, 16] and is explored in complex circuits [17]. Due to the non-minimum phase behaviour of the switched electrical system, an indirect control technique is employed, which controls the output voltage to the fixed value *via* input inductor current [13].

The PBC technique is also employed for the battery charging application using a bi-directional buck-boost converter [18]. The PBC in the Hamiltonian framework has been studied for several switched power converters in literature [19 - 21]. To improve the robustness of the controllers, an adaptive PBC methodology has been proposed [22 - 24]. In the adaptive passivity-based control technique, the system stabilises using adaptation laws with the help of the state estimators of uncertain parameters [23]. In a study [25], an adaptive sliding mode control scheme has been employed for a DC-DC converter with an unknown load.

Like non-linear controllers, passivity-based controllers also require accurate average dynamic equations of the system. Several efforts have been made for the mathematical modelling of nonlinear electrical networks using a power-based approach [26 - 28]. Initially, mathematical modelling of DC-DC power converters was presented by Middlebrook and Ćuk [26]. In a paper [27, 28], the classical Euler-Lagrange (EL) and Hamiltonian-based methodologies have been discussed.

The main contributions of this chapter include (i) the design of an adaptive PBC for the TL boost PFC converter, which facilitates regulated DC output voltage and improves power qualities like low THD and nearly unity power factor operation; (ii) Furthermore, stability analysis, eigenvalues and frequency response analysis are accomplished. (iii) The developed control law is validated through Simulink/MATLAB as well as through OPAL RT simulator. (iv) Additionally, the comparative discussion of the proposed adaptive PBC against the PI controller is included in terms of efficiency, THD, and various control parameters.

This chapter is structured in the following manner. In Section I, a brief introduction regarding the TL boost converter, EV battery charger, power factor correction, and PBC technique, along with the objective of the paper, are discussed. Section II explains the system configuration, modes of operation, and the dynamics of the TL boost converter. The adaptive PBC is introduced in section III. The stability analysis, eigenvalues, and frequency response of the system are also included in section III. Simulation results and comparative study, along with the test results, are discussed in section IV. Further, the conclusion is provided in section V.

SYSTEM CONFIGURATION

A schematic diagram of the proposed system with the adaptive PBC is depicted in Fig. (1). The adaptive PBC is implemented in the anticipated system to provide controlled DC output voltage along with improved power quality. The adaptive controller includes adaption laws, which make the converter insensitive to parameter variations.

Topology

The above circuit diagram (Fig. 1) includes a single-phase diode bridge rectifier (DBR), a TL boost converter, a load (resistive or battery), and an adaptive PBC. The single-phase DBR is used to obtain a rectified sine wave $E(t)$, from sinusoidal input source voltage, which acts as an input source for the TL boost converter.

The proposed TL boost converter contains storage inductor (L) output capacitors (C_1, C_2), diodes (D_1, D_2) and switches (S_1, S_2). The duty ratio of both switches is the same but is shifted by 1800 , reducing the ripple contents in passive elements.

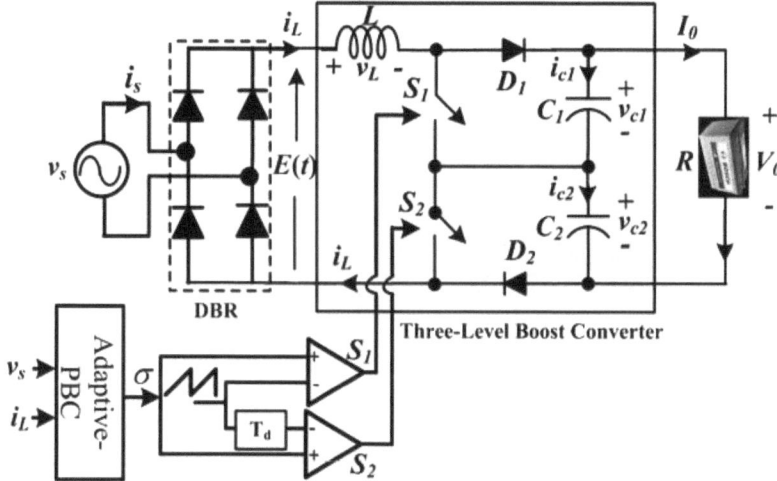

Fig. (1). A schematic diagram of TL boost PFC converter.

The duty cycle changes to either $\sigma < 0.5$ or $\sigma > 0.5$ in each sampling time as the rectified voltage $E(t)$, keeps on changing from zero to its peak value. The switching waveforms for both duty ratios ($\sigma < 0.5$ and $\sigma > 0.5$) are shown in Fig. (2).

A Lagrangian Formulation of TL Boost Converter

This section discusses the dynamic equation of the TL boost converter, which has been derived using an Euler-Lagrange [17] dynamics approach as given below:

$$\frac{d}{dt}\left\{\frac{\partial L}{\partial \dot{q}}(q,\dot{q})\right\} - \frac{\partial L}{\partial q}(q,\dot{q}) = -\frac{\partial D}{\partial \dot{q}}(q,\dot{q}) + A(q)\lambda + F_q, \qquad \textbf{(1a)}$$

$$L(q,\dot{q}) = T(q,\dot{q}) - V(q,\dot{q}). \qquad \textbf{(1b)}$$

Where $(\dot{q})$ is the current vector, represented by $\dot{q}_1,......,\dot{q}_n$. $D(q,\dot{q})$ is the dissipation function and λ is the Lagrange multiplier.

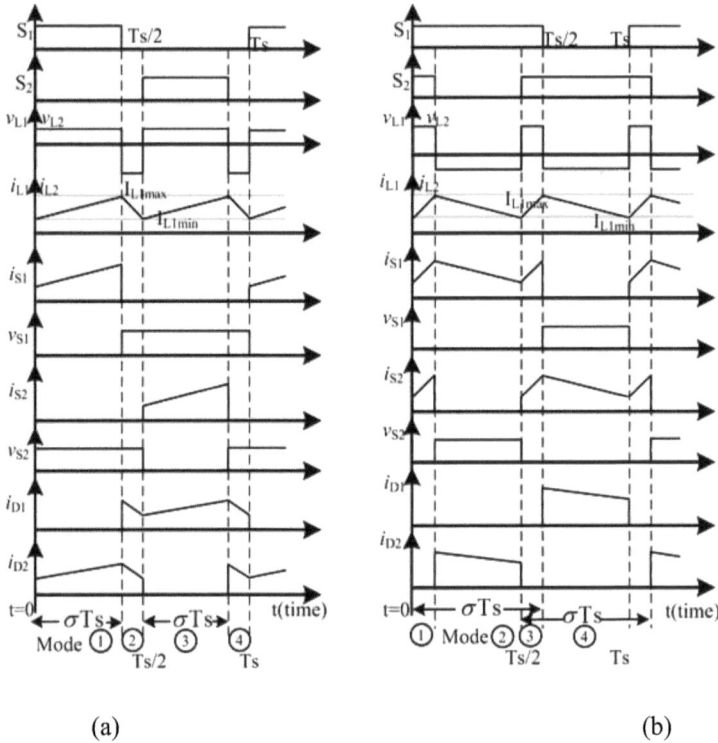

(a)   (b)

Fig. (2a and b). Switching waveform of TL boost converter over one cycle.

Here, the dynamic equation of the TL boost converter is established by using the Lagrangian formulation. So, first, we should obtain EL parameters using EL Eq. (**1**) for all possible switching states in one switching cycle. The switching states for both switches (σ_1, σ_2) are identified as '1' as 'ON' and '0' as 'OFF'.

Although the dissipation function $\mathcal{D}(\dot{q}_R)$ and forcing functions of the proposed system are same for all modes as given below.

$$\mathcal{D}(\dot{q}_R) = \frac{1}{2} R \dot{q}_R^2,$$

$$\mathcal{F}_{q_L} = E; \mathcal{F}_{q_{C1}} = 0; \mathcal{F}_{q_{C2}} = 0.$$

Meanwhile, the Lagrangian is a variant function with switching states, as discussed below. Let the switches be at position (1, 0) *i.e.* switch (S_1 : *ON*) and (S_2 : *OFF*), and concerned power diodes (D_2 : *ON*) , (D_1 : *OFF*) as shown in Fig. **3(a)**. The EL parameters for switching states (1, 0) are as follows.

Fig. (3). Equivalent circuits of TL boost converter under various switching states.

$$\mathcal{L}^{(1,0)}(q_L, \dot{q}_L) = \frac{1}{2} L \dot{q}_L^2 - \frac{1}{2C_1} q_R^2 - \frac{1}{2C_2}(q_L - q_R)^2, \quad \dot{q}_R = \dot{q}_L - \dot{q}_{C2}, \quad \dot{q}_R = \dot{q}_L - \dot{q}_{C2}.$$

When the switches are at position (0, 1), *i.e.* switch, (S_1 : *OFF*) and (S_2 : *ON*) and power diode (D_1 : *ON*) and (D_2 : *OFF*) as depicted in Fig. **3(b)**. The EL parameters for switching states (0, 1) are:

$$\mathcal{L}^{(0,1)}(q_L, \dot{q}_L) = \frac{1}{2} L \dot{q}_L^2 - \frac{1}{2C_1}(q_L - q_R)^2 - \frac{1}{2C_2} q_R^2, \quad \dot{q}_R = \dot{q}_L - \dot{q}_{C1}, \quad \dot{q}_R = \dot{q}_{C2}.$$

For the switches position (1, 1), both switches (S_1, S_2 : *ON*) and corresponding diodes, as shown in Fig. **3(c)**, and the EL parameter for switching states (1, 1) are as follows:

$$\mathcal{L}^{(1,1)}(q_L, \dot{q}_L) = \frac{1}{2} L \dot{q}_L^2 - \frac{1}{2C_1} q_R^2 - \frac{1}{2C_2} q_R^2, \quad \dot{q}_R = \dot{q}_{C1}, \quad \dot{q}_R = \dot{q}_{C2}.$$

Considering the switches at position (0, 0), both switches (S_1, S_2) are OFF and power diodes (D_1, D_2) are conducting as depicted in Fig. **3(d)**. Hence, the EL parameters for switching states (0, 0) are:

$$\mathcal{L}^{(0,0)}(q_L, \dot{q}_L) = \frac{1}{2} L \dot{q}_L^2 - \frac{1}{2C_1}(q_L - q_R)^2 - \frac{1}{2C_2}(q_L - q_R)^2, \quad \dot{q}_R = \dot{q}_L - \dot{q}_{C1}, \quad \dot{q}_R = \dot{q}_L - \dot{q}_{C2}.$$

The above-mentioned EL parameters for various switching states can be generalized in terms of switching states (σ_1, σ_2) as given below:

$$\mathcal{L}^{(\sigma_1,\sigma_2)}(q_L, \dot{q}_L) = \frac{1}{2} L \dot{q}_L^2 - \frac{1}{2C_1}((1-\sigma_1)q_L - q_R)^2 - \frac{1}{2C_2}((1-\sigma_2)q_L - q_R)^2,$$

$$\mathcal{D}^{(\sigma_1,\sigma_2)}(\dot{q}_R) = \frac{1}{2} R \dot{q}_R^2, \quad \mathcal{F}_{q_L} = E; \mathcal{F}_{q_{C1}} = 0; \mathcal{F}_{q_{C2}} = 0,$$

$$\dot{q}_{C1} = (1-\sigma_1)\dot{q}_L - \dot{q}_R, \quad \dot{q}_{C2} = (1-\sigma_2)\dot{q}_L - \dot{q}_R, \quad \dot{q}_R = \frac{q_{C1}}{RC_1} + \frac{q_{C2}}{RC_2}.$$

Substituting the above equations in the EL Eq. **(1)**, the above boils down to

$$L\ddot{q}_L = -\frac{(1-\sigma_1)}{C_1} q_{C1} - \frac{(1-\sigma_2)}{C_2} q_{C2} + E,$$

$$\frac{\dot{q}_{C1}}{C_1} = \frac{1}{C_1}\left((1-\sigma_1)\dot{q}_L - \frac{q_{C1}}{RC_1} - \frac{q_{C2}}{RC_2}\right),$$

$$\frac{\dot{q}_{C2}}{C_2} = \frac{1}{C_2}\left((1-\sigma_2)\dot{q}_L - \frac{q_{C1}}{RC_1} - \frac{q_{C2}}{RC_2}\right).$$

(2)

$$\begin{bmatrix} \dot{z}_1 \\ \dot{z}_2 \\ \dot{z}_3 \end{bmatrix} = \begin{bmatrix} 0 & -\dfrac{(1-\sigma)}{L} & -\dfrac{(1-\sigma)}{L} \\ \dfrac{(1-\sigma)}{C_1} & -\dfrac{1}{RC_1} & -\dfrac{1}{RC_2} \\ \dfrac{(1-\sigma)}{C_2} & -\dfrac{1}{RC_1} & -\dfrac{1}{RC_2} \end{bmatrix} \begin{bmatrix} z_1 \\ z_2 \\ z_3 \end{bmatrix} + \begin{bmatrix} \dfrac{1}{L} \\ 0 \\ 0 \end{bmatrix} E.$$

Where, z_1 is the average inductor current through the inductor (L). z_1 and z_2 are the average capacitor voltages across capacitors (C_1) and, (C_2) respectively.

CONTROLLER DESIGN

In this section, consider that the resistive load is constant but unknown in the proposed circuit. In order to handle the uncertainty in parameters, an adaptive PBC controller is designed to inject virtual damping factors [22].

Proposition 1: Consider the average dynamics of the TL boost converter Eq. **(2)**, where $L > 0$, $C_1 = C_2 > 0$, $E(t) > 0$, are known parameters whereas $R > 0$ is the unknown parameter. The adaptive PBC control law of the proposed converter is described by Eq. **3 (A-D)**.

$$\sigma = 1 - \frac{[E - L\dot{z}_1^* + R_1 z_{1e}]}{(z_2^* + z_3^*)}, \tag{3A}$$

$$\dot{z}_2^* = \frac{1}{C_1}\left[(1-\sigma)z_1^* - \hat{\theta}(z_2^* + z_3^*)\right], \tag{3B}$$

$$\dot{z}_3^* = \frac{1}{C_2}\left[(1-\sigma)z_1^* - \hat{\theta}(z_2^* + z_3^*)\right], \tag{3C}$$

$$\dot{\hat{\theta}} = -kz_2^*(z_2 - z_2^*); \quad k > 0, \tag{3D}$$

Where $\theta = G = \frac{1}{R}$, is the unknown load and $\hat{\theta}$ is the estimated load. is the control design parameter known as adaptive gain.

Proof: Let the value of an unknown parameter $\theta = G = \frac{1}{R}$, of the aforesaid circuit. The above-derived average state-space Eq. **(2)** can be presented in the given matrix form.

$$M\dot{z} + (1-\sigma)Jz + R_i z = E_i,$$

$$M = \begin{bmatrix} L & 0 & 0 \\ 0 & C_1 & 0 \\ 0 & 0 & C_2 \end{bmatrix}, \quad J = \begin{bmatrix} 0 & 1 & 1 \\ -1 & 0 & 0 \\ -1 & 0 & 0 \end{bmatrix}, \quad R_i = \begin{bmatrix} 0 & 0 & 0 \\ 0 & \theta & \theta \\ 0 & \theta & \theta \end{bmatrix}, \quad E_i = \begin{bmatrix} 1 \\ 0 \\ 0 \end{bmatrix} E. \tag{4}$$

The system has a non-minimum phase nature. Therefore, output voltage is controlled through an indirect control method in which the desired output voltage is controlled through the input inductor current [16]. Hence, the control reference current in terms of unknown load parameters is given below.

Let the error state variables, $z_e = z - z^*$ and z^* is the desired state vector, *i.e.*

Substituting $z_e - z\text{-}z^*$ in Eq. **(4)**, yields the Eq. **(5)**.

$$M\dot{z}_e + (1-\sigma)Jz_e + R_i z_e = E_i - (M\dot{z}^* + (1-\sigma)Jz^* + R_i z^*). \tag{5}$$

Here, the virtual damping injection (R_{inj}) is injected to achieve the equilibrium point.

$$M\dot{z}_e + (1-\sigma)Jz_e + R_t z_e = \psi,$$

$$\psi = E_i - (M\dot{z}^* + (1-\sigma)Jz^* + R_i z^* - R_{inj}z_e). \tag{6}$$

$$R_t = R_i + R_{inj}, \quad \text{where} \quad R_{inj} = \begin{bmatrix} R_1 & 0 \\ 0 & 0 \end{bmatrix}, \quad R_1 > 0.$$

In adaptive PBC, the load estimation error causes perturbation in the error dynamics system [22]. Hence, the perturbed term is taken as follows.

$$\psi = \begin{bmatrix} 0 \\ -(z_2^* + z_3^*)\tilde{\theta} \\ -(z_2^* + z_3^*)\tilde{\theta} \end{bmatrix},$$

where $\tilde{\theta} = \theta - \hat{\theta}$.

Hence, Eq. (**6**) can be re-written as:

$$M\dot{z}_e + (1-\sigma)Jz_e + R_t z_e = \begin{bmatrix} 0 \\ -(z_2^* + z_3^*)\tilde{\theta} \\ -(z_2^* + z_3^*)\tilde{\theta} \end{bmatrix}. \tag{7}$$

From Eqs. (**6** and **7**), the following equation yields:

$$L\dot{z}_1^* + (1-\sigma)z_2^* + (1-\sigma)z_3^* - R_1 z_{1e} = E,$$

$$C_1\dot{z}_2^* - (1-\sigma)z_1^* + \theta(z_2^* + z_3^*) = -(z_2^* + z_3^*)\tilde{\theta},$$

$$C_2\dot{z}_3^* - (1-\sigma)z_1^* + \theta(z_2^* + z_3^*) = -(z_2^* + z_3^*)\tilde{\theta}.$$

The control law is obtained by solving the above equations. A PI controller is added to the adaptive PBC to improve the robustness of the adaptive PBC controller. The obtained control law after adding the PI controller is given by:

$$\sigma = 1 - \frac{[E - L\dot{z}_1^* + R_1 z_{1e}]}{(z_2^* + z_3^*)} + k_p e(t) + k_i \int e(t)dt, \tag{8A}$$

$$\dot{z}_2^* = \frac{1}{C_1}\left[(1-\sigma)z_1^* - \hat{\theta}(z_2^* + z_3^*)\right], \tag{8B}$$

$$\dot{z}_3^* = \frac{1}{C_2}\left[(1-\sigma)z_1^* - \hat{\theta}(z_2^* + z_3^*)\right], \tag{8C}$$

Where k_p, k_i are the gain of the PI controller, $e(t) = V_{ref}$-V_o is the output voltage error in CV mode, and $e(t) = I_{ref}$-I_o is the output current error in the CC mode.

Stability Analysis

Consider the total error energy function of the above-said system as follows:

$$\mathcal{H}_t = \frac{1}{2} z_e^T M z_e + \frac{1}{2} \frac{\tilde{\theta}^2}{k}.$$

Furthermore, the above equation becomes,

$$\dot{\mathcal{H}}_t = z_e^T (\psi - (1-\sigma) J z_e - R_t z_e) + \frac{1}{k} \tilde{\theta} \dot{\tilde{\theta}}. \tag{9}$$

Consider $\dot{\tilde{\theta}} = \dot{\hat{\theta}}$, and from Eqs. (**3** and **9**), yields Eq. (**10**),

$$\dot{\mathcal{H}}_t = -z_e^T R_t z_e = -z_e^T (R_i + R_{inj}) z_e < 0. \tag{10}$$

Eq. (**10**) satisfies the Lyapunov stability criteria [29]; henceforth, the system is asymptotically stable.

Eigenvalue and Frequency Response Analysis

The eigenvalues and frequency response of the above-mentioned system are attained to determine stability. The eigenvalues are (-59.99, -0.106, -0.106), which fulfilled the stability conditions [30]. Further, the frequency response of the proposed system is deployed in Fig. **4(a)**, which shows that the considered system is stable.

RESULTS AND DISCUSSIONS

The simulation study of an adaptive passivity-based control strategy for three-level boost PFC is carried out through MATLAB/Simulink and validated *via* OPAL RT simulator. The schematic diagram of the proposed controller is displayed in Fig. **4(a)**. The circuit parameters for simulation are selected as AC input source voltage (v_s):230V, 50Hz, inductors (L_1, L_2) : 10mH, output capacitor, and 2.5kHz, switching frequency. The robustness of the developed controller is assessed through steady-state and dynamic performance with battery load.

Here, a lithium-ion battery with a 35Ah rating is charged using CC-CV charging techniques. Initially, it is charged with c/5-rate in CC mode, and after 70% of the

State of Charge (SOC), the battery is charged with a constant voltage of 400V in CV mode. A phase and frequency plot is displayed in Fig. **4(b)**.

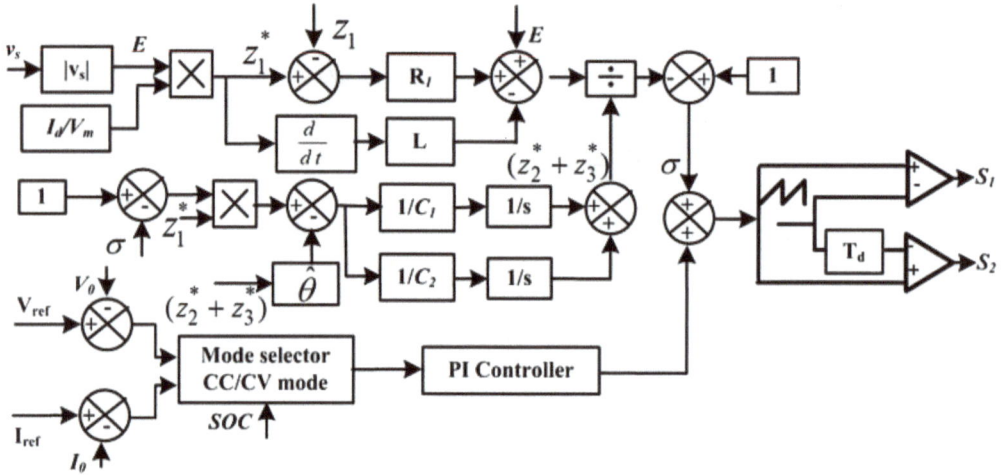

(a)

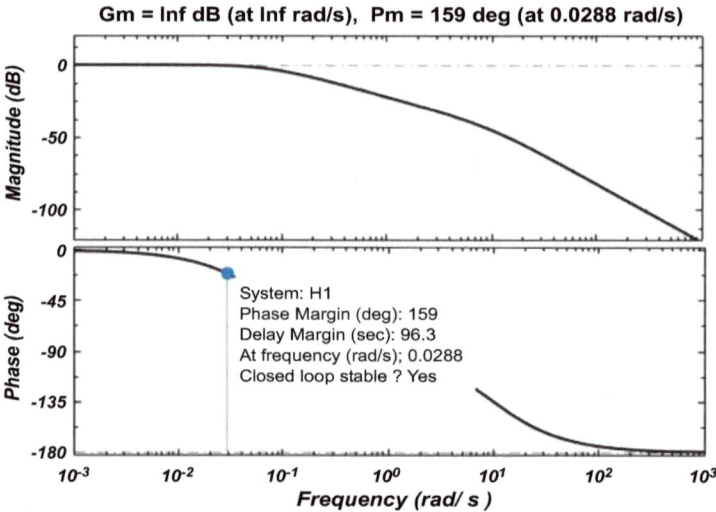

(b)

Fig. (4). (a) Schematic block diagram of adaptive PBC (b) Phase and frequency plot.

As can be noticed in Fig. **(5)**, the output current is achieved at 7A and remains constant in CC mode, and after 70% SOC, a constant voltage of 400 V is achieved in the CV mode. In both cases, the input current is sinusoidal and is in phase with the input voltage source, which depicts operation at unity power factor. The THD of input source current is 3.07% and 4.66% for CC and CV mode as presented in Fig. **5(a)** (ii) and Fig. **5(b)** (ii), respectively.

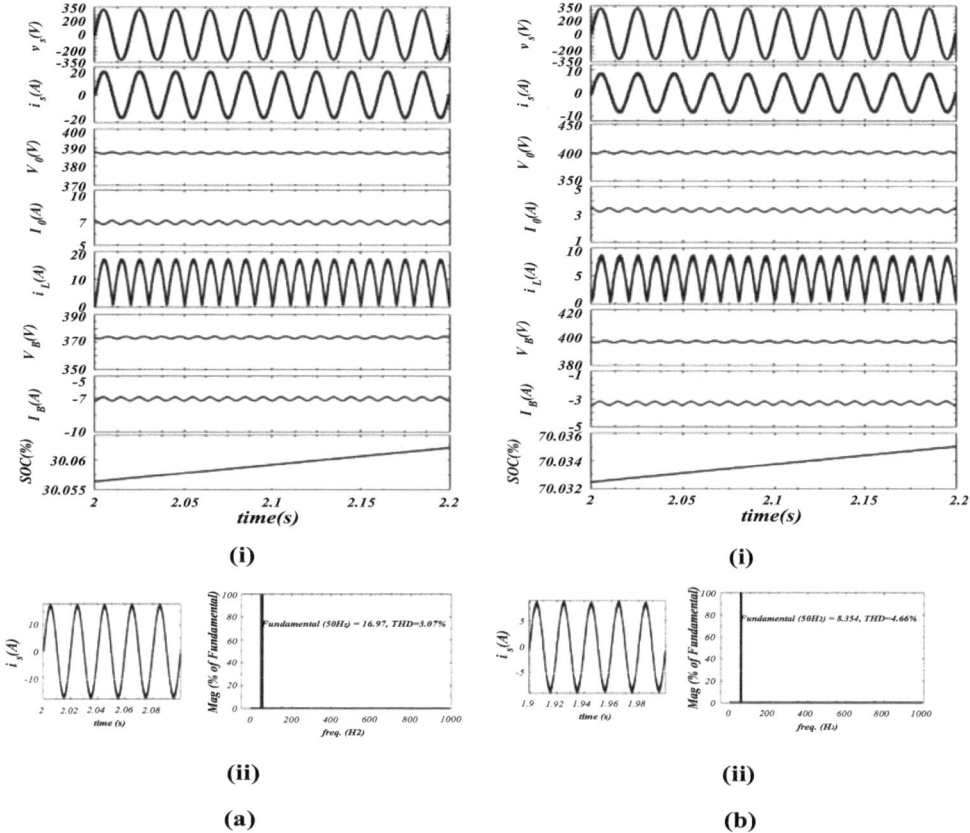

Fig. (5). Steady state waveforms feeding battery load (i) v_s, i_s, V_0, I_0, i_L, V_B, I_B, and SOC (ii) Harmonic spectra of input current (a) CC mode (b) CV mode.

The dynamic performance of the system under input voltage variations is examined, and the obtained results are presented in Fig. (6). The input source voltage decreases by 10% at t=2.5s and increases by 10% of nominal voltage (230) at *t*=3s. Under these source voltage variations, the battery is smoothly charged with 7A in the CC mode and 400V in the CV mode, along with nearly UPF, as presented in Fig. **6(a)** and Fig. **6(b)**, respectively.

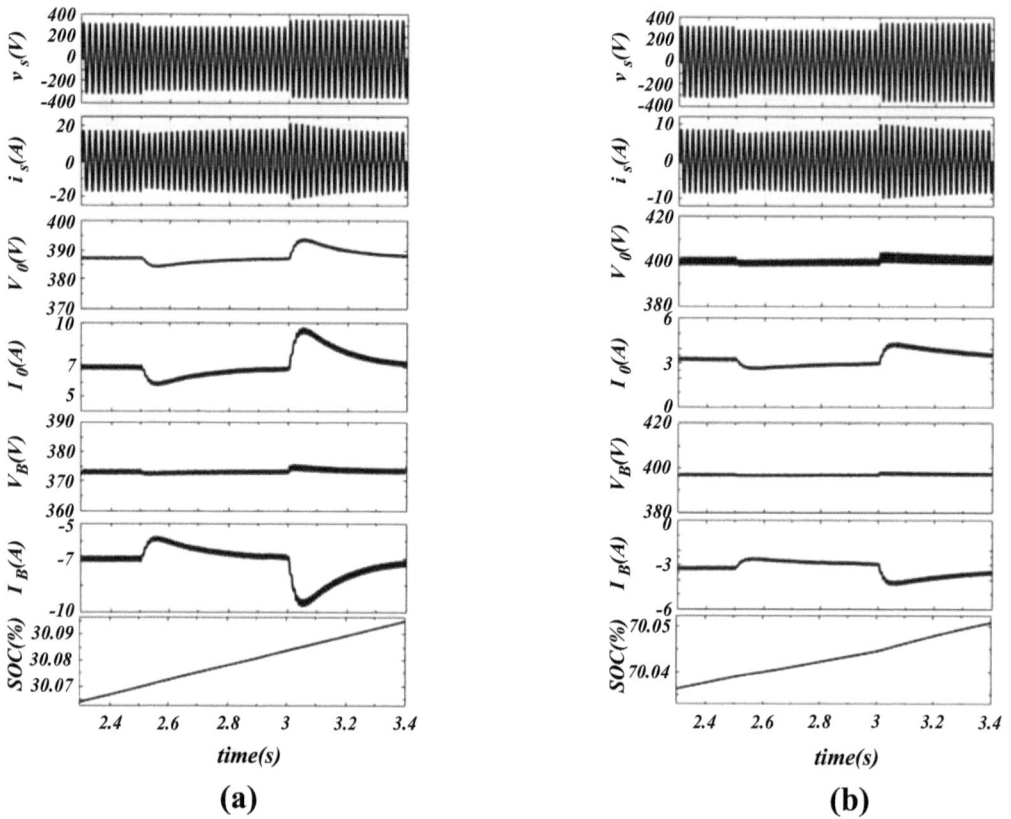

Fig. (6). Dynamic performance feeding battery load against input variations (a) CC mode (b) CV mode.

The simulation results are validated *via* the OPAL-RT simulator with specifications similar to those of the simulation parameters. Fig. (7) displays the photograph of the prototype setup. The adaptive-PBC algorithm through an FPGA-based XC3S5000 series processor with 10μs sampling time is used, and the test results are recorded under various conditions.

The test performance of the proposed converter under battery load with adaptive PBC at single-phase AC supply of *230V, 50Hz* is examined and presented in Fig. (8). It is noticed that the battery is constantly charged along with the nearly UPF in steady state condition and under input source variation (±10% from nominal voltage 230V) as shown in Fig. 8(iii and iv) for both CC and CV mode, respectively.

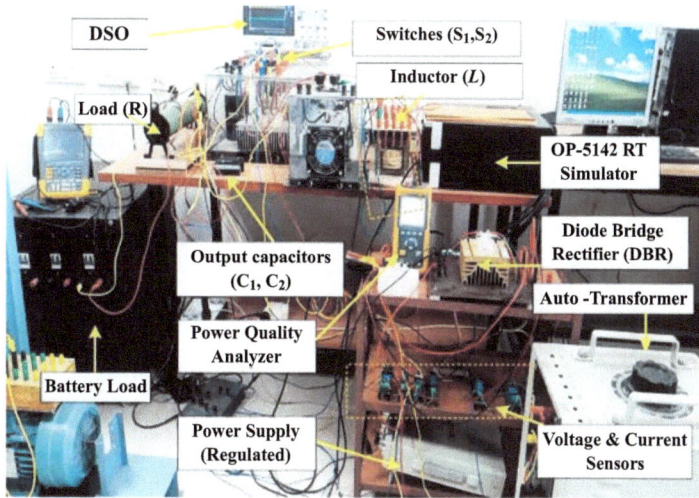

Fig. (7). Photograph of the experimental setup.

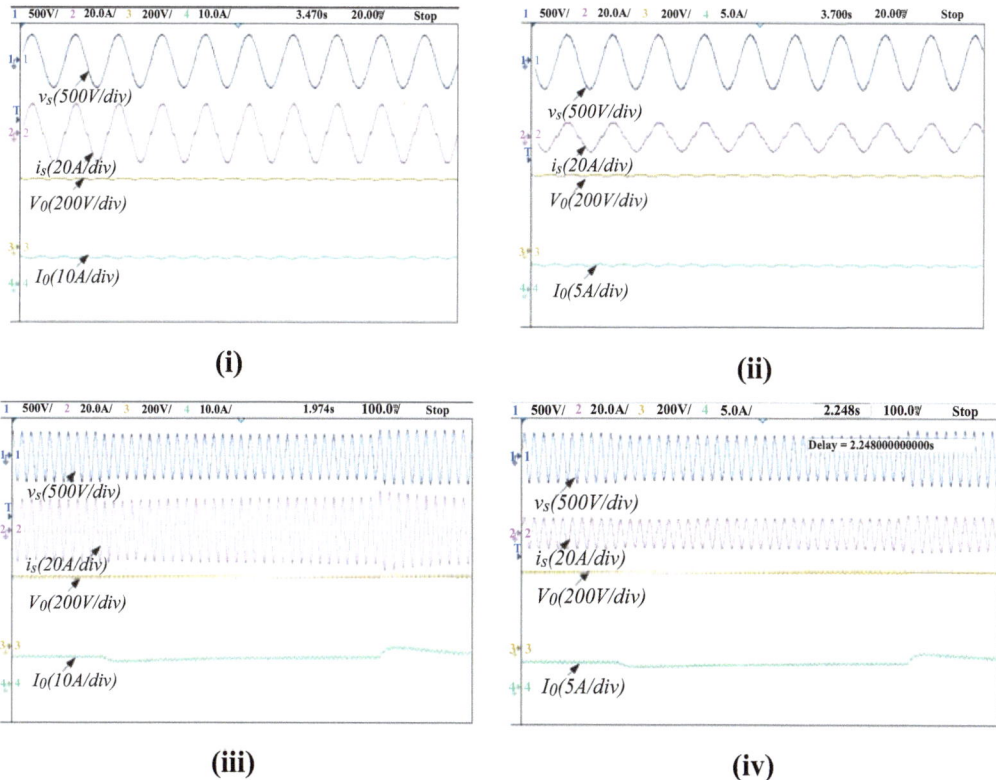

Fig. (8). Waveforms of test results feeding battery load, (i) v_s, i_s, V_0, and I_0, under CC mode (ii) v_s, i_s, V_0, and I_0, under CV mode (iii) dynamic performance against input variations under CC mode (iv) dynamic performance against input variations under CV mode.

The FFT spectrum of supply voltage (v_s and source current (i_s are presented in Fig. (**9**). It is noticed that THD in source voltage (v_s and source current (i_s are 0.4% and 3.6% respectively under R-load. In the CC mode, THD in v_s and i_s are 0.6% and2.8% respectively as presented in Fig. **9(b)**. In the CV mode of battery charging, the THD in v_s and i_s being 0.4% and 4.5% is presented in Fig. **9(c)**, respectively.

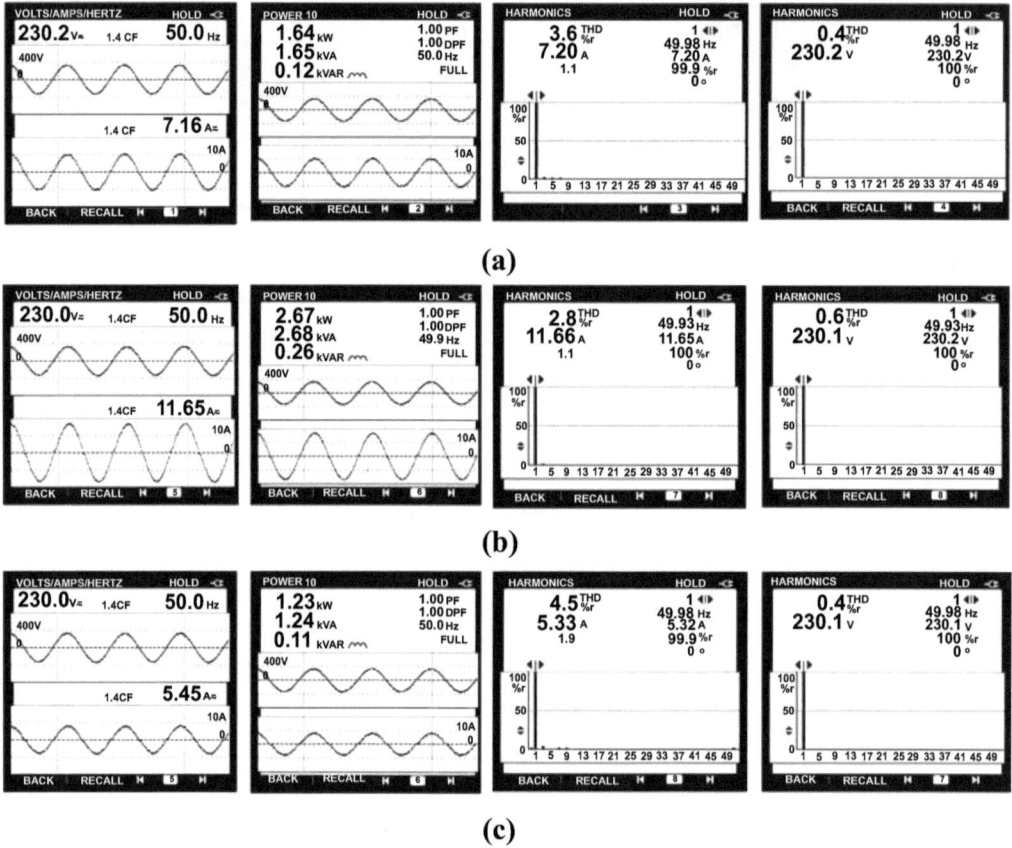

(a)

(b)

(c)

Fig. (9). Power Quality assessment (a) resistive load (b) CC mode (c) CV mode.

COMPARATIVE STUDY

The comparison of the adaptive PBC methodology with the PI controller has been done and depicted in Figs. **10(a-d)**. It can be noticed that the adaptive PBC has higher efficiency than the PI controller under uncertainty conditions, see Figs. **10(a-b)**. It is also noticed that the THD under the adaptive PBC lies in the range of 5%, see Figs. **10(c-d)**. The performance curve of the aforesaid system with the proposed controller is presented in Fig. (**11**) for both charging modes. It is noticed that efficiency varies around 98-99% against a large variation of input voltage in CC mode, and for CV mode, it is 97-98%.

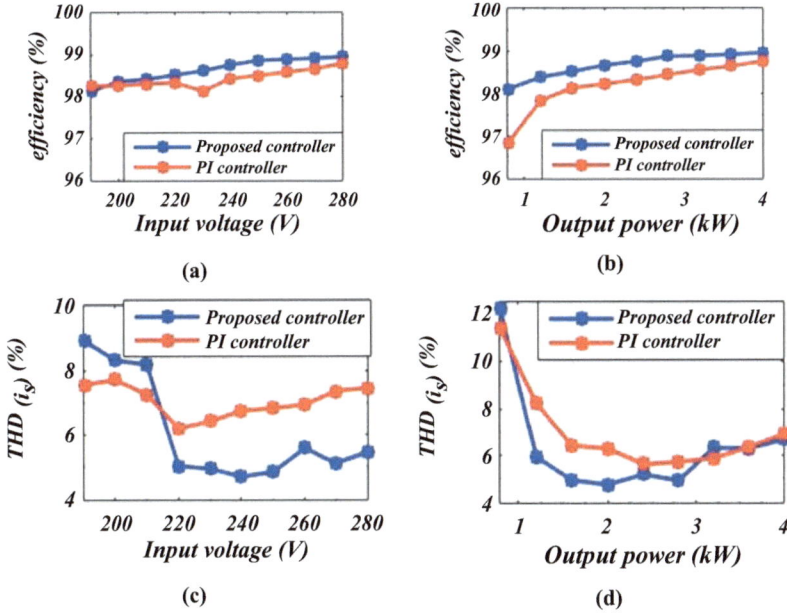

Fig. (10). Comparative performance of TL boost converter feeding resistive load (a) efficiency *vs.* input voltage (b) efficiency *vs.* output power (c) THD (i_s) *vs.* input voltage (d) THD(i_s) *vs.* output power.

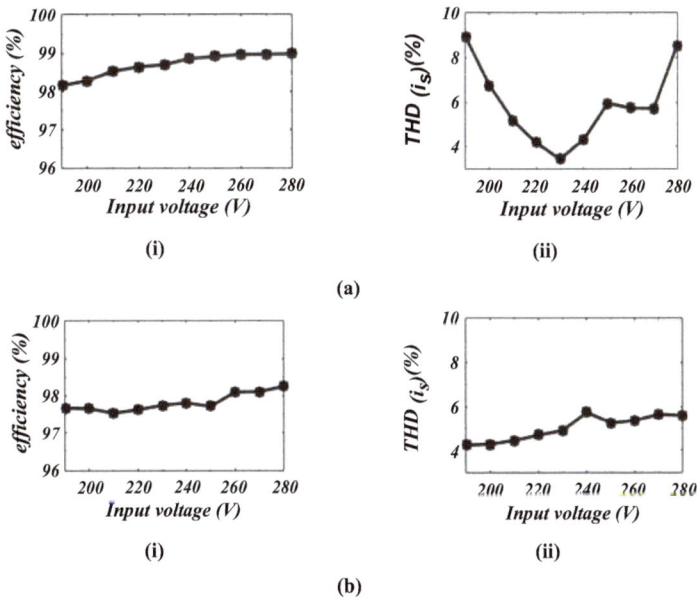

Fig. (11). Performance curves of TL boost converter feeding battery load (a) CC mode (b) CV mode.

The plot of THD against input voltage for battery load is also displayed in Fig. (**11**). It is clearly shown in Tables **1** and **2** that the power factor is nearly unity under the variation of input voltage and load current. The comparative analysis through different control parameters is also carried out and summarized in Tables **3** and **4**.

Table 1. System performance against input variation.

Input Volt (V)	Adaptive PBC			PI Controller		
	THD (%)	Input p. f.	Efficiency (%)	THD (%)	Input p. f.	Efficiency (%)
220	5.04	0.9991	98.49	8.96	0.9994	98.34
230	4.95	0.9991	98.78	5.14	0.9995	98.14
240	4.71	0.9993	98.39	10.04	0.9995	98.44

Table 2. System performance against output power variation.

Output Power (kW)	Adaptive PBC			PI Controller		
	THD (%)	Input p. f.	Efficiency (%)	THD (%)	Input p. f.	Efficiency (%)
2.0	4.76	0.9993	98.66	8.92	0.9995	98.23
2.4	5.20	0.9995	98.76	8.53	0.9996	98.33
2.8	4.93	0.9995	98.86	8.73	0.9996	98.45

Table 3. A comparative study with input variation.

Controllers	Input Volt (V)	M_P (%)	t_r (sec)	t_p(sec)	t_s (sec)
Adaptive PBC	220	20.00	0.015	0.058	0.46
	230	21.25	0.010	0.046	0.46
	240	22.75	0.010	0.038	0.45
PI Controller	220	42.35	0.025	0.038	0.40
	230	43.75	0.024	0.038	0.41
	240	43.75	0.027	0.038	0.41

Table 4. A comparative study with output power.

Controllers	Output Power (kW)	M_P (%)	t_r (sec)	t_p (sec)	t_s (sec)
Adaptive PBC	1.6	21.25	0.010	0.046	0.46
	2.0	18.50	0.010	0.046	0.46
	2.4	15.75	0.010	0.048	0.45

(Table 4) cont.....

Controllers	Output Power (kW)	M_p (%)	t_r (sec)	t_p (sec)	t_s (sec)
PI Controller	1.6	43.75	0.024	0.038	0.41
	2.0	42.35	0.026	0.037	0.39
	2.4	41.50	0.026	0.037	0.39

CONCLUSION

In this chapter, the adaptive PBC in the Lagrangian framework, based on an average TL boost converter mathematical model, is designed and implemented. The mathematical modelling of the TL boost PFC is developed to design the proposed controller. Furthermore, the stability analysis is carried out. In order to achieve a robust controller, a PI controller is added in parallel to the proposed adaptive PBC. The effectiveness of the proposed control scheme for battery load under numerous operating conditions has been studied through Simulink/ MATLAB and verified through the OPAL-RT simulator. Moreover, the superiority and effectiveness of the system are also assessed through THD and it provides less than 5% THD, which lies in the range prescribed by international harmonic standard IEC 61000-3-2 Class C. Based on the simulation studies, the comparative discussions of the above-mentioned controller with the PI controller has been demonstrated through various efficiency curves and various control parameters. It is noticed that the proposed adaptive PBC is appropriate for both loads (resistive and battery) and robust against perturbations of input source and load current.

This chapter would be of interest to practitioners aspiring to refine controllers for EV technology. This chapter is geared towards understanding the adaptive passivity control of switched electrical networks in the Lagrangian framework as well.

REFERENCES

[1]   S.S. Williamson, *Energy management strategies for electric and plug-in hybrid electric vehicles.* Springer: New York, NY, USA, 2013.
      [http://dx.doi.org/10.1007/978-1-4614-7711-2]

[2]   J. Larminie, and J. Lowry, *Electric vehicle technology explained.* John Wiley & Sons: Swindon, UK, 2012.
      [http://dx.doi.org/10.1002/9781118361146]

[3]   N. Mohan and T. M. Mohan, *Power Electronics,* vol. 3 New York: John Wiley & Sons, 1995.

[4]   R.W. Erickson, and D. Maksimovic, *Fundamentals of power electronics.* 2nd ed. Kluwer: New York, USA, 2001.
      [http://dx.doi.org/10.1007/b100747]

[5]   O. García, J.A. Cobos, R. Prieto, P. Alou, and J. Uceda, "Single phase power factor correction: a survey", *IEEE Trans. Power Electron.,* vol. 18, no. 3, pp. 749-755, 2003.
      [http://dx.doi.org/10.1109/TPEL.2003.810856]

[6]   J. Linares-Flores, H. Sira-Ramirez, J. Reger, and S. Hernández-Marcial, "A boost unity power factor pre-compensator", *IEEE Power Electronics Specialists Conference,* pp. 3623-3627, 2008.

[7]   Xinbo Ruan, Bin Li, Qianhong Chen, Siew-Chong Tan, and C.K. Tse, "Fundamental considerations of three-level DC–DC converters: topologies, analyses, and control", *IEEE Trans. Circuits Syst. I Regul. Pap.,* vol. 55, no. 11, pp. 3733-3743, 2008.
[http://dx.doi.org/10.1109/TCSI.2008.927218]

[8]   W.Y. Choi, and S.J. Lee, "Three-Level SEPIC with Improved Efficiency and Balanced Capacitor Voltages", *Journal of Power Electronics,* vol. 16, no. 2, pp. 447-454, 2016.
[http://dx.doi.org/10.6113/JPE.2016.16.2.447]

[9]   H. Sira-Ramirez, "Nonlinear P-I controller design for switchmode DC-to-DC power converters", *IEEE Trans. Circ. Syst.,* vol. 38, no. 4, pp. 410-417, 1991.
[http://dx.doi.org/10.1109/31.75397]

[10]   B.B. Naik, and A.J. Mehta, "Sliding mode controller with modified sliding function for DC-DC Buck Converter", *ISA Trans.,* vol. 70, pp. 279-287, 2017.
[http://dx.doi.org/10.1016/j.isatra.2017.05.009] [PMID: 28577974]

[11]   M. Saleh, Y. Esa, Y. Mhandi, W. Brandauer, and A. Mohamed, "Design and implementation of CCNY DC microgrid testbed," *IEEE Industry Applications Society Annual Meeting,* pp. 1-7, 2016.
[http://dx.doi.org/10.1109/IAS.2016.7731870]

[12]   Tsai-Fu Wu, Chien-Hsuan Chang, and Yu-Hai Chen, "A fuzzy-logic-controlled single-stage converter for PV-powered lighting system applications", *IEEE Trans. Ind. Electron.,* vol. 47, no. 2, pp. 287-296, 2000.
[http://dx.doi.org/10.1109/41.836344]

[13]   H. Sira-Ramirez, R.A. Perez-Moreno, R. Ortega, and M. Garcia-Esteban, "Passivity-based controllers for the stabilization of Dc-to-Dc Power converters", *Automatica,* vol. 33, no. 4, pp. 499-513, 1997.
[http://dx.doi.org/10.1016/S0005-1098(96)00207-5]

[14]   R. Ortega, J.A.L. Perez, P.J. Nicklasson, and H.J. Sira-Ramirez, *Passivity-based control of Euler-Lagrange systems: mechanical, electrical and electromechanical applications.* 1st ed. Springer Science-Verlag London, 1998.
[http://dx.doi.org/10.1007/978-1-4471-3603-3]

[15]   H.J. Sira-Ramirez, and R. Silva-Ortigoza, "Control design techniques in power electronics devices", *Springer Science-Verlag London,* 2006.

[16]   R. Leyva, A. Cid-Pastor, C. Alonso, I. Queinnec, S. Tarbouriech, and I. Martinez-Salamero, "Passivity-based integral control of a boost converter for large-signal stability," *IEEE Proceedings-Control Theory and Applications,* vol. 153, no. 2, pp. 139-146, 2006.
[http://dx.doi.org/10.1049/ip-cta:20045223]

[17]   J.M. Scherpen, D. Jeltsema, and J.B. Klaassens, "Lagrangian modeling and control of switching networks with integrated coupled magnetics", *Proceedings of the 39th IEEE Conference,* pp. 4054-4059, 2000.
[http://dx.doi.org/10.1109/CDC.2000.912349]

[18]   O.D.M. Giraldo, A.G. Ruiz, I.O. Velázquez, and G.R.E. Pérez, "Passivity-Based control for battery charging/discharging applications by using a buck-boost DC-DC converter", *IEEE Green Technologies Conference (GreenTech),* pp. 89-94, 2018.
[http://dx.doi.org/10.1109/GreenTech.2018.00025]

[19]   R. Ortega, A. van der Schaft, B. Maschke, and G. Escobar, "Interconnection and damping assignment passivity-based control of port-controlled Hamiltonian systems", *Automatica,* vol. 38, no. 4, pp. 585-596, 2002.
[http://dx.doi.org/10.1016/S0005-1098(01)00278-3]

[20]   B. Wang, and Y. Ma, "Research on the passivity-based control strategy of buck-boost converters with

a wide input power supply range", *Proceedings of 2nd IEEE International Symposium on Power Electronics for Distributed Generation Systems,* pp. 304-308, 2010.
[http://dx.doi.org/10.1109/PEDG.2010.5545830]

[21] J. Zeng, Z. Zhang, and W. Qiao, "An interconnection and damping assignment passivity-based controller for a DC–DC boost converter with a constant power load", *IEEE Trans. Ind. Appl.,* vol. 50, no. 4, pp. 2314-2322, 2014.
[http://dx.doi.org/10.1109/TIA.2013.2290872]

[22] K. Shipra, S.N. Sharma, and R. Maurya, "Passivity-based controllers for ZVS quasi-resonant boost converter", *IET Control Theory Appl.,* vol. 14, no. 20, pp. 3461-3475, 2020.
[http://dx.doi.org/10.1049/iet-cta.2020.0129]

[23] G. Escobar, D. Chevreau, R. Ortega, and E. Mendes, "An adaptive passivity-based controller for a unity power factor rectifier", *IEEE Trans. Control Syst. Technol.,* vol. 9, no. 4, pp. 637-644, 2001.
[http://dx.doi.org/10.1109/87.930975]

[24] S.I. Seleme Jr, A.H.R. Rosa, L.M.F. Morais, P.F. Donoso-Garcia, and P.C. Cortizo, "Evaluation of adaptive passivity-based controller for power factor correction using a boost converter", *IET Control Theory Appl.,* vol. 6, no. 14, pp. 2168-2178, 2012.
[http://dx.doi.org/10.1049/iet-cta.2011.0218]

[25] M.R. Mojallizadeh, and M.A. Badamchizadeh, "Adaptive passivity-based control of a photovoltaic/battery hybrid power source via algebraic parameter identification", *IEEE J. Photovolt.,* vol. 6, no. 2, pp. 532-539, 2016.
[http://dx.doi.org/10.1109/JPHOTOV.2016.2514715]

[26] L. Shen, D.D.C. Lu, and C. Li, "Adaptive sliding mode control method for DC–DC converters", *IET Power Electron.,* vol. 8, no. 9, pp. 1723-1732, 2015.
[http://dx.doi.org/10.1049/iet-pel.2014.0979]

[27] R. Middlebrook, and S. Cuk, "A general unified approach to modelling switching-converter power stages", *Proceedings of IEEE Power Electronics Specialists Conference,* pp. 18-34, 1976.
[http://dx.doi.org/10.1109/PESC.1976.7072895]

[28] H. Sira-Ramirez, and M.D. deNieto, "A Lagrangian approach to average modeling of pulsewidth-modulation controlled DC-to-DC power converters", *IEEE Trans. Circ. Syst. I Fundam. Theory Appl.,* vol. 43, no. 5, p. 427, 1996.
[http://dx.doi.org/10.1109/81.502217]

[29] H. K. Khalil, *Nonlinear Systems,* 3rd ed. New Jersey, USA: Prentice-Hall, 2006..

[30] S. Bittanti, A. J. Laub, and J. C. Willems, *The Riccati Equation.* Berlin: Springer-Verlag, 1991. [Online]. Available:
[http://dx.doi.org/10.1007/978-3-642-58223-3]

CHAPTER 7

Vehicle-to-Grid (V2G) Battery Charging System for Electric Vehicles

Anurag Dwivedi[1], **Vidhi Dubey**[1,*] and **Vaibhav Tripathi**[1]

[1] *Department of Electrical Engineering, Bansal Institute of Engineering and Technology, Lucknow, Uttar Pradesh, India*

Abstract: This study introduces a groundbreaking Vehicle-to-Grid (V2G) battery charging system tailored specifically for Electric Vehicles (EVs), accompanied by a comprehensive analysis and design methodology. The innovative technology facilitates bidirectional power flow, allowing energy to be transferred from the EV back to the grid or other interconnected devices, alongside conventional charging capabilities for EV batteries. This bidirectional functionality not only enhances the adaptability and efficiency of EV charging infrastructure but also holds significant promise for enhancing the resilience and stability of the grid. By enabling EVs to not only draw energy from the grid but also contribute surplus energy back when needed, the V2G system transforms EVs into flexible energy storage units. This capability can play a crucial role in mitigating grid imbalances caused by fluctuations in renewable energy generation or unexpected demand spikes. Moreover, during peak demand periods or emergencies, EVs can act as distributed energy resources, providing valuable support to the grid and reducing strain on traditional power generation facilities. The deployment of such a V2G system represents a paradigm shift in the way we approach both EV charging and grid management. It offers a sustainable solution to enhance grid resilience, reduce reliance on fossil fuels, and accommodate the growing demand for electric mobility. Additionally, the bidirectional power flow capability opens up opportunities for new revenue streams for EV owners through participation in energy markets or grid services.

Keywords: Battery, Electric grid, Optimization, Two-way communication, Vehicle fleet, Vehicle-to-Grid (V2G).

INTRODUCTION

In response to the growing demand for sustainable transportation solutions, Electric Vehicles (EVs) have gained considerable attention in recent years. As the EV market continues to expand, there is a pressing need for innovative charging infrastructure capable of accommodating the diverse requirements of EV owners

---

* **Corresponding author Vidhi Dubey:** Department of Electrical Engineering, Bansal Institute of Engineering and Technology, Lucknow, Uttar Pradesh, India; Tel: 7753873811; E-mail: dubeyvidhi619@gmail.com

Nitesh Tiwari, Shekhar Yadav and Sabha Raj Arya (Eds.)

and grid operators. Electric vehicles (EVs) emit less carbon dioxide, and the price of fossil fuels is rising; they are now more competitively priced than conventional internal combustion engine vehicles [1]. However, a number of drawbacks, including high car costs, lack of adequate charging infrastructure, and short all-electric drive range, prevent EVs from being widely used in the market [2]. Furthermore, there are many difficult problems when EVs are integrated into the power system. For example, a high degree of EV charging penetration results in higher power grid loading. The revolutionary concept of Vehicle-to-Grid (V2G) involves the use of Electric Vehicle (EV) batteries for energy storage. V2G enables regulated power injection into the grid based on predetermined schedules and pricing structures, allowing EV owners and power utilities to interact dynamically in contrast to normal EV charging. There are several advantages to this mutually beneficial interaction between EVs and grids. When considering V2G from the perspective of power utilities, several benefits are introduced, such as load levelling, harmonic attenuation, reactive power supply, active power regulation, and mitigation of peak loads. Simultaneously, by charging for grid involvement, EV owners can monetize the energy stored in their cars [3 - 5]. The majority of EV chargers that are sold commercially are now made to operate in only one way, which limits their use for slow or fast charging. However, for V2G to be implemented, specific EV chargers that can transfer power in both directions between the EV batteries and the grid are needed. This study proposes a revolutionary bidirectional EV battery charger with a creative control scheme in response to this need. The four operational modes that can be achieved using the proposed control technique are fast charging, rapid discharging, slow charging, and gradual discharging. This adaptability allows for a variety of charging circumstances to ensure effective grid integration and optimal energy management [6, 7].

The Vehicle-to-Grid (V2G) Battery Charging System is a disruptive technology that enables bidirectional energy flow between electric vehicles and the power grid. Unlike traditional charging systems that only draw power from the grid, V2G systems allow EVs to send excess stored energy back to the grid. This capability supports energy efficiency, grid stability, and the integration of renewable energy sources, making it a cornerstone for the future of sustainable energy systems.

The primary functionality of V2G systems is to act as energy consumers and suppliers. When grid demand is low, EVs can charge their batteries, usually benefiting from lower electricity prices. Conversely, in peak demand or emergencies, they can discharge stored energy back into the grid when used as mobile energy storage. This bidirectional energy flow helps stabilize the grid, reduces reliance on fossil-fuel-based power plants during high demand, and improves the overall efficiency of energy systems.

A V2G system usually consists of advanced hardware, such as bi-directional chargers, and software that handles the energy flow. Communication protocols, like ISO 15118, will allow for smooth interaction between the EV, the charging infrastructure, and the grid. Smart charging capabilities will allow these systems to optimize energy usage based on the needs of the grid, the cost of electricity, and the needs of the user for their travel, so the vehicle is always ready when it is needed.

One of the main benefits of V2G technology is the opportunity to deliver economic advantages to EV owners. In that manner, selling unused energy back to the grid allows the owner to offset costs from charging. Moreover, the role of V2G systems is important for boosting grid reliability. When an outage or disruption occurs, it is capable of providing backup power to residences and commercial establishments.

Despite the many benefits of V2G technology, there are a number of challenges. The investment needed for V2G-compatible infrastructure is quite high, and charge-discharge cycles are known to accelerate battery degradation. Regulatory frameworks and market structures to support V2G are still developing, and consumer awareness about the technology is limited. These will be critical in ensuring that V2G systems become widely adopted.

Looking ahead, V2G technology is going to shift the very thinking about energy systems and change everything in a very short period of time. Growing investments in smart grids, renewable energy, and battery technologies give V2G better sustainability and efficiency in making energy systems. As barriers continue to be overcome together by governments, automakers, and energy providers, integration of V2G systems could likely be an integral part of the global energy transition.

AGGREGATOR TECHNOLOGY GRID-BASED VEHICLE

Aggregator Strategy

Scholars in academia and industry are investigating various Vehicle-to-Grid (V2G) aggregation strategies [8]. The particular goals of the control system usually determine the aggregation approach that is chosen. The goal of optimal aggregation solutions is to minimize cost functions related to energy bills for preset grid utilities, or in other words, to lower the charging costs for owners of electric vehicles (EVs). Various ancillary service markets, such as regulation, peak power management, and overall cost reduction, are often considered using these methods.

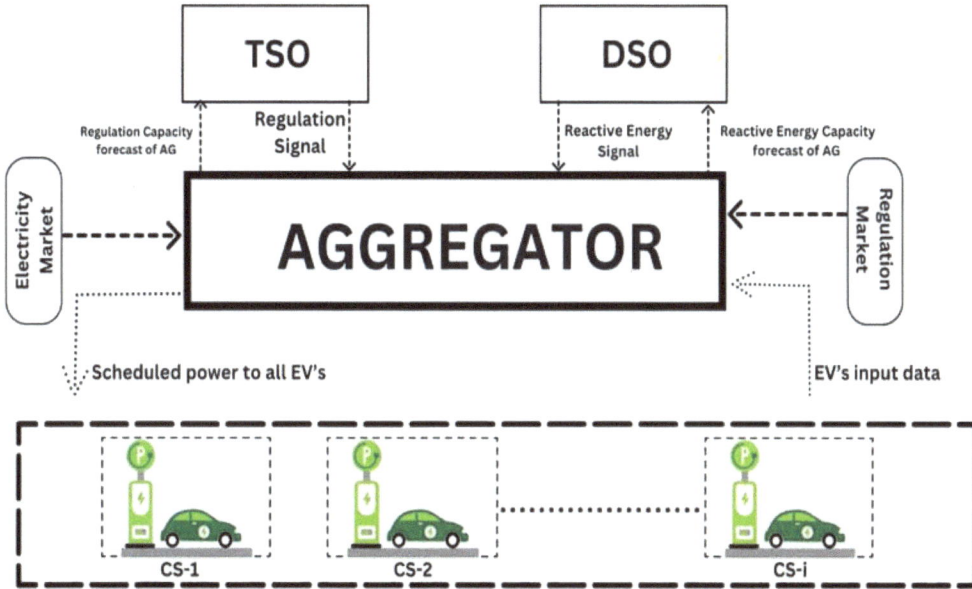

Fig. (1). Aggregator schemes as a grid operator and electric vehicle fleet interface.

The suggested frequency and voltage service aggregator structure, shown in Fig. (**1**) [9], was carefully chosen because of its high degree of adaptability and ease of administration. The information flow that is vital for effective system optimization between Electric Vehicle (EV) fleets, aggregators, and power system operators is depicted in Fig. (**1**). In this design, the aggregator uses the received data to decide which commands to issue for charging and discharging a group of electric vehicles. The Transmission System Operator (TSO) and Distribution System Operator (DSO) regulatory references, as well as regulation market pricing (*e.g.,* £/kWh), are important considerations in these decisions. The model notably assumes that a single aggregation organization is responsible for managing EVs at different charging stations, which is in line with previous studies [9]. Regulation signals primarily consist of "regulation up" and "regulation down" directives, corresponding to scenarios in which energy production falls short of consumption or exceeds it. During periods of vehicle connection, EVs possess the capability to undertake various actions aimed at responding to these distinct regulatory signals (Fig. **2**). In essence, this architecture facilitates effective coordination between the EV fleets, aggregators, and power system operators, enabling dynamic responses to regulatory signals for optimized system performance.

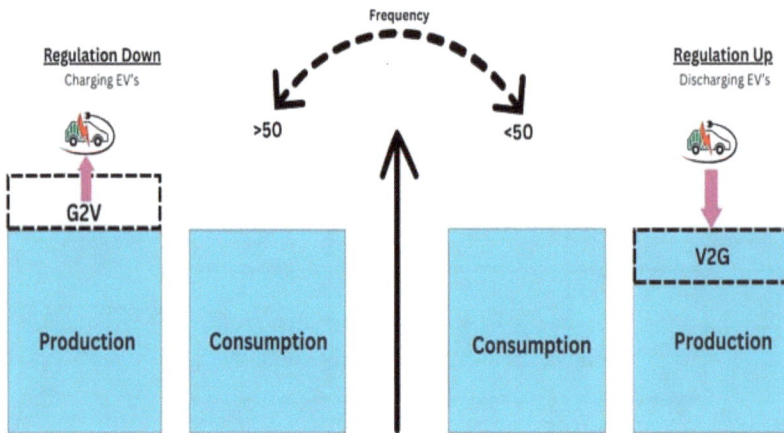

Fig. (2). Regulation signal informs the aggregator's decision.

Vehicle-to-Grid Architecture

The Vehicle-to-Grid (V2G) infrastructure primarily consists of electric cars (EVs) and bidirectional charging stations, with additional facilities for communication and charging. The charging stations are arranged in a way that allows them to monitor and group together all the EV/V2G chargers, as shown in Fig. (**3**) system architecture. This arrangement ensures that, when they are added together, they have sufficient energy to have a substantial effect on the power grid. As discussed earlier [10], to aggregate and provide/absorb energy at the megawatt-hour (MWh) scale, a significant number of EVs, typically several hundred, are required. Examples of this type of aggregation with 500–1500 EVs have been reported in a number of studies. This can be further understood by considering the fact that approximately 25 Nissan Leaf vehicles, each with a 40-kWh battery, can store 1 MWh of energy. Therefore, a matching charging station can be placed in each EV parking spot. Because of this, electricity trading is made easier for EVs that are parked and can easily connect to the smart grid. Vehicle-to-Grid (V2G) infrastructure facilitates the bidirectional flow of energy between Electric Vehicles (EVs) and the grid. This creates a mutually beneficial relationship in which EVs support grid resilience and stability, while simultaneously using optimal charging and energy management features.

The aggregator and charging stations are directly connected to a hierarchical structure (Fig. **3**). The energy aggregator is responsible for managing the entire system and coordinating transactions on behalf of Electric Vehicles (EVs) in response to fluctuating market pricing and/or energy requirements from grid operators. Each Charging Station (CS) is tasked with the duty of immediately monitoring EVs parked within its immediate neighborhood, as batch data communication methods are known to be successful in monitoring high numbers of EVs. Subsequently, the CS sends the collected information to the aggregator, including the EV State of Charge (SOC), arrival and departure times, and the final SOC. Fig (**3**) shows the flow of information and electricity, which are the two fundamental fluxes inside the smart grid. Key technical data, such as battery State of Charge (SOC), financial factors, such as electricity pricing, and statistical information, such as power availability, are typically included in the information flow [11]. The aggregator receives demands from the smart grid operator and sends them to the EVs, telling them to discharge and return stored energy to the grid, among other things. Although the availability of specific EV plugs may differ, statistics on traffic or road usage can be used to approximate the availability of hundreds of EVs, as mentioned in [12]. As an illustration, a typical American car is driven for only one hour per day [13], meaning that over 92% of cars are parked and can be used to power the grid even during rush hour [14].

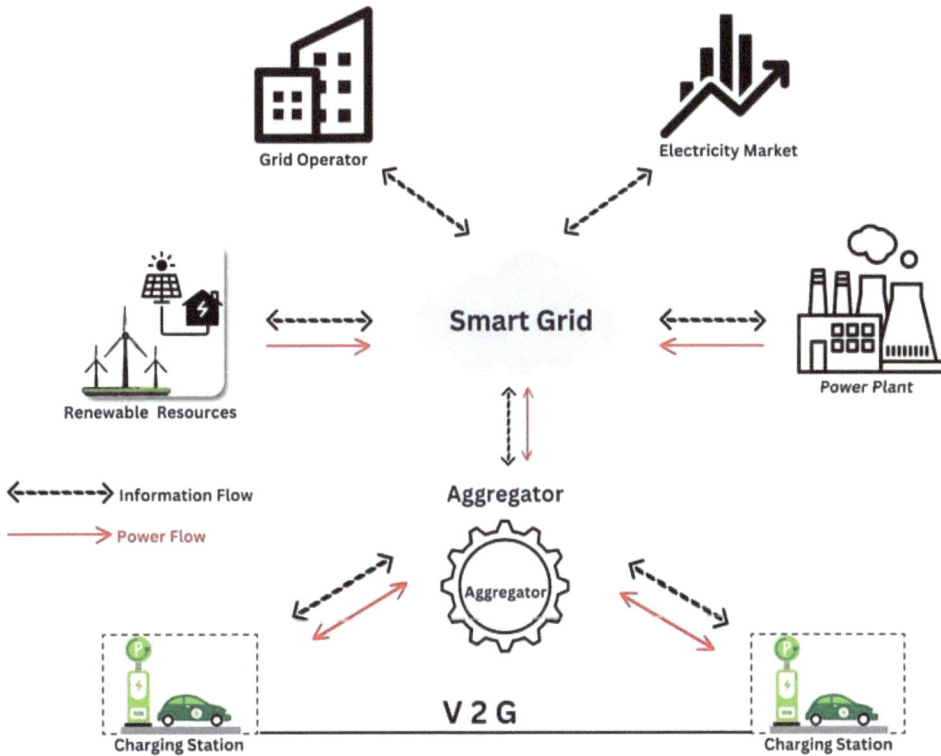

Fig. (3). Vehicle-to-grid system architecture.

V2G APPROACH: SOLUTION OR DELAY

It is common knowledge that electric cars (EVs) are charged overnight using grid infrastructure during off-peak hours. However, this perspective fails to consider a substantial opportunity presented by the fact that more than 90% of cars are parked. Distributed energy resources have the potential to offer significant grid services when linked to the grid, particularly using Vehicle-to-Grid (V2G) technology [15]. There are two ways to examine the idea of using the energy stored by Electric Vehicles (EVs) and then putting it back into the grid [15 - 17]. The industry does not see much movement from the second viewpoint on electric cars (EVs). This is mostly because it portrays EVs as liabilities for system managers, rather than as tools that can help create a more intelligent grid architecture. This viewpoint also tends to reduce consumers' enthusiasm for buying electric vehicles. However, the Vehicle-to-Grid (V2G) concept presents a strong argument against it. By selling extra energy stored in EV batteries back to the grid, car owners can profit from V2G. By doing this, we can reduce the time it takes to recover your investment and partially offset the high initial cost of buying and maintaining an electric vehicle. V2G offers system operators the opportunity to use EVs to supply grid services from a supply standpoint. Raising consumer awareness and building the required infrastructure and incentives on the supply side are the key to achieving mutual satisfaction between car owners and system operators. This entails informing customers of the advantages of V2G and putting laws and technology in place that will encourage its uptake.

Owners of Electric Vehicles (EVs) are hesitant to let the grid use their cars for system services because they are worried about how the use of EV batteries would affect them over time. Nonetheless, the idea of Vehicle-to-Grid (V2G) offers EV scheduling and management opportunities in a dynamic economic market, particularly in smart grid architectures [18, 19]. The integration of EVs into electric markets requires a control and communication system that can quickly and accurately react to signals from the central grid operator. This emphasizes how crucial smart grid technologies make it easier for EVs to be integrated into different electricity markets. Furthermore, the broad commercialization of electric vehicles is essential for realizing this concept (EVs). The low energy-storage capacity of vehicles makes a sizable fleet of vehicles necessary for the integration of Vehicle-to-Grid (V2G) systems to deliver grid services. Manufacturers must also concentrate on developing battery storage to power electronic equipment suitable for V2G applications.

In addition, the focus needs to be placed on improving grid infrastructure [20]. Dealing with various concerns, some of which go beyond the advancement and technology of vehicles, makes the management of these challenges difficult. Consequently, implementing this strategy is a difficult task requiring thorough answers. Moreover, there is a significant discrepancy between consumers' expectations about the capabilities of Electric Vehicles (EVs) and the actual state of what EVs can accomplish today. Customers generally expect EVs to be more economical, have a longer charging range, and cost less than automakers currently sell. The reality is that current EV products only satisfy the aspirations of a small percentage of the population (between 2 and 4 percent) in any particular country. The U.S. Department of Energy (DOE) has provided a cautious estimate of the market penetration of Electric Vehicles (EVs) in its 2009 Annual Energy Outlook predictions. Fig. (**3**) shows respondents' buy likelihood scores after looking over vehicle details based on a research conducted by a Southern U.S. corporation. However, given the current variations in power markets among nations, it is also feasible that certain power markets would not benefit from V2G. In the German market, for instance, using this technology is not thought to be as beneficial as in the US market [14]. Consequently, EVs can be employed for unidirectional storage rather than for grid services [15]. This makes it easier to contribute to the market, requires less new communication equipment, and is more well-liked by consumers [15]. In addition, it can improve the initial experience with EVs by entering the power market before utilizing them as a distributed energy supply.

The following questions arise when developing this model:

• How might V2G systems be optimized for grid stability and bi-directional energy flow?

The major issue with V2G systems is how to balance the grid's needs with the EV owner's preferences. For example, how would you make sure there was enough power available for the grid when users needed their cars without drawing down the batteries of EVs? It can be pretty tricky to get the EVs and the grid to communicate due to a lack of standard protocols [21].

The key will be the use of advanced control systems that are capable of predicting energy demand and controlling flow dynamically, thus keeping the grid stable. Standardization of communication protocols, such as ISO 15118, would facilitate easier integration. The contributions of EV owners also need to be encouraged with incentives, such as discounts or payments for feeding into the grid. Simultaneously, smart battery management systems would safeguard the battery by appropriately controlling the energy flow.

• What are the problem areas with phase-shifted full-bridge converters in fast charging and how to avoid them?

Phase-shifted full-bridge converters are widely used in EV chargers, but they have the disadvantages of high power losses at light loads, electromagnetic interference, and voltage stress on components. Over time, it can also affect the battery.

To overcome these challenges, engineers are exploring soft-switching techniques to reduce power losses. Proper EMI filtering and using wide bandgap semiconductors like Silicon Carbide (SiC) can handle voltage stress better while improving efficiency. These technologies make fast charging safer and more efficient, which also helps in extending battery life [22].

- How can advancements in photovoltaic technology enhance solar-based EV charging?

The challenge with solar-powered charging is that it is intermittent, so what then when it's cloudy or nighttime? Besides, current solar panels don't convert sunlight into energy as efficiently as we'd like, and their environmental footprint during manufacturing is another concern.

This is changing with the new photovoltaic technologies, such as perovskite solar cells and bifacial panels. They provide greater efficiency under low-light conditions and a better output when not available. The systems combined with the energy storage solution such as batteries can guarantee an adequate and constant power supply when the sun is not available. Further innovation involves attaching solar panels to charging stations for EVs [23].

- How can adaptive passivity-based controllers be applied to enhance battery management in EVs?

Battery Management Systems (BMS) play a critical role in maintaining the performance and longevity of the EV battery. However, due to environmental conditions like temperature and usage patterns, the challenge arises. Adaptive passivity-based controllers can be designed to adapt dynamically to the changing conditions.

For example, these controllers can regulate charging and discharging in real-time, preventing overheating or overcharging. By continuously adapting to the battery's state of health and external conditions, they maximize efficiency while extending battery life. Implementing them effectively requires precise modelling of battery behaviour and robust testing under real-world conditions [24].

LITERATURE REVIEW

With the help of V2G technology, electric cars (EVs) and the grid may exchange energy in both directions. This allows EV batteries to store grid energy and release it when required. This technique could improve the integration of renewable energy sources, stabilize the grid, and financially benefit EV owners. Research (*e.g.,* Kempton and Tomi [25]) showed that V2G can reduce grid instability by using aggregated EV batteries to provide frequency-regulation services. Regarding how V2G affects battery deterioration and overall system reliability, issues remain. Energy arbitrage, auxiliary services, and peak shaving are three ways that V2G involvement can generate income streams for EV owners, according to economic models (*e.g.,* research by Zhang *et al.* [26]). Regulations, market arrangements for electricity, and the expense of battery degradation have a significant impact on the viability of V2G. Studies that have examined the environmental advantages of V2G (*e.g.,* Moura *et al.* [27]) have shown that it can lower greenhouse gas emissions by facilitating a greater uptake of renewable energy sources. The creation of batteries, sources of charging, and grid emissions should all be considered in environmental impact assessments. Widespread V2G implementation is hampered by technical obstacles, such as communication protocols, interoperability standards, and concerns about battery deterioration. Overcoming these obstacles will require advancements in battery management systems and car-to-grid connections (such as vehicle telematics and smart charging algorithms). Supportive legislative and regulatory environments are necessary for the deployment of the V2G technology to encourage investment and guarantee grid stability. Successful V2G adoption has been demonstrated in case studies (such as in Denmark and Japan), which were made possible by legislative changes, pilot programs, and government initiatives. Market adoption depends on an understanding of customer attitudes, interests, and behaviors regarding V2G. Market adoption depends on an understanding of customer attitudes, interests, and behavior regarding V2G. The desire of Electric Vehicle (EV) owners to engage in V2G programs has been investigated through surveys and experimental investigations (Sierzchula *et al.,* 2014). These considerations include financial incentives, convenience, and technological trust [28]. Developments in the grid infrastructure, battery technology, and policy support are critical to the viability of V2G. Technical, economic, and social aspects of V2G require further investigation. This includes standardization initiatives, public involvement plans, and implementation studies conducted in real-world settings.

FUTURE SCOPE

Future energy management and sustainability could greatly benefit from Vehicle-to-Grid (V2G) charging of Electric Vehicles (EVs). When EVs use V2G technology, they can actively participate in the grid ecosystem, which allows bidirectional energy flow between EVs and the electric grid. This novel strategy offers several advantages.

First, by enabling EVs to function as mobile energy-storage devices, V2G charging can reduce the load on the electrical grid. EVs may send excess energy back into the grid during times of peak demand, which lowers the need for more power generation capacity and improves the system's stability. On the other hand, EVs can recharge using less expensive off-peak electricity prices when the demand is low. Moreover, V2G may make it easier for renewable energy sources to be fully integrated into the grid. When renewable energy production peaks, EV batteries may store the extra energy produced and then return it to the grid when needed, thereby balancing supply and demand and encouraging the use of clean energy.

In addition, V2G technology provides EV owners with access to new revenue sources. EV owners can profit from their car's battery capacity and support the resilience and dependability of the grid by participating in grid services such as demand response, peak shaving, and frequency control. This encourages the use and acceptance of EVs, eventually accelerating the shift to a more efficient and sustainable energy system. Furthermore, the increased energy resilience during emergencies and natural disasters could be a benefit of V2G charging. By providing backup power to critical facilities, residential areas, and emergency services in cases where traditional power infrastructure is compromised, fleets of electric vehicles equipped with variable-voltage generators (V2G) can augment community resilience and expedite disaster-response operations.

However, to fully utilize V2G charging, several infrastructure, legislative, and technical issues must be resolved. The main obstacles to be addressed are grid compatibility, cybersecurity issues, standardization of communication protocols, and interoperability of V2G devices. Furthermore, legal frameworks must be changed to allow for the integration of V2G technology and provide equitable payments to electric vehicle owners who use grid services. Despite these obstacles, V2G charging is expected to have a bright future. The potential for V2G to completely transform the way we create, distribute, and use energy, and open the door to a more resilient and sustainable energy future, is immense, provided that stakeholders work together to overcome implementation challenges and technological advancements.

CONCLUSION

In conclusion, EV Vehicle-to-Grid (V2G) charging offers a viable way to maximize energy efficiency and maintain grid stability. With the help of V2G technology, which enables bidirectional energy flow and permits EV batteries to both draw and supply electricity to the grid, effective energy management is possible, potentially alleviating strain during periods of peak demand. Furthermore, V2G systems encourage EV owners to participate in demand response programs by providing them with the opportunity to profit from selling extra energy back to the grid during periods of high demand. However, before they are widely used, issues such as battery deterioration and compatibility requirements must be resolved. V2G has enormous potential for improving grid resilience and maximizing the advantages of owning an electric car.

REFERENCES

[1] J. Gallardo-Lozano, M.I. Milanés-Montero, M.A. Guerrero-Martínez, and E. Romero-Cadaval, "Electric vehicle battery charger for smart grids", *Electr. Power Syst. Res.,* vol. 90, pp. 18-29, 2012.

[2] D.B. Richardson, "Electric vehicles and the electric grid: a review of modelling approaches, impacts, and renewable energy integration", *Renew. Sustain. Energy Rev.,* vol. 19, pp. 247-254, 2013.

[3] Z. Wang, and S. Wang, "Grid power peak shaving and valley filling using vehicle-to-grid systems", *IEEE Trans. Power Deliv.,* vol. 28, no. 3, pp. 1822-1829, 2013.

[4] J. Gallardo-Lozano, M.I. Milanés-Montero, M.A. Guerrero-Martínez, and E. Romero-Cadaval, "Three-phase bidirectional battery charger for smart electric vehicles", *7th International Compatibility and Power Electronics Conf.-Workshop,* pp. 371-376, 2011.

[5] K. Bao, S. Li, and H. Zheng, "Battery charge and discharge control for energy management in EV and utility integration", *IEEE Power and Energy Society General Meeting,* pp. 1-8, 2012.

[6] S. Li, T.A. Haskew, Y.K. Hong, and L. Xu, "Direct-current vector control of three-phase grid-connected rectifier–inverter", *Electr. Power Syst. Res.,* vol. 81, no. 2, pp. 357-366, 2011.

[7] M. Yilmaz, and P.T. Krein, "Review of the impact of vehicle-to-grid technologies on distribution systems and utility interfaces", *IEEE Trans. Power Electron.,* vol. 28, no. 12, pp. 5673-5689, 2013.

[8] K. Kaur, M. Singh, and N. Kumar, "Multi objective Optimization for Frequency Support Using Electric Vehicles: An Aggregator-Based Hierarchical Control Mechanism", *IEEE Syst. J.,* vol. 13, no. 1, pp. 771-782, 2019.

[9] R. Wang, Y. Li, P. Wang, and D. Niyato, "Design of a V2G aggregator to optimize PHEV charging and frequency regulation control," in Proc. *IEEE Int. Conf. Smart Grid Comm.,* 2013, pp. 127–132.

[10] S.I. Vagropoulos, and A.G. Bakirtzis, "Optimal bidding strategy for electric vehicle aggregators in electricity markets", *IEEE Trans. Power Syst.,* vol. 28, no. 4, pp. 4031-4041, 2013.

[11] Z. Yang, S. Yu, W. Lou, and C. Liu, "P2: privacy-preserving communication and precise reward architecture for V2G networks in smart grid", *IEEE Trans. Smart Grid,* vol. 2, no. 4, pp. 697-706, 2011.

[12] W. Su, H. Eichi, W. Zeng, and M.Y. Chow, "A survey on the electrification of transportation in a smart grid environment", *IEEE Trans. Industr. Inform.,* vol. 8, no. 1, pp. 1-10, 2012. [http://dx.doi.org/10.1109/TII.2011.2172454]

[13] S.E. Letendre, and W. Kempton, *The V2G concept: a new model for power?* Public Utilities Fortnightly, 2002, pp. 16-26.

[14] Fang X, Misra S, Xue G, Yang D. "Smart grid – the new and improved power grid: a survey" *IEEE Commun Surveys Tuts*, 14(4): 944-80, 2012.

[15] S. Letendre, P. Denholm, and P. Lilienthal, "Electric & Hybrid Cars: New Load or New Resource?," *Public Utilities Frotnightly*, 2006.

[16] S.B. Peterson, J.F. Whitacre, and J. Apt, "The economics of using plug-in hybrid electric vehicle battery packs for grid storage", *J. Power Sources,* vol. 195, no. 8, pp. 2377-2384, 2010. [http://dx.doi.org/10.1016/j.jpowsour.2009.09.070]

[17] *Accenture's study, "Betting on Science: Disruptive Technologies in Transport Fuels",* 2009, Available from: http://www.accenture.com/us-en/Pages/insight-disruptive-technologies

[18] J. Fluhr, K-H. Ahlert, and C. Weinhardt, "A Stochastic Model for Simulating the Availability of

Electric Vehicles for Services to the Power Grid", *IEEE Conference on System Science,* pp. 1-10, 2010.
[http://dx.doi.org/10.1109/HICSS.2010.33]

[19]   R. Freire, J. Delgado, J.M. Santos, and A.T. de Almeida, "Integration of renewable energy generation with EV charging strategies to optimize grid load balancing", *IEEE Conference on Intelligent Transportation Systems (ITSC),* pp. 392-396, 2010.

[20]   C. Quinn, D. Zimmerle, and T.H. Bradley, "The effect of communication architecture on the availability, reliability, and economics of plug-in hybrid electric vehicle-to-grid ancillary services", *J. Power Sources,* vol. 195, no. 5, pp. 1500-1509, 2010.
[http://dx.doi.org/10.1016/j.jpowsour.2009.08.075]

[21]   D. Dallinger, D. Krampe, and M. Wietschel, "Vehicle-to-Grid Regulation Reserves Based on a Dynamic Simulation of Mobility Behavior", *IEEE Trans. Smart Grid,* vol. 2, no. 2, pp. 302-313, 2011.
[http://dx.doi.org/10.1109/TSG.2011.2131692]

[22]   E. Sortomme, and M.A. El-Sharkawi, "Optimal Charging Strategies for Unidirectional Vehicle-t--Grid", *IEEE Trans. Smart Grid,* vol. 2, no. 1, pp. 131-138, 2011.
[http://dx.doi.org/10.1109/TSG.2010.2090910]

[23]   Deloitte, *"Unplugged: Electric vehicle realities versus consumer expectations,"* Sept. 2011. [Online].

[24]   *Energy Power Research Institute (EPRI), "Characterizing Consumers' Interest in and Infrastructure Expectations for Electric Vehicles: Research Design and Survey Results,"* 2010. [Online].

[25]   W. Kempton, and J. Tomić, "Vehicle-to-grid power implementation: From stabilizing the grid to supporting large-scale renewable energy", *J. Power Sources,* vol. 144, no. 1, pp. 280-294, 2005.
[http://dx.doi.org/10.1016/j.jpowsour.2004.12.022]

[26]   S. Zhang, J. Wu, Y. Huang, and J. Hu, "Electric vehicle-to-grid (V2G) operation strategy considering battery life degradation", *Appl. Energy,* vol. 184, pp. 1194-1205, 2016.

[27]   S.J. Moura, H.K. Fathy, D.S. Callaway, and J.L. Stein, "Stochastic modeling of PHEV-Grid integration", *IEEE Trans. Vehicular Technol.,* vol. 59, no. 2, pp. 588-599, 2010.

[28]   W. Sierzchula, S. Bakker, K. Maat, and B. van Wee, "The influence of financial incentives and other socio-economic factors on electric vehicle adoption", *Energy Policy,* vol. 68, pp. 183-194, 2014.
[http://dx.doi.org/10.1016/j.enpol.2014.01.043]

CHAPTER 8

IoT Based Floor Cleaning Electric Vehicle Robot with Live Streaming Camera

Paritosh Kumar Rai[1,*], **Rachit Srivastava**[1], **Arun Kumar Yadav**[1], **Sahil Ramazan**[1], **Palak Gaur**[1] and **Anuradha Tiwari**[1]

[1] *Department of Electrical Engineering, Bansal Institute of Engineering & Technology, Lucknow, Uttar Pradesh, India*

Abstract: The integration of Internet of Things (IoT) technology in domestic automation has revolutionized household applications, including floor cleaning. Automated Floor cleaning is a very useful application in the field of Electrical Vehicle technology that is helpful in household as well as industrial applications. This paper presents a brief overview of the basic structure and components of a floor-cleaning vehicle. Also, this paper presents a detailed literature review on various topologies involved in robots for floor cleaning systems. The ultimate objective is to engineer an independent cleaning solution that not only excels at thorough and efficient floor cleaning but also provides users with the ability to monitor the process in real-time. The proposed system harnesses a sophisticated array of sensors, microcontrollers, and a Wi-Fi module, establishing a seamless channel of communication between the cleaning robot and a remote user interface. The cleaning mechanism is designed to incorporate precision brushes and powerful vacuum functionality, ensuring the effective removal of dust and debris from a wide range of floor surfaces. Moreover, the integration of a live streaming camera on the robot presents users with the unique opportunity to closely observe the cleaning process as it unfolds, accessible *via* a user-friendly mobile application or web interface. Key features of the system include efficient path planning, obstacle detection and avoidance, and remote monitoring *via* live streaming. This research contributes to the field of smart home technology by offering a practical and innovative solution for automated floor cleaning. In the future, machine learning algorithms will be developed in the proposed system.

Keywords: Automated floor cleaning robot, Electric vehicle, Microcontroller, Robot.

INTRODUCTION

The rapid advancement of electrical vehicle-based robotic cleaners has gained significant attention in the field of robotics. These innovative devices have proven

---

* **Corresponding author Paritosh Kumar Rai:** Department of Electrical Engineering, Bansal Institute of Engineering & Technology, Lucknow, Uttar Pradesh, India; E-mail: paritoshrai0214@gmail.com

Nitesh Tiwari, Shekhar Yadav and Sabha Raj Arya (Eds.)

to be highly effective in aiding humans with floor-cleaning tasks in various settings such as homes, hotels, restaurants, offices, hospitals, workshops, warehouses, and universities. Robotic cleaners excel in diverse cleaning abilities, including floor mopping and dry vacuuming. While some models utilize simple obstacle avoidance with infrared sensors, others employ more advanced laser mapping techniques. The cleaning and operating mechanisms of robotic floor cleaners each have unique benefits and drawbacks. For instance, robots using laser mapping are faster, more efficient, and save energy, but can be costly. On the other hand, obstacle avoidance-based robots are more affordable but may be less energy-efficient and time-consuming due to random cleaning patterns.

The main objective of this work is to discuss the basic structure of a typical floor-cleaning robot and provide a literature review on various types of floor-cleaning robots for the household as well as industrial applications. Along with that, this paper proposes a floor-cleaning robot that provides a considerable solution to the problem of manufacturing robotic cleaners utilizing local resources while keeping low costs. In this work, a "live streaming smart floor cleaning robot" has been intended for customer or organization purposes. The proposed design has the facility of livestreaming, by which, a user can monitor the process from a remote place.

This paper is organized into five sections. The first section is committed to the introduction of the floor-cleaning robot. The second section is dedicated to the basic structure of a floor-cleaning robot. In the third section, a brief review of floor-cleaning robots is discussed. In the fourth section, a brief on the proposed live-streaming robot has been discussed. The fifth and the last section is dedicated to the conclusions of the work.

METHODOLOGY

Fig. (**1**) presents the decisive steps taken in the development of the robot prototype. The autonomous floor cleaning system features an array of sensors strategically positioned around and beneath the robot chassis. Notably, these sensors consist of one ultrasonic sensor and three infrared sensors, providing robust guidance to the robot for effective collision avoidance.

To ensure efficient cleaning, wipers are powered by a motor, while a water pump delivers water to the mop at regular intervals for mopping. The entire robotic system operates on a rechargeable battery and can be controlled *via* Android-based or other applications, allowing for remote operation within a range of about 10 m. Once the cleaning is complete, the dirt container is emptied, and the mop cloth is replaced. Fig. (**2**) illustrates the various components used in the prototype, with detailed descriptions provided in the following sections.

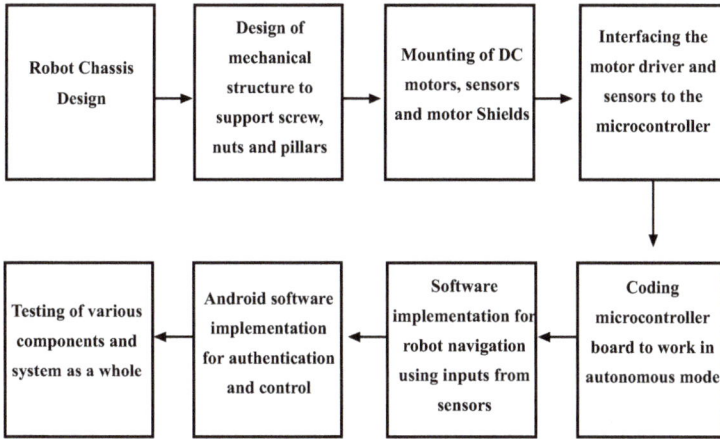

Fig. (1). Steps involved in the implementation of electrical vehicle-based robotic cleaners.

Fig. (2). Components Involved in Electrical Vehicle-Based Robotic Cleaners.

Microcontroller

Node MCU boards have become indispensable for the implementation of cutting-edge robotics and IoT projects. They integrate a microcontroller and an Integrated Development Environment (IDE) for seamless programming. The Node MCU, as a low-cost, open-source IoT platform, harmoniously combines the ESP8266 Wi-Fi SoC from Expressive Systems with the Node MCU firmware, making it a versatile and powerful choice for our work.

Battery

A rechargeable LiPo battery is employed to supply direct current to the circuit. Given the size constraints of the chassis, a compact and lightweight battery is chosen to deliver sustained current for a minimum of one hour.

Servo Motor

The Servo Motor is a powerful and compact motor ideal for robotics, model making, and various hobbyist projects. Its small size makes it perfect for lightweight and space-efficient robotic designs.

Motor Driver

The motor drivers are a popular module for controlling DC and stepper motors using a microcontroller or other digital controllers. The module can handle high current requirements for motor control. The motor driver connects the motor to the driver's output pins and then connects the driver to your microcontroller's output pins. The motor drivers have several control inputs that allow you to control the direction and speed of the motor.

Ultrasonic Sensor

The ultrasonic sensor is a crucial component for guiding the robot and ensuring it avoids collisions with walls or obstacles. By emitting ultrasonic waves and measuring the distance to the wall through the reflected wave, the sensor accurately detects its surroundings. This distance measurement is achieved by precisely timing the emission and reception of the waves. The sensor uses a high-frequency sound wave to measure the distance from an object. When the trigger pin is high, the sensor sends an ultrasonic pulse, which then bounces off an object and returns to the sensor as an echo. The time taken for the pulse to return is used to calculate the distance to the object.

Relay Module

A relay module is an electromagnetic switch that operates on simple electromagnetic induction principles. It controls circuits by using magnetic flux generated when an electric current passes through its coil. Applying voltage to the electromagnetic coil of the relay generates an electromagnetic field, pulling the metal contacts together and enabling current flow. This relay module functions as a controllable switch, perfect for digital circuits and microcontrollers.

LITERATURE REVIEW

The household floor cleaning robot has had a significant social impact as a convenient and efficient cleaning solution. Gutmann, Jens-Steffen, *et al.,* have researched the automatic cleaning robot, which both sweeps and mops hard-surface floors using dusting and mopping cloths and navigating homes to systematically clean them. Since its commercial introduction in mid-2010, hundreds of thousands of these cleaning robots are now in use. Their study delves into the social impact of this robot by examining customer attitudes and their influence on their lifestyle. The robot offers two cleaning methods: dry and wet. In dry mode, it brushes the floor in a neat and parallel line direction, while in wet mode, it mops the floor in forward and backward directions [1].

In another study, Hendriks Bram *et al.* explored the behavior of robot vacuum cleaners based on gesture, sound, and luminosity. They operated a vacuum cleaner robot using a Bluetooth link and observed the user experience to understand how people want to interact with this new cleaning appliance. Reviews were conducted to determine the desired personality for a future robot vacuum cleaner, shaping its behavior based on the gathered knowledge [2].

Vibha Burman and Ravinder Kumar suggested a revolutionary technology that combines dry cleaning and wet cleaning in one. The Internet of Things framework is the most appropriate for obtaining precise sensor findings and carrying out necessary operations. Interfacing sensors to produce outcomes with very high connectivity is made possible by IoT. The connectivity of the sensor does not lessen its capacity for value measurement and analysis. The Wi-Fi module is included to allow regulating communications across great distances [3].

Julia Fink *et al.* conducted a comprehensive study on people's perception of robots and their evolving roles in daily routines, cleaning tool usage, and social activities. They integrated their findings into an existing domestic robot adoption framework, highlighting both similarities and differences. Moreover, they identified key factors that either facilitate or hinder the adoption of domestic service robots and provided recommendations to enhance human-robot interactions and improve the design of home robots for long-term acceptance [4].

Burman Vibha and Ravinder Kumar introduced an innovative system that combines wet and dry cleaning methods. They emphasized the effectiveness of an IoT framework in providing accurate sensor results and facilitating necessary tasks. By integrating IoT technology with a Wi-Fi module for long-distance communication, their cleaning robot offers enhanced functionality and smarter cleaning capabilities [5].

Kaur Manreet and Preeti Abrol have developed an innovative robot for floor cleaning that offers both automatic and manual modes. In the automatic mode, the robot autonomously handles all operations, including adjusting lanes to avoid obstacles. The Manual mode allows for remote control using an RF module, with obstacle detection information displayed on an LCD screen [6].

A sample of seven robots was examined by F. Vaussard to determine how important technologies—like the navigation system—affect technical performance. To determine the demands of the users, they carried out an ethnographic investigation on nine houses for the second study. With the use of this creative strategy, it is possible to suggest several practical enhancements that attempt to meet user needs by utilizing existing technology to open up opportunities [7].

M. L. Walters demonstrated a trial that varied the robot voice styles according to participants' initial comfort levels while approaching. Three speech types were selected for the robot: a male voice, a female voice, and a (synthesized) neutral voice to investigate the impacts of robot voice gender. The control condition was the inability to speak [8].

Lee Hyunsoo and Amarnath Banerjee's research tackles the scheduling of vacuum cleaning robots for multiple cleaning cycles. While previous studies have addressed path generation for such devices, they found that the paths in each cycle often ended up being similar due to motion planning being based on a single tour of the target space. Their predictive model offers constraints for various mathematical programming models during the optimization phase. Their proposed framework is seen as an effective scheduling method for minimizing redundant paths while keeping dust levels within acceptable limits across multiple cleaning cycles [9].

Yatmono, S., *et al.* have engineered an innovative floor-cleaning robot with the ability to autonomously navigate, effectively clean dust, and polish floors. Their study employed Pressman's meticulous research and development methods, encompassing thorough analysis, comprehensive design, meticulous implementation, and rigorous testing [10].

Bhingare Komal Manoj *et al.* have designed a vacuum cleaner using Arduino and IoT. The system is connected to the internet using the Wi-Fi module which will help the user to turn on or turn off the machine from remote places. Using IoT users can also keep the records of the on-time and off-time of the robot. This can help the user operate or monitor the robot from any distance [11].

Parmar Harshvardhansinh, *et al.* have developed an innovative system that allows for efficient floor and surface cleaning using an Android device and sensors. This technology includes a mop attached to a robot, which is equipped with a water container and a mini water pump to ensure thorough cleaning. By enabling both manual and automatic control, this system aims to enhance people's quality of life [12].

Garud M. J. *et al.* have introduced a cutting-edge robot for floor cleaning, featuring an IR sensor for obstacle detection and an automatic water sprayer pump. With four motors dedicated to cleaning and water spraying, this technology is designed for optimal performance using a dual relay circuit [13].

In his research paper, Raj Vishaal presents a versatile robot equipped with an electric ducted fan and support ropes to facilitate cleaning not only glass walls but also floors. The incorporation of a vacuum pump for spraying cleaning solution ensures both dry and wet cleaning capabilities, making this robot highly effective for a range of cleaning tasks [14].

The house cleaning robot, developed by Abhishek Pandey *etal.*, utilizes a microcontroller to identify obstacles and adjust its path based on the data received from infrared sensors positioned at the front, right, and left sides of the robot. Alternatively, it can also rely on the digital signal processor for this purpose [15].

Burman, Vibha, and Ravinder Kumar have introduced an innovative system that combines wet cleaning and dry cleaning processes. The IoT framework is identified as the most suitable for obtaining precise sensor results and performing essential tasks. IoT offers high-connectivity interfacing capabilities for sensor data [16].

Das NabamitaRamkrishna, along with collaborators from the Mechanical, Electrical, and Electronic fields, utilizes a range of rigid components such as chassis, motors, and electromechanical devices in their systems [17].

R. Bhoopathi *et al.,* have developed a remotely controllable floor cleaner, designed and tested under various load conditions. The cleaner features an Aluminum 6061 frame, and Nylocast plastic wheels crafted using a lathe machine, and is powered by two 12V 100 rpm DC motors regulated by a motor driver L293D. To operate the cleaner, a mobile device is used in conjunction with a Wi-Fi module ESP8266 [18].

The literature survey of floor cleaners, and hardware parts, *i.e.*, wireless mediums, sensors, and microcontrollers are summarized in the tabular form listed as Tables **1-5**.

Table 1. Categories of floor cleaners.

Flore Cleaner Technique	References
Wet cleaners	[1, 4 - 7, 15]
Dry cleaners	[1 - 6, 10 - 12, 14 - 18]

Table 2. Sensors involved for floor cleaners.

Sensors	References
IR sensor	[7, 12]
Infrared sensor (TSOP1738)	[16]
Dust sensor (DSM501)	[10]
Ultrasonic sensor	[12, 14, 17, 18]
Level sensor	[12]
IR sensor	[7, 12]

Table 3. Motor drivers involved in floor cleaners.

Motor Drivers	References
L293D	[7, 15, 17, 18]

Table 4. Microcontrollers involved for floor cleaners.

Microcontrollers	References
AT89S52	[7]
PIC 16F877A	[14]
Arduino UNO	[11,15.16]
Arduino Mega	[15]
ATMEGA 328P	[17]

Table 5. Communication Mediumnvolved for floor cleaner.

Communication Medium	References
RF modules	[7]
IoT	[10]
Bluetooth	[12, 15, 18]
Wi-Fi	[12, 14]

OBJECTIVE

An IoT-based floor cleaning robot with a live streaming camera aims to integrate advanced robotics with Internet of Things (IoT) technology to provide a comprehensive, efficient, and user-friendly solution for maintaining clean floors. The primary objectives include:

Automated Cleaning

• The robot autonomously navigates and cleans the floor, reducing the need for manual labor.
• It uses sensors to detect obstacles, and dirt, and optimize cleaning paths.

Live Monitoring

• The live streaming camera allows users to monitor the cleaning process in real time from remote locations.
• It provides visual feedback on areas that need extra attention or verification that the robot is functioning correctly.

Remote Control and Management

• Through a connected app or web interface, users can start, stop, or schedule cleaning sessions from anywhere.
• Users can also manually control the robot if needed, using the live camera feed for navigation.

Data Collection and Analytics

• The robot collects data on cleaning patterns, frequency, and effectiveness.
• Users can review cleaning logs and performance statistics to optimize future cleaning schedules and ensure thorough maintenance.

Integration with Smart Home Systems

• Easily integrate the robot with other smart home devices to create a fully automated and seamless home experience.
• It can work in conjunction with other IoT devices like smart locks, lights, and security systems to enhance home automation.

Enhanced Security and Surveillance

• The live streaming camera can also function as a mobile security camera, providing surveillance of different areas of the home.

- Users can receive alerts and view the live feed if unusual activity is detected during the robot's operation.

User-Friendly Interface

- The system is designed to be easy to use, with intuitive controls and clear feedback on the robot's status and cleaning progress.
- User notifications and alerts keep the user informed of any issues or completed tasks.

Energy Efficiency

- The robot is designed to optimize energy usage, reducing power consumption while ensuring effective cleaning.
- It can return to its charging station autonomously when the battery is low or after completing a cleaning cycle.

Customization and Adaptability

- Users can customize cleaning modes, set specific areas for focused cleaning, and adjust the robot's behavior based on their preferences and home layout.
- The robot can adapt to different floor types and cleaning requirements.

Overall, the IoT-based floor cleaning robot with a live streaming camera aims to provide a smart, efficient, and versatile solution for maintaining a clean and secure home environment.

PROPOSED METHODOLOGY

The proposed Floor-Cleaning Robot (FCR) will feature separate components for both dry and wet cleaning processes, as depicted in Fig. (3).

The system's block diagram showcases the relationship between the microcontroller, motor driver, and power supply. The microcontroller will transmit control signals to the motor driver, which will then activate the left and right motors to execute vacuuming, mopping, sprinkling, and fan operations. Fig. (3) serves to visualize the information flow within the FCR system, highlighting the microcontroller's pivotal role in activating the motor driver and controlling the various cleaning functions.

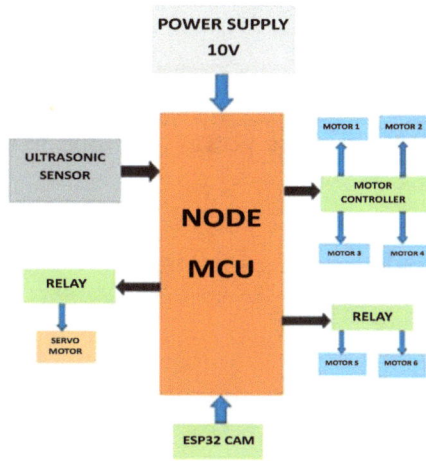

Fig. (3). Block diagram of the proposed FCR.

MODELS VIEW

An IoT-based floor cleaning robot with live streaming involves multiple steps. The robot design should encompass various components, including the chassis, motors, sensors, microcontroller, camera module, and connectivity modules [19]. Below is a basic guide to outline the key components and features of such a design:

Chassis Design

• The chassis should be sturdy and spacious enough to house all the components.
• Includes mounting points for motors, wheels, and casters for smooth movement.

Motor and Wheel Assembly

• Place two DC motors with wheels for movement.
• Include a couple of caster wheels for balance and smooth turning.

Sensor Placement

• Ultrasonic or infrared sensors for obstacle detection.
• Line sensors if line-following capabilities are needed.

Microcontroller

• A compartment to securely mount the microcontroller, such as Arduino or Raspberry Pi.

Camera Module

• A camera module for live streaming.

• Position the camera at an angle that provides a clear view of the robot's path.

Power Supply

• Battery compartment and wiring for power distribution to all components.

Connectivity

• Wi-Fi or Bluetooth module for IoT capabilities.
• Antennas and necessary slots for connectivity modules.

Cleaning Mechanism

• Brushes or mop pads for cleaning.
• Vacuum system if required.

Other Components

• Additional sensors or modules as per the required functionality (*e.g.*, dustbin level sensor).

Front View: Fig. (**4**) illustrates the front view of an electrical vehicle-based floor-cleaning robot. In this robot, we can assemble an ESP32 Cam for live streaming, which provides real-time updates to users, Moppers (2-series moppers) with water sprinklers that can be used to provide water for mopping. Moppers can operate with the help of gear motors for mopping up the floor. These moppers are operated with the help of a relay module; the relay module works as an automatic switch. It allows the control of moppers using a microcontroller. The HC-SR04 Ultrasonic sensor used for obstacle detection is often utilized to find out the distance to an entity.

Fig. (4). Front view of the Bot.

Back View: Fig. (**5**) illustrates the back view of the electrical vehicle-based floor-cleaning robot. On the back side of the electrical vehicle-based floor-cleaning robot, a roller is assembled with a servo motor. This servo is used to move the roller up and down. In order to use the roller, we can pull down the robot with the use of the servo motor and after completing that work, we can place it up with the help of the servo motor. This servo motor is connected with the Relay Module 2, which allows the control of the servo motor using a microcontroller.

Fig. (5). Back view of the Bot.

Right Side View: Fig. (**6**) illustrates the right-side view of an electrical vehicle-based floor-cleaning robot. On this side of the robot assembled, Relay Module-2 is used for operating the moppers automatically for mopping up the floor. It allows the control of moppers using a microcontroller and the right side of the driving wheels with gear motors of this robot.

Fig. (6). Right-side view of the Bot.

Left Side View: Fig. (**7**) illustrates the left side of the floor cleaning robot. This view shows the left side of the driving wheels with the gear motors of the robot. Here, Relay Module-1 is used for operating the water pump and servo motor.

Fig. (7). Left side view of the Bot.

This servo motor is utilized to move the roller up and down and dry the wet area, caused by water sprinklers, and the water pump is used to provide water to sprinklers from the water tank, which can be mounted on the top of this robot.

Top View: Fig. (**8**) illustrates the top of the robot. The top of the robot illustrates all the circuitry of the floor cleaning robot, which helps to operate this robot. In this circuitry, we can use ESP8266 Node MCU, L298N Dual H-Bridge Motor Driver, Two Relay Module, Water Pump, SCRF-310 Pump, s90 micro servo motor 12 V Battery and Water tank. In this Node, MCU is used to operate the whole system automatically with the help of the Blynk IoT application.

Fig. (8). Top view of the Bot.

Bottom Side View: Fig. (**9**) shows the bottom view of the robot. The bottom of the robot shows four driving wheels, four driving gear motors, and a mopper for mopping up the floor. These driving wheels are used to move our robot according to our requirements automatically with the help of Node MCU. This Node MCU is directly connected to the Blynk IoT application.

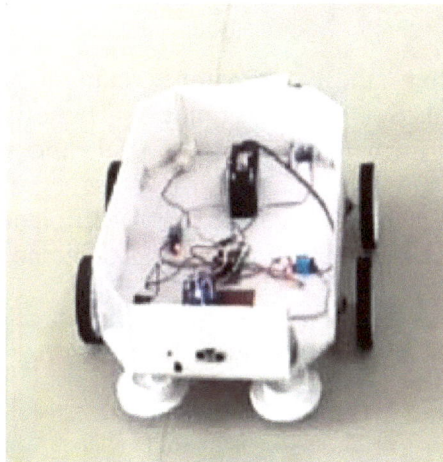

Fig. (9). Bottom view of the Bot.

WORKING PROCESS

The revolutionary floor cleaning model's operational flow is depicted in the following block diagram. To execute cleaning, the system employs a DC motor coupled with wipers. For mopping, a DC water pump ensures regular water supply to a mop cloth. A 12V rechargeable battery powers the entire robotic system. Using an Android app, users can control the floor cleaner or set it to autonomous mode, offering a remote operating range of approximately 10 meters. Upon completion of the cleaning process, the dirt container is emptied and the mop cloth is replaced. Refer to Fig. (**4**) for an overview of the prototype's various components, with detailed descriptions provided in the subsequent sections. . The flow of information in the proposed FCR is shown in Fig. (**10**).

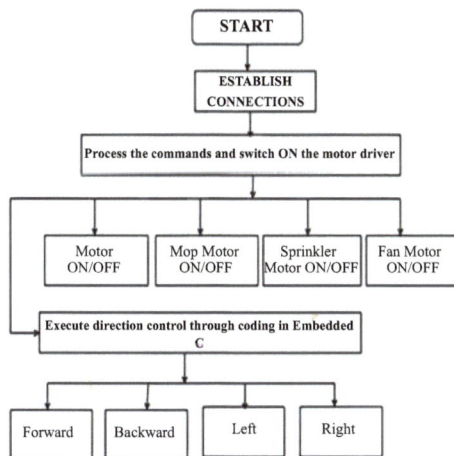

Fig. (10). Flow of information in the proposed FCR.

RESULTS AND ANALYSIS

Integrating IoT technology and live streaming camera functionality into a floor cleaning robot encompasses a wide range of benefits, including enhanced efficiency, cleaning performance, remote control, and monitoring capabilities, customizable cleaning modes, data analytics insights, smart home integration, user-friendly interface, scalability, and cost-efficiency, culminating in a compelling value proposition for users seeking advanced cleaning solutions.

Automatic electric vehicle floor cleaning systems have been examined in real environment conditions. Before cleaning the floor, our floor was dusted, this shown in Fig. (**11**).

Fig. (11). Picture view of Dusted Floor before the Cleaning Process.

Fig. (**12**) shows a picture view of the floor after cleaning process. From the observations, it has been observed that our floor was cleaned.

The integration of IoT technology into floor cleaning robots has revolutionized their efficiency by enabling remote monitoring and control, which dramatically reduces the need for manual intervention and boosts productivity. By incorporating a live streaming camera, users can monitor the cleaning process in real time, gaining critical insights into the robot's performance and facilitating immediate adjustments when necessary.

The data gathered through IoT sensors and the live streaming camera can be thoroughly analyzed to uncover patterns, trends, and areas for enhancement, empowering decision-makers to optimize cleaning processes and allocate resources more effectively. Users enjoy the freedom of controlling the robot remotely and tracking cleaning progress from any location, significantly boosting user satisfaction and engagement with the product. The automation and efficiency gains provided by IoT-driven floor cleaning robots result in impressive cost savings for businesses by cutting labor expenses, reducing resource waste, and extending the lifespan of cleaning equipment.

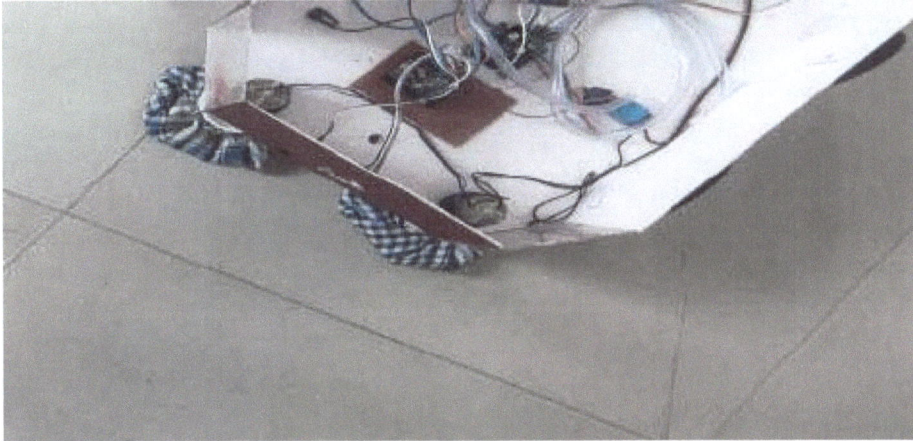

Fig. (12). Picture view of Cleaned Floor after Cleaning Process.

By optimizing cleaning processes and resource usage, IoT-enabled robots play a crucial role in promoting environmental sustainability by minimizing energy consumption and decreasing reliance on chemical cleaning agents. The modular design combined with IoT integration ensures that the floor cleaning robot is both scalable and adaptable to a wide range of environments and cleaning needs, guaranteeing versatility and long-term usability. As IoT technology continues to advance, there is immense potential for further enhancements in the functionality and capabilities of floor-cleaning robots, including features like predictive maintenance, autonomous navigation, and seamless integration with smart home systems.

In summary, the integration of IoT technology and live streaming camera functionality into floor cleaning robots delivers undeniable advantages, including significantly enhanced efficiency, real-time monitoring, and critical data-driven insights. These benefits transform the user experience, yield substantial cost savings, and reinforce a commitment to environmental sustainability. Furthermore, the scalability of these robots, along with their immense potential for future innovation, cements their status as a groundbreaking solution in the cleaning technology landscape.

CONCLUSION AND FUTURE SCOPE

An automatic electric vehicle floor cleaning system is a very important application of automation in household appliances. In this paper, a detailed literature survey has been conducted on floor cleaning systems. Along with that, a live streaming-based floor cleaning system has also been proposed. This work can be used for the survey of floor cleaning systems and applications in various household and industrial areas. The innovative design architecture offers comprehensive cleaning assistance for people from all walks of life. Our automatic floor cleaner is capable of both dry and wet cleaning, making it a versatile solution. Not only is our design cost-effective and user-friendly, but we also have plans to develop and test a prototype in real-life conditions. Additionally, our robot designed for human-robot interaction can be seamlessly integrated with the Blynk application. To cater to individual needs, the hardware fabrication for this project can incorporate various sensors.

AUTHORS' CONTRIBUTION

Paritosh Kumar Rai: Analyzed and interpreted the data; Wrote the paper.

Rachit Srivastava: Study conception and design

Arun Kumar Yadav: Study conception and design

Anuradha Tiwari: Wrote the paper

Sahil Ramazan: Contributed materials, analysis tools or data

Palak Gaur: Contributed materials, analysis tools or data

REFERENCES

[1]   J-S. Gutmann, "The social impact of a systematic floor cleaner", *IEEE Workshop on Advanced Robotics and its Social Impacts (ARSO),* 2012.
[http://dx.doi.org/10.1109/ARSO.2012.6213398]

[2]   B. Hendriks, B. Meerbeek, S. Boess, S. Pauws, and M. Sonneveld, "Robot vacuum cleaner personality and behavior", *Int. J. Soc. Robot.,* vol. 3, no. 2, pp. 187-195, 2011.
[http://dx.doi.org/10.1007/s12369-010-0084-5]

[3]   V. Burman, and R. Kumar, "IoT-enabled automatic floor cleaning robot", *International Conference on Recent Advancements in Mechanical Engineering,* 2020.

[4]   J. Fink, V. Bauwens, F. Kaplan, and P. Dillenbourg, "Living with a vacuum cleaning robot: A 6-month ethnographic study", *Int. J. Soc. Robot.,* vol. 5, no. 3, pp. 389-408, 2013.
[http://dx.doi.org/10.1007/s12369-013-0190-2]

[5]   N. Singh, A. Sharma, Dwivedi , and N. Tiwari, "Internet of things (IoT) based home automation: A review", *I-Managers Journal on Digital Signal Processing,* vol. 6, no. 4, pp. 20-27, 2018.

[6]   Manreet Kaur, *Int. J. Comput. Appl.,* vol. 97, p. 19, 2014.

[7]   F. Vaussard, J. Fink, V. Bauwens, P. Rétornaz, D. Hamel, P. Dillenbourg, and F. Mondada, "Lessons learned from robotic vacuum cleaners entering the home ecosystem", *Robot. Auton. Syst.,* vol. 62, no. 3, pp. 376-391, 2014.
[http://dx.doi.org/10.1016/j.robot.2013.09.014]

[8]   M.L. Walters, "Human approach distances to a mechanical-looking robot with different robot voice styles", *RO-MAN 2008-The 17th IEEE international symposium on robot and human interactive communication,* 2008.
[http://dx.doi.org/10.1109/ROMAN.2008.4600750]

[9]   H. Lee, and A. Banerjee, "Intelligent scheduling and motion control for household vacuum cleaning robot system using simulation-based optimization", *Winter Simulation Conference (WSC),* 2015.
[http://dx.doi.org/10.1109/WSC.2015.7408242]

[10]   Yatmono, S., *et al.* "Development of intelligent floor cleaning robot." *Journal of Physics: Conference Series*, Vol. 1413. No. 1. IOP Publishing, 2019.

[11]   K.M. Bhingare, "Vacuum cleaner using microcontroller", *Open Access Int J Sci Eng,* vol. 3, pp. 15-17, 2018.

[12]   H. Parmar, "Automatic smart mop for floor cleaning", *International Research Journal of Engineering and Technology,* vol. 6, no. 4, pp. 3159-3165, 2019.

[13]   M.J. Garud, "A review wireless floor cleaning robot", *Int. J. Sci. Res. Comput. Sci. Eng. Inf. Technol.,* vol. 3, pp. 648-652, 2018.

[14]   R. Vishaal, R. P, R. R, S. Michael, and M.R. Elara, "Design of dual-purpose cleaning robot", *Procedia Comput. Sci.,* vol. 133, pp. 518-525, 2018.
[http://dx.doi.org/10.1016/j.procs.2018.07.065]

[15]   A. Pandey, "A technological survey on autonomous home cleaning robots", *International Journal of Scientific and Research Publications,* vol. 4, no. 4, pp. 1-7, 2014.

[16]   N. Tiwari, R. Chander, V. Dubey, Upadhyay , A.P. Singh, P.K. Srivastava, and S. Yadav, "Hardware designing and modeling of joystick based electric wheelchair drive", *International Conference on Frontiers in Desalination, Energy, Environment and Material Sciences for Sustainable Development,* pp. 241-247, 2023.

[17]   Das, NabamitaRamkrishna, *et al.* "Robotic automated floor cleaner." *International Research Journal of Engineering and Technology*, 2019.

[18]   R. Bhoopathi, "Fabrication of Automated Scrap Collector Cum Scrubber for Production Industries", *Advances in Manufacturing Technology: Select Proceedings of ICAMT,* 2019.
[http://dx.doi.org/10.1007/978-981-13-6374-0_18]

[19]   S. Dubey, "An FPGA-based service Robot for floor cleaning with autonomous navigation", *2016 International Conference on Research Advances in Integrated Navigation Systems (RAINS),* 2016.
[http://dx.doi.org/10.1109/RAINS.2016.7764425]

Electric Vehicle Technologies, 2025, 175-201   **175**

Hardware Design and Modelling of Solar based Wireless Electric Vehicle Charging Station

Nitesh Tiwari[1,*], **Ajay Kumar Maurya**[1], **Ankesh Kumar Mishra**[1], **Aditya Chaurasia**[1] and **Shubham Gupta**[1]

[1] *Department of Electrical Engineering, KIPM College of Engineering and Technology, Gida, Gorakhpur (UP), India*

Abstract: This chapter proposes a model for a wireless charging station for Electric Vehicles (EVs), eliminating the need for conventional charging plugs and wires. The system operates based on the principle of mutual induction, utilizing two coils: a transmitter (primary coil) and a receiver (secondary coil). In this setup, the primary coil is powered by a high-frequency AC supply source/inverter, and EMF is automatically in the IC field. When the secondary coil, located in the vehicle, comes into proximity with the primary coil, an Electromagnetic Force (EMF) is induced in the receiver coil, allowing energy transfer without physical contact. A key feature of this model is that the two coils are not co-located. The primary coil is installed at the charging station, while the secondary coil is integrated into the electric vehicle. For the system to work, the vehicle must be equipped with this secondary coil. Once energy is transferred from the primary to the secondary coil, it is used to charge the vehicle's batteries. In addition to facilitating wireless charging, the station is powered primarily by solar energy, making it an eco-friendly solution by utilizing renewable energy sources. Importantly, electric vehicles without the secondary coil installed will not be compatible with this wireless charging system, underscoring the need for integration of this technology into the vehicle design.

Keywords: Compensation, Green renewable source, Inductive power transfer, Resonant power transfer, WPT.

INTRODUCTION

Electric vehicles around the world are being charged by wired charging methods at various electric charging stations. All these stations have overhead electricity or diesel generators as their input source of energy. Diesel engines were already a responsible source of pollution, and the grid's inputs just supported the pollution level because about 50 percent of electrical energy is still generated by conven-

---

[*] **Corresponding author Nitesh Tiwari:** Department of Electrical Engineering, KIPM College of Engineering and Technology, Gida, Gorakhpur (UP), India; E-mail: niteshwr1994@gmail.com

Nitesh Tiwari, Shekhar Yadav and Sabha Raj Arya (Eds.)

tional non-renewable resources. Most people think that just using electric vehicles and charging stations reduces the pollution in the environment, but it is not 100% true. This is because if you are taking energy from charging stations from the grid supply, then there is no difference in the level of pollution as electricity is eventually generated by coal and some other conventional sources [1]. You are just converting dispersed pollution into concentrated one without any reduction in level. If we go deep, we see that the overall pollution increases despite being reduced. It is because there are losses at various stages of transmission and distribution, and the generating station has to feed those losses, too. So, coal consumption increases for the same energy at the vehicle level, and thus, pollution and carbon emissions slightly increase. The only way to truly reduce pollution is by using non-conventional or renewable sources. These sources have no meaning to coal or the grid, and they can be autonomous sources with net zero emission of carbon and their subsidiaries [2].

This charging station uses the energy of a green renewable source, *i.e.*, solar energy, as the input and converts it into AC electricity after some controller circuitry and devices. This minimizes the energy intake and dependency on electric vehicles to charge electricity to utility companies alone [3]. Electricity is transferred from the station to the vehicle through inductive and resonant wireless charging in AC form, which is further rectified and regulated by the vehicle's internal circuitry. It also employs the overhead AC utility provided by the government in case solar rays are unavailable. This increases the reliability of the station [4].

An electric vehicle is a means of transport that needs electricity as the input fuel to the system. Since electric vehicles, instead of using an inter-combustion engine, employ electric motors for the propulsion, and this motor can be DC/AC, which is fed by the series and parallel combination of batteries through various power electronic converters, they depend most severely on charging infrastructure [5]. Batteries used in vehicles are lead storage in most EVs, but some hi-tech EVs can use a huge combination of lithium-ion batteries. The advantage of lithium-ion batteries is their high energy density. It also has the challenge of proper charging and discharging maintenance, as these batteries are more prone to explosions. That's why proper BMS is employed in those systems that employ Li-ion batteries to store electricity [6].

The charging station has both steady and quick charging features, such as level 1 and level 2 charging, respectively. Fast or level 2 charging can be done for vehicles in an emergency. However, steady charging is far better than quick charging from the battery's life point of view. This is because if we charge the battery rapidly, it takes up a lot of current and produces heat inside the battery.

Chemical reactions are fast and quick, which leads to a decrease in the storage capacity of the batteries [7]. The life of batteries is often recognized by a number of cycles, *i.e.* no. of charge and discharge in a battery's life, and it is much affected by the way a battery is charged and used. For the best performance and results with longevity, steady charging with a proper battery management system is required. Talking about lithium batteries (whether it be lithium ion or lithium polymer), they have high risks of explosions. This is because lithium is the most reactive metal element in the periodic table. However, it has a very high energy density and efficiency with lesser weight per unit of energy and power compared to other storage devices (batteries). This is the reason why most EV manufacturers use and promote lithium batteries. The lithium sector has undergone a new revolution after the discovery of lithium sources in the United States of America and China [8].

In the charging infrastructure, an inverter section connects DC and AC links. This is basically a high-frequency inverter with a ferrite core transformer. It is somewhat different from conventional domestic inverter. It is because it does not produce output at power frequency. It has its output at super higher frequencies at some kilohertz or megahertz. Using higher frequency is the demand of the charging station in order to make wireless power transfer efficient. At higher frequencies, the required flux for the mutual induction decreases, and thus, the loss of flux is also minimized [9]. In order to make this system further efficient, a technology called resonant wireless power transfer is used. It makes coupling between the primary transmitter and secondary receiver coils *via* resonance. Both coils resonate at the same frequency, and it gives maximum efficiency. Moreover, it supports multiple secondaries at the same time. There is a compensation network that includes capacitors and inductors in both the transmitter and receiver in order to match the impedances exactly [10]. Various measuring instruments are used to measure the output voltage, current, power, and energy. Measuring energy is the most crucial thing when building a project like a charging station because consumers have to pay bills for the electrical energy they use to charge their vehicles [11].

The charging pad design is important as it transfers the power to the vehicle's receiver coil. For the transmitter and receiver coil, a litz wire with a proper diameter and cross-sectional area according to the requirement is used. This wire is hollow from the inside, and it is important in this application. Whenever we use alternating current, we observe that current density is higher, mostly near the surface of the wire, and almost zero at the center. In other words, we can say that most of the current flow through the surface, and this alternating current effect is called the skin effect. This is mainly due to the inductance and inductive reactance, which are directly proportional to supply frequency. So, to better utilize the conductor material, either stranded or hollow conductors are often used for AC supply. Since the frequency of this project is much higher than the normal power frequency, it is a must to use a hollow conductor for transmitter and receiver coils. If it were solid, it would just be a waste of a lot of conductor material at high frequency due to the skin effect, and also, it offers more weight, making the system bulkier [12].

The new innovations one can consider as contributions are three things mainly. The first and foremost thing is that a new technology has been introduced, *i.e.*, the wireless charging of vehicles. This is a progressive step towards automation as it eliminates the need for human labour and the need for plugging those heavy wires and cables in vehicles and so on. The second thing is that solar energy has been taken into account. This not only reduces the level of carbon emission but also promotes research in the renewable energy sector for optimum efficiency. The third and last thing is that the research is implemented physically and found to be working as per estimations.

METHODOLOGY

The various methods and diagrams with explanations are:

Block Diagram of Charging Station

The block diagram of the charging station is shown in Fig. (1).

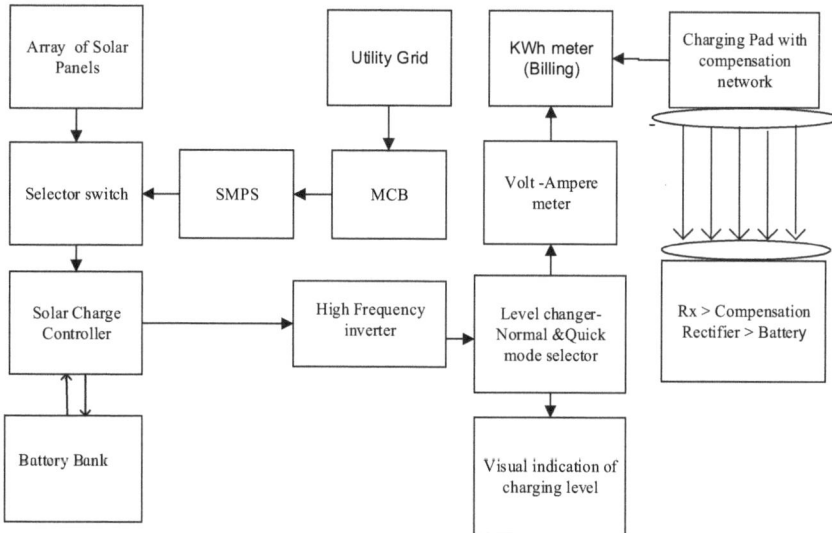

Fig. (1). Block diagram of charging station.

As shown in the above block diagram, solar panels get sunlight from the sun and convert it into direct current electricity, which goes to one of the inputs of the selector switch. Meanwhile, grid electricity (AC) is fed to the full bridge rectifier through MCB. The full bridge rectifier converts 220 V AC into 12 V DC, which goes to another input of the selector switch. By default, the selector switch is connected to the solar panel. The output of the selector is fed to the charge controller. This charge controller has these features:

- It can monitor the charge level of the battery and charge the battery accordingly.
- It regulates the voltage level for proper charging.
- It protects the battery from getting overcharged and deep discharge.
- It has an internal low-voltage against short-circuit [13].

The battery bank contains a lot of batteries connected in parallel. These are lead storage batteries. These all get charged by the charge controller. Simultaneously, a parallel connection is made with the high-frequency inverter. The inverter converts 12 V DC into high-frequency high voltage and alternating current, which is 300 V AC (RMS) at 25 kHz. Here, a high-frequency inverter is used to minimize magnetic losses and increase transmission efficiency [14].

Next, the output high-frequency transformer of the inverter has two tapings – one for Level 1 (normal charging at 250 V) and another for Level 2 (fast charging at 300 V). This transition in the level of voltage is switched by a changer switch connected to the transformer [15]. After this, voltage and current are measured by measuring the device at output. Since the charging station supplies energy to the consumer vehicle, it is required to bill the number of units consumed while charging and calculating money. An energy meter is also used to do so [16]. Finally, power is fed to the transmitter coil through compensation, and it is transferred wirelessly to the vehicle's coil. The vehicle has its own rectifier and voltage regulator circuit to monitor the battery and its charge. This is how this charging station works.

MATHEMATICAL MODELLING

The methodology contains various sections and subsections, which are discussed below:

Technology Integration

Technologies such as solar power generation, dual (Alternate) power sources, wireless power transfer, high-frequency inversion, and transformation are used in this research project. These technologies promote green energy usage and increase reliability due to alternate sources.

Solar Power Generation

Solar power generation is a method of generating direct current from the solar radiation. It uses an array of photovoltaic cells within which photoelectric phenomena happen, and direct current is generated at the output terminals. This is the cheapest technique used to extract the hidden energy of nature (which is the sun here) when compared to other renewable energy resources like hydropower generation, geothermal power generation, wind power generation, tidal, *etc.* All other sources of this category require high installation capital and maintenance costs, while the current requires only panels to be installed in the proper land area [17]. Schematics of solar power generation are shown in Fig (**2**).

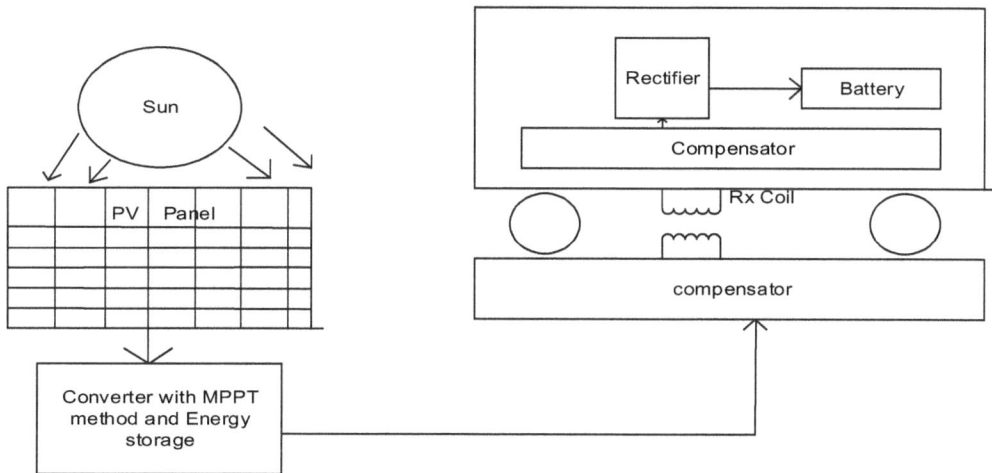

Fig. (2). Solar power generation.

Since the number of panels used can be expressed as Eq. (**1**),

$$n = P/p \quad (1)$$

The total land area required is denoted by Eq. (**2**),

$$A = n*a \quad (2)$$

Or, rearranging, we get Eq. (**3**) as the total land area required,

$$A = P*a/p \quad (3)$$

Here, A, a, P, p, and n are the total, denoting the installation of solar panels, the area of individual solar panels, the total power of the system, the power of the individual solar panel, and the number of panels required, respectively.

Photovoltaic Cell

Photovoltaic cells are devices that contribute to semiconductors' manufacturing process. Trivalent and pentavalent semiconductor materials make their junction at the incidence of photons or light. It produces an electron-hole pair at the junction of the two materials and disbalances the potential of both sides. This generates a direct current in the closed circuit [18]. The point to be noted is that it behaves like a current source with an upper limit of power and voltage. Unlike a voltage source (DC battery), where output power is inversely proportional to the resistance of the circuit, its power utilization is proportional to the value of the resistance of the circuit. It is because the current in the circuit is independent of the resistance (or load) until it goes beyond the maximum power rating of the solar cell/panel. When it exceeds, the current gets reduced in order to make the output power and voltage constant at upper loads. Ohm's law is followed in each case [19]. Power across load is mentioned as per Eq. (**4**). For a fixed value of load resistance, the terminal voltage is given by Eq. (**5**). For a solar panel, power output,

$$P = I^2 * R \ (4)$$

The output terminal voltage across the load is,

$$V = I * R \text{ or } P/I \ (5)$$

Here, P, I, R, and V are the output power of the panel, the maximum current rating of the solar panel, the resistance of the load connected across the panel and the closed-circuit voltage across the load, respectively. But there is the threshold value of resistance above which a solar panel or photovoltaic cell changes its behavior from current sources to the constant power source. In other words, exceeding the threshold value of load resistance, the output solar-generated current starts decreasing in order to maintain the output power constant, and this is equal to the maximum power rating of the photovoltaic cell [20]. The threshold value or maximum allowable value of load resistance is given by Eq. (**6**),

$$R_{max} = P_{rated}/\text{sqrt}(I) \ (6)$$

Here, R_{max}, P_{max}, and I are the maximum resistance that can be added for a constant rated current, power rating of the photovoltaic cell and rated current of the photovoltaic cell, respectively.

Arrangement of Panels

Arranging the panels in the array is essential for systematic installation. The number of solar panels used depends on the power rating of the charging station.

For a 1 kW system, 25 solar panels of 40 watts each are required. They can be arranged/connected in series or parallel configurations depending on the voltage and current rating of the controller. Controllers are rated based on current incoming from the solar array. For the proposed 1 kW system here, the controller should be able to withstand the current of around 90 (exactly 83.33 but including a safety factor of 1.08) Amperes if all 25 panels are connected in parallel. This was just a 12 Volt system. For parallel connected arrays, net current and net voltage are given in Eqs. (**7 and 8**), respectively. Similarly, for series connected arrays, net voltage and net current are according to Eqs. (**9 and 10**), respectively.

For parallel connection of panels, net current,

$$I_{net} = I_{rated} * N \quad (7)$$

Net voltage,

$$V_{net} = V \quad (8)$$

Similarly, for series connection, net voltage,

$$V_{net} = V * N \quad (9)$$

Net current,

$$I_{net} = I_{rated} \quad (10)$$

Here, I_{net}, I_{rated}, N, V_{net}, and V are the resultant current of the array, the current rating of one solar panel, the number of solar panels in the parallel connection, and the resultant voltage of the array and voltage across any individual panel, respectively.

Power Densities and Efficiencies

Generally, solar cells have different power densities according to their types. These are:

Monocrystalline solar panels have a power density of approximately 183 watts per square meter and an efficiency of 21.2%.

Polycrystalline solar panels – These have a power density of approximately 172 watts per square meter with an efficiency of 15%.

Thin film solar panels – These have about 62 watts per square meter of power density and conversion efficiency ranging from 7 – 12% [21].

Out of these all, the most efficient is the monocrystalline one, which is used. So, for a 1 kW system, the area of land or roof for solar panel installation will be 5.5 square meters. The maximum efficiency is 21.2%, which is for mono-crystalline panels [22]. MPPT method or maximum power point tracking method is often used in such systems, which increases the all-day efficiency of panels. This is an inbuilt feature of some good quality charge controllers [23].

Dual (Alternate) Power Source

The charging station has the feature of dual sources of input energy. These sources are Solar arrays & Grid utilities. In both of them, the principal source is the solar array, but grid utility is also added for some emergency cases, such as rainy and cloudy weather. Also, sometimes, in the winter season, there are very low levels of UV indexes, lowering the power density of solar panels. So, for these circumstances, an auxiliary source, *i.e.* grid utility, is concerned. One more benefit of this is that it also increases the overall reliability of the charging station [24.] The grid has a negligible share of input power to the charging station during the sunny summer season. Its share increases in rainy and winter seasons, which is estimated to go up to 50% (estimated) per day. A block diagram of SMPS used for the conversion of grid AC supply into DC is given in Fig. (**3**).

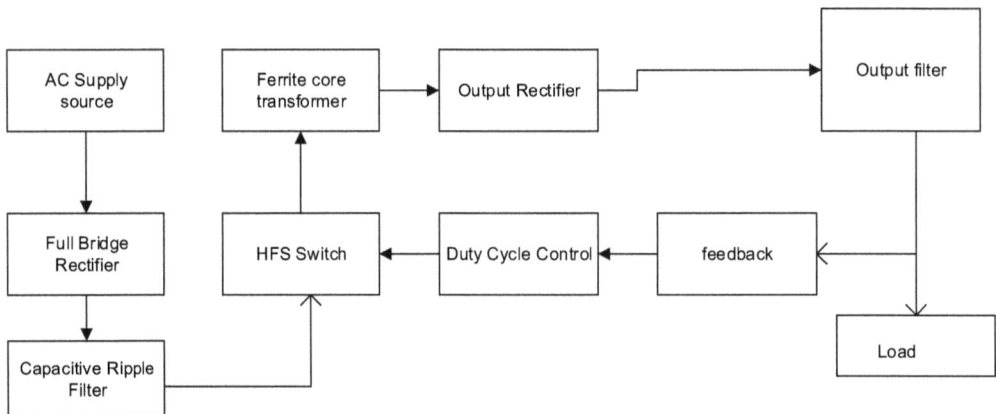

Fig. (3). Block diagram of SMPS.

Wireless Power Transfer

Wireless power transfer is the technology that is the backbone of this project. The whole project is set to replace conventional wired charging with wireless technology. There are various technologies for the transmission of power without electrical connection, out of which two technologies are the mains, which are Inductive coupling WPT & Resonant coupling *WPT* [25].

Inductive Coupling WPT

Inductive coupling is the same as how a normal transformer works. It simply has input power at the primary coil, which produces alternating flux. If flux interacts with the secondary coil, EMF is induced by the mutual induction principle [26]. It has no additional circuits like compensation or else.

The induced EMF is given by Eq. (**11**):

$E = -Ndf/dt$ (**11**)

Here, E, N, f, and df/dt are an electromotive force induced by Faraday's law of electromagnetic induction, the number of conductors, flux linked to N conductors, and the rate of change flux, respectively. The negative sign in the above expression denotes Lenj's law, according to which induced EMF has polarity in such a direction that it always opposes the cause of its generation. In case of mutually induced EMF through inductive coupling, the following Eqs. (**12 – 20**) sit well,

$E_1 = V_2 - I_1Z_1$ (**12**)

$E_2 = I_2Z_2 + V_2$ (**13**)

$Z_1 = R_1 + jX_1$ (**14**)

$Z_2 = R_2 + jX_2$ (**15**)

$E_1 = -N_1df/dt$ (**16**)

Since, $f = f_m sin wt$,

$E_1 = -N_1f_m cos wt$ (**16**)

or

$E_1 = N_1 wf_m \sin (wt - 90)$ (**18**)

Similarly, for E_2,

$E_2 = -N_2 df/dt$ (**19**)

Again, $f = f_m sin wt$,

$E_2 = -N_2 wf_m cos wt$ (20)

$E_2 = N_2 wf_m \sin (wt - 90)$

Where E_1, E_2, V_1, V_2, Z_1, Z_2, R_1, R_2, X_1, X_2, N_1, N_2, w & t are EMF induced in the primary coil, EMF induced in the secondary coil, AC voltage applied at the primary side, AC terminal voltage obtained across the load at the secondary side, the overall impedance of the primary side, the overall impedance of the secondary side, resistance of the primary side, the resistance of the secondary side, the inductive reactance of the primary winding, inductive reactance of the secondary winding, number of turns in primary side, number of turns in secondary side, angular velocity in radians per seconds and time respectively. These induced electromotive forces at both sides of mutual inductance phenomena were average values. In order to get the root mean square (RMS) value, we use Eq. (**21**),

$V_{rms} = V_m/\text{sqrt}2$ (**21**)

So, we get Eq. (**22**) as,

$E_{1rms} = E_{1(m)}/\text{sqrt}2$ (**22**)

Since, for E_{1m}, sin $(wt - 90) = 1$,

Hence, putting values, we get Eqs. (**23** and **24**),

$E_{1rms} = wN_1f_m/\text{sqrt}2$ (**23**)

$E_{1rms} = 4.44ff_mN_1$ (**24**)

Similarly, for E_2, the expression is in Eq. (**25**),

$E_{2rms} = 4.44ff_mN_2$ (**25**)

But, being simple circuitry, it suffers in applications other than transformation. It has the drawback of its very low efficiency even when the receiver coil is a few centimetres from the transmitter one. It requires a minimum air gap to have greater efficiencies. Orientation also affects the ratio of utilization. Since severely less air gap is not possible for EV charging, this method is not used in this charging station [27].

Resonant Coupling WPT

It is another method of wireless power transfer that makes some modifications to the inductive coupling WPT method. Mutual induction is the same principle acting here also but one extra thing here is resonance. The two coils in this system are coupled in such a way that both resonate at the same frequency. To achieve this, an additional compensation circuit has been used. This circuit basically contains inductors and capacitors to make the impedance exactly, what is required for the resonance to happen at any particular frequency [28]. The same type of circuit is also used when the vehicle is getting charged. First, the effective inductance and capacitance of the transmitter circuit decide the frequency of resonance, which can be expressed as shown in Eq. (**26**),

$$f_1 = 1/ (2\pi * sqrt (L_1 * C_1))$$ (**26**)

The receiver resonance frequency is given in Eq. (**28**),

$$f_2 = 1/ (2\pi * sqrt(L_2 * C_2))$$ (**27**)

For the resonance between the two coils, the condition is according to Eq. (**28**),

$$f_1 = f_2 = f_r$$ (**28**)

It is expressed as Eq. (**29**),

$$f_r = 1/ (2\pi * sqrt (L_r * C_r)$$ (**29**)

Here, L_1, C_1, L_2, C_2, L_r, and Cr are the inductance of the transmitter coil, the capacitance of the transmitter coil, the inductance of the receiver coil, the capacitance of the receiver coil, the required inductance for the given capacitance with a resonance frequency and required capacitance for the given inductance with resonance frequency respectively [29]. Both coils are tuned in such a way that their resonance frequency becomes equal, and an AC supply of the same resonance frequency is applied at the primary side or transmitter coil. To maximize the efficiency (as efficiency is reduced in coreless coupling), the quality factor is maximized. The quality factor is given by Eqs. (**30 and 31**),

$$Q = X/R$$ (**30**)

$$Q = wL/R$$ (**31**)

where *w*, L, X and R are angular velocity in radians per second, inductance, inductive reactance, and resistance, respectively. Usually, a higher value of inductance is required for the compensation of reduced efficiency in wireless power transfer. In case of resonance, the air gap does not affect as it was in inductive coupling. Also, there is not much foundation of the secondary coil. It has the feature that it can supply power wirelessly to multiple secondaries. Thus, this method has been adopted in this charging station [30].

High-frequency Inverter

Since resonant coupling is included in the project, it requires frequencies above 10 kHz. For such a high-frequency AC supply, a high-frequency inverter is obviously required. The inverter is an electrical device or power electronic circuit that converts Direct Current (DC) power into Alternating Current (AC) power. It performs this action by the use of switching devices like MOSFETs, IGBTs, and transistors [31]. These devices form an H-bridge (depending on the number of phases in the output AC supply), which is triggered by a proper gate control mechanism. This triggering allows these switching devices to turn ON and OFF continuously in a periodic manner, and finally, the AC wave is realized at the output section.

Power of Inverter

It is given in terms of voltage, current, power factor, *etc.*, on both sides, as well as input and output. Input power to inverter (P_i) is given by Eq. (**32**),

$$P_i = V_{dc} * I_{dc} \text{ (32)}$$

The output power of the inverter (P_o) is given by Eq. (**33**),

$$P_o = V_o * I_o * \cos(phi) \text{ (33)}$$

Here, V_{dc}, I_{dc}, V_o, I_o, cos(phi), and (phi) are the input DC voltage to the inverter, input DC current in the inverter, output rms AC voltage across the load, output rms AC current in the load, power factor of output load and phase difference between rms voltage and rms current at output, respectively. However, inverters are always rated in Volt-Ampere (VA). It is because active power output depends on power factor and power factor is dependent on load. The maximum active power that an inverter can deliver is equal to the rated volt-ampere value or apparent power of the inverter, and this happens only at the unity power factor [32].

Losses in Inverter

No power electronic circuit is completely loss-free. Loss always exists due to switching electronic switches, such as MOSFETs, IGBTs, and some other factors. When an electronic switch turns ON or OFF, a dynamic voltage drop exists across it, and current flows through it. This causes a power drop across the switch, referred to as switching loss. Further, there are conduction and stray losses also in the circuit [33]. Switching loss (L_s) is given by Eq. (**34**),

$$L_s = E_{Lavg} * f \text{ (34)}$$

Where E_{Lavg} and f are the average energy loss across the switch and frequency of switching, respectively. Conduction loss (L_c) in the switch is given by Eq. (**35**),

$$L_c = (I_{ds}^2) * R_{ds} \ (35)$$

where I_{ds} and R_{ds} are drained to source current of MOSFET (used here) and ON state drain to source resistance of MOSFET, respectively. Stray losses in the inverter are random and depend on multiple factors like current, temperature, frequency, *etc.* It can be determined only when total losses, as well as conduction losses and switching losses, are already known [34]. Hence, the total losses (L_t) in an inverter can be expressed as in Eq. (**36**),

$$L_t = L_s + L_c + \text{stray losses} \ (36)$$

Apart from these, there are also some triggering losses in the circuit, but those are a very small fraction of the above losses.

Efficiency

Efficiency is given by Eqs. (**37** and **41**),

$$\eta = P_o/P_i \ (37)$$

$$\eta = (P_i - \text{total losses} \ (L_t))/P_i \ (38)$$

$$\eta = (P_i - (L_s + L_c + \text{stray losses}))/P_i \ (39)$$

$$\eta = (Pi - (E_{Lavg} * f + (I_{ds}^2) * R_{ds} + \text{stray losses}))/P_i \ (40)$$

or

$$\% \ \eta = *100 \ (41)$$

Here, = efficiency of the inverter.

Gate Triggering

The triggering circuit plays a vital role in the inverter as it controls when a MOSFET conducts and when it does not. It acts like the brain of the inverter. The triggering circuit of MOSFETs depends on the type of output waveform required. Here, for the sinusoidal output, the gate is triggered with SPWM signals. SPWM stands for sinusoidal pulse width modulation. It is a series of square pulses with varying duty cycles of each pulse in a cycle. The duty cycle is minimum at the start, *i.e.*, o degree, maximum at 90 degrees, and again minimum at 180 degrees. This, in turn, gives the realization of the sine function [35].

Here, the SPWM wave for gate triggering is generated by comparing a sine wave and fast sawtooth wave generated by CD4047 and 555 timer IC, respectively. For PWM, modulation index (m) is given in Eq. (**42**),

$$m = V_o/V_c \text{ (42)}$$

Here, V_o and V_c are the amplitude of the original or fundamental sine wave and the amplitude of the carrier wave, respectively. The modulation index's value is always equal to or less than 1 for proper modulation. Here, the modulation index is taken as 1. The frequency output of a stable oscillator CD4047 (f) used is given by Eq. (**43**),

$$f = 1/(4.4R*C) \text{ (43)}$$

where R & C are the resistance and capacitance connected to the CD4047 oscillator. Here, f = 25000Hz, C = 10000 pF, hence,

$$R = 1/ (4.4*25000*0.00000001),$$

$$R = 910 \text{ ohms.}$$

A resistor of 1 kiloohms can be used without much problem. The frequency of the fast sawtooth wave generated by 555 IC (f_s) is given by Eq. (**44**).

$$f_s = 1/ (0.69*C_1*R_2*(2 + R_1)) \text{ (44)}$$

where C_1, C_2 & R_1, and R_2 are capacitances and resistances connected to 555 timers.

High-frequency Transformer

A high-frequency transformer is used at the output of the inverter and just before the transmitter coil. This transformer utilizes a ferrite core in order to avoid any saturation and hysteresis problems at high frequencies. Usually, ATX cores are used to hold the windings of such transformers [36]. The various parameters of transformer design, such as core flux, area, number of turns on both sides of winding, size (diameter) of conductor used, *etc.*, depending on the supply frequency, VA rating, voltage, and current rating [37].

<u>Calculation of Core Flux</u>

The area of the transformer core is given in terms of the total flux and flux density of the transformer. It is given by Eq. (**45**),

$$a =/b \text{ (45)}$$

where a, , and b are core area, flux linkage, and flux density in the core, respectively. For ATX core, b = 1800 Gauss (it can work well in the range of 1500 – 2500 Gauss). Hence, a = *10000/1800 m^2 . Here, the chosen area of the cross-section of the core = 20mm *10mm. Thus, the value of flux,

= 20*10*1800/10^{10} Wb

= 0.000036 Wb.

Calculation of Number of Turns

From the EMF equation of the transformer, the induced EMF in any winding is given by Eq. (46),

E = 4.44***N*f (46)

Rearranging, we see these in Eq. (47),

N = E/(4.44*f*) (47)

Hence for the primary number of turns, the expression is in Eq. (48),

N$_1$ = V$_1$/(4.44*f*) (48)

The secondary number of turns is given in Eq. (49),

N$_2$ = V$_2$/(4.44*f*$_)$) (49)

In this project, V$_1$ = 12 V, V$_2$ = 300 V, f = 25000 Hz, = 0.000036 Wb. So,

N$_1$ = 12/ (4.44*25000*0.000036),

N$_1$ = 3 turns.

and

N$_2$ = 300/ (4.44*25000*0.000036)

N$_2$ = 75 turns.

Calculation of Conductor Dimension

For the calculation of the conductor's diameter or cross-sectional area, the first current at both sides of the winding is required to be determined. The current is determined with the help of the power and voltage of that side. The primary side current of the high-frequency transformer is given by Eq. (50),

$I_1 = S/V_1$ **(50)**

Since this project is intended for 1KVA or 1000 VA and $V_1 = 12$ V,

$I_1 = 1000/1_2,$

$I_1 = 83.33$ A.

Here, I_1, S, and V_1 are the primary side current, kVA or VA rating of the transformer and primary side voltage, respectively. Now, secondary current is given in Eq. **(51)**,

$I_2 = N_1*I_1/N_2$ **(51)**

$I_2 = 3*83.33/75,$

$I_2 = 3.33$ A.

Here, I_2, N_1, and N_2 are the secondary side currents, the number of turns on the primary side, and the number of turns on the secondary side, respectively. Now, using the standard conductor chart for current *vs.* cross-sectional area and diameter, the required dimension for the primary conductor is as follows,

diameter, $d_1 = 6.54$ mm &

area, $a_1 = 33$ mm^2

Similarly, for secondary conductors,

diameter, $d_2 = 1.29$ mm &

area, $a_2 = 1.31$ mm^2

Components and Specifications

Since various types of controlling, converting and compensation circuits are employed, it contains a lot of components in its implementation. Components and their specifications are tabulated in Table **1**:

Table 1. Components with their ratings and quantities.

S. No.	Component's Name	Specification	Qty
1.	Solar panels	40 W, Monocrystalline	25
2.	Charge controller	90 A, inbuilt MPPT method	1
3.	Batteries	32 Ah, Lead storage battery	10

(Table 1) cont.....

S. No.	Component's Name	Specification	Qty
4.	Charging pad	1 kWh, 25 kHz Copper coil	2
5.	MCB	220 V, 5A	1
6.	Indicators	220 V operated, Red	2
7.	Volt-Amp display	Digital	1
8.	Energy meter	Digital with reset function	1
9.	Diodes	1N5458	20
10.	Capacitor	50 V, 3000 μF, Polar	2
11.	Capacitor	400 V, 10 μF, Mica	5
12.	MOSFET	IRFZ44N, N channel, Enhancement	12
13.	Heatsink	Copper	4
14.	555 IC	DIP, timer	1
15.	CD4047 IC	DIP, Oscillator	1
16.	741 IC	Op-Amp, Comparator	1
17.	Relay	DPDT, 300 V AC, 5 A	2
18.	Changer	5A, Two way	1
19.	7812 IC	Linear voltage regulator	1
20.	Zener diode	5 V, 1.5 W	5
21.	Resistors	10 kΩ, 1kΩ, 220 Ω	2, 5, 7
22.	Litz wire	Toroidal	2
23.	ATX core transformer	25 kHz, 1800 Gauss, E-type core, 1 kVA	1

Apart from these above-listed components and devices, some other structural components, such as iron frames, woodwork, steel, fibre, *etc.*, are also required for the physical implementation of the project.

CONTROLLERS

Controllers are always required if we want precision and accuracy in the system, whether it be a PID controller of higher order or just a normal controller. Based on their properties, they are employed in worldwide applications belonging to the power sectors. Here, the controllers are used to maximize the harvested output energy from renewable nature and to vary the magnitude and rate of charging. The controllers and devices used are given below for control purposes.

Solar Charge Controller

• It can sense the input voltage level and current generated by the photovoltaic array. If it is overvoltage, it will trip the circuit to ensure the overvoltage protection of the upcoming equipment. Talking about the current, it has a maximum rated value of current which can be controlled easily by this. When the input current exceeds the rated value, it again opens the circuit to safeguard upcoming circuits.

- If the generated currents and voltage and currents are low, as is much more obvious on rainy, cloudy, and winter days, it compares the value with a minimum set value of current and voltage and decides accordingly whether to trip or not. This minimum value is actually the threshold value for the cut-off of the circuit.

- The control operation is not only on the source side, but it also monitors the load status connected to its output terminals. A short circuit has a chance of occurring on this side. It (the solar charge controller) has features called overload cut-off and short circuit protection. Using the current and voltage sensors embedded in the controller, both of the above protection control actions are performed.

- If the battery or bank of batteries is connected to it for charging purposes, it monitors the charge level and status of the current. It has a feature that regulates the charge rate and auto-cuts and the output power of the battery once it is fully charged. It also protects the batteries from getting deeply discharged.

MPPT Technology

MPPT stands for 'maximum power point tracking'. A charge controller is used along with tracking arrays of solar panels; it is a must that the controller should be equipped with maximum power point tracking technology. This is because tracking arrays are designed to get most of the incident radiations falling on them. MPPT helps achieve maximum efficiency [38]. It extracts the maximum possible energy from the panels by allowing the variation in the duty cycles of switches so that the panel or solar module can see the impedance corresponding to the maximum power point all the time. It maximizes the all-day efficiency and the amount of energy generated by using even fewer panels comparatively. In other words, it increases the energy generated per unit area occupied by the system. In this way, it is very beneficial [39]. The block diagram of MPPT is shown in Fig. (4).

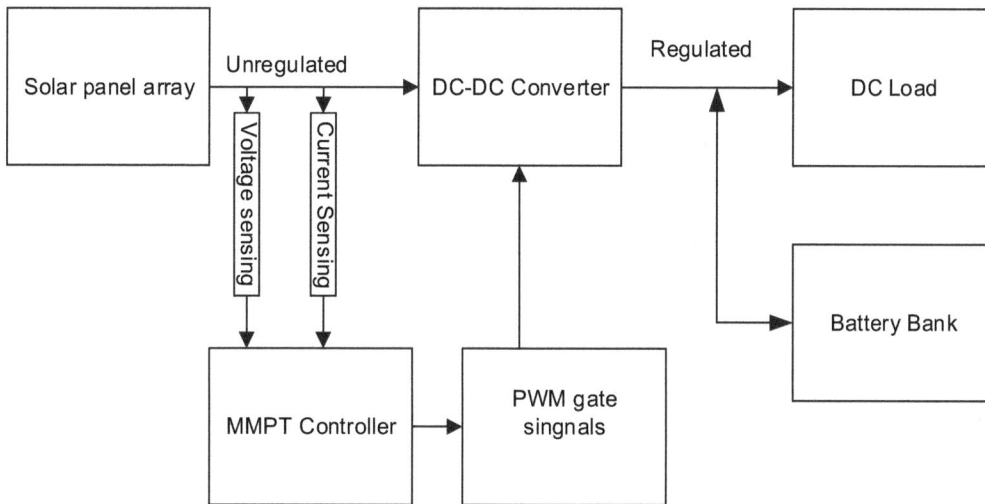

Fig. (4). MPPT Technology.

Voltage Level Changer

In this project, a voltage level changer is basically a changeover switch that has the ability to switch two-way. The output transformer of the high-frequency inverter is a ferrite core transformer that has two tapings on the high-voltage side. The changeover switch only has the duty to switch the output voltage between these two taps in a safe manner. This is used to change the charging rate based on user and vehicle demand. For example, heavy-power electric vehicles need fast charging in order to minimize their charging time, while light-power vehicles can be charged at the normal rate at the same time due to their low battery storage capacity. The charging rate also depends on the type of battery used inside the electric vehicle. However, there are multiple other methods to change voltage levels, too. One of them is using AC voltage controllers. However, it suffers from the problem of waveform distortion and generates harmonics, which is not desirable in any case [40]. Moreover, these methods are considered when there is a transformer absent in the system, but here, the transformer must step up the output voltage of a high-frequency inverter, so it will be best to use tapping for voltage level control.

HARDWARE MODELLING

Proper design of the station and charging pad area are required for a systematic view of the station. Along with a good look, there is enough space in which vehicles can be parked for charging.

Station's Architecture and Panel's Position

The station architecture is such that a solar panels array is used to build the roof of the station. These panels are actually mounted on iron frames, making the total squared area 5.5 square meters. There are 5 rows and 5 columns in arrangement. Each row has 5 panels, and combining 5 such rows, a total of 25 panels are there. Under the roof, there are enough spaces and a centre where the charging pad is installed on the ground. There is a proper distance of about 2 meters from the panel mounting to the pad. All the circuitries are behind the panel. Some indicators and switches are embedded, which can be observed and operated from the front side of the station panel. The measuring devices are also mounted on the same panel, which reads the voltage, current and energy used during the duration of vehicle charging.

Design of Charging Pad

The shape of the charging pad is circular. It has a thick copper coil and 12 turns in the pad. It is arranged such that the ferrite core will not saturate. The core used is the ferrite core. Since 25 kHz frequency is used, it requires fewer turns and also flux density remains very low. Application of this frequency reduces the core area by far means. This is because the required area of the core is inversely proportional to frequency. For the coil, the Litz copper coil is used by the manufacturer itself to minimize skin effect losses. This arrangement is within a casing whose diameter is greater than that of the coil and core. Just like the transmitter coil inside the charging pad, the receiver coil also has the same number of turns. The physical structure and assembly of the circuit are shown in Fig. (5-7).

Fig. (5). Physical structure of charging station.

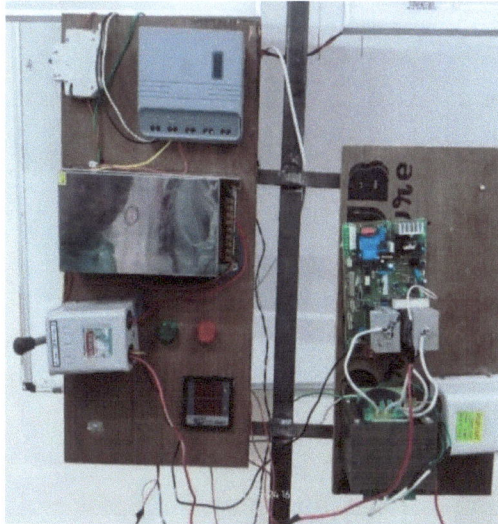

Fig. (6). Circuit on board.

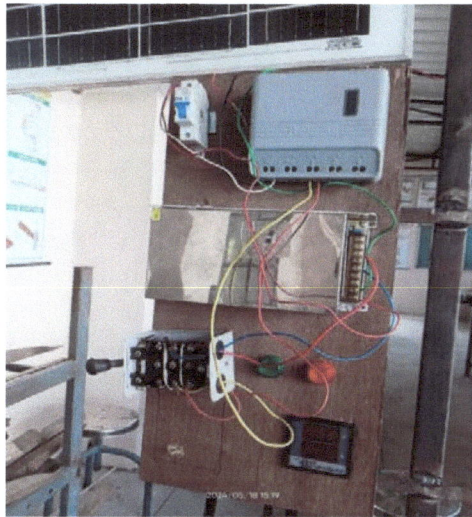

Fig. (7). Controller and SMPS.

It is mounted beneath the front wheel axles of the vehicle. In other words, both coils are identical in nature.

RESULTS AND DISCUSSION

After the physical implementation of the proposed model, the output voltage was tested across the high-frequency ATX transformer and across the receiver coil. Voltage was within the limit with a tolerance of 5% in the value. Since the transformer was handmade and wound, there was little noise from it, but the output was perfect. Since there was a much higher current at the low voltage side of the ATX transformer, MOSFETs were getting a bit hotter but were protected by the heatsinks used. The current little amount was continuously flowing. This was actually a kind of leakage current for various semiconductor switching circuits used. A charger, when used to change the charging level during the ongoing charging process, creates a spark. This was due to large inductance. A sudden interruption of a large current created a huge voltage, which caused sparking in the changer. The energy meter displayed the amount of active energy transferred to the secondary while testing. For billing purposes, further rates can be applied to recorded units. Before starting the charging of the next vehicle, the energy meter is manually reset. So, the project was tested successfully, and the results were as per estimations.

CONCLUSION

Wireless power transfer was the motive of this work carried out. It replaced the plugging system. The frequency of the wireless power transfer circuit was 25 kHz. The resonant method was used to transfer electricity in the vehicle as this method allows more clearance and air gap between the transmitter and receiver coils than inductive power transfer. Also, resonant power transfer does not bind for the same orientation of primary and secondary coils. The only term that affects its efficacy is quality factor, which can be improved by proper design. For years and decades, many scientists and researchers have indulged in this field because this is the future of the global transportation system. However, the issue has not been resolved completely, and many programs are still in practice. Some work is on material optimization in order to enhance magnetic and hysteresis properties, while some innovators are innovating circuits that have the minimum possible harmonic contents in the various power electronic conversion and transmission processes. A modification or upgradation that can be done in this system is the use of a hydraulic system. It will lift the transmitter coil up to the vehicle's receiver and then start charging. The inclusion of this technique will minimize the air gap between the transmitter and receiver coils, reducing the leakage flux as well. Overall, the efficiency of the system will tend to increase.

Nowadays, engineers are innovating techniques to make major use of green, sustainable energy, *i.e.* renewable energy resources. This highly impacts our environments and surroundings as well as our upcoming generation's livelihood and it is a good step to sustain our future. All possible efforts have been made in this project according to finances and available resources, it is not the last because success is never lasting. More innovations in the model can lead to more degree of success. Here, some other stuff that can be added is the application of hydraulic lift, sensing of vehicle presence nearby, displaying bills in currency directly, full charge alarm or buzzer, *etc.* If we further tend to a smart system, it can include online payment and then charging/supplying the units according to paid money as per the user's demand. The hydraulic system should be tried because, using this, the air gap between the transmitter and receiver coils can be minimized after the vehicle has stood over the pad area. Thus, it increases the power transmission efficiency of the charging station.

AUTHOR CONTRIBUTION

Nitesh Tiwari: Analyzed and interpreted the data.

Ajay Kumar Maurya: Study conception and design, and wrote the paper.

Ankesh Kumar Mishra: Study conception and design.

Aditya Chaurasia: Wrote the paper.

Shubham Gupta: Contributed materials, analysis tools or data.

REFERENCES

[1]   S. Pareek, A. Sujil, S. Ratra, and R. Kumar, "Electric vehicle charging station challenges and opportunities: A future perspective", *International Conference on Emerging Trends in Communication, Control and Computing (ICONC3)*, pp. 1-6, 2020.
[http://dx.doi.org/10.1109/ICONC345789.2020.9117473]

[2]   S.P. Holland, E.T. Mansur, N.Z. Muller, and A.J. Yates, "Distributional effects of air pollution from electric vehicle adoption", *J. Assoc. Environ. Resour. Econ.*, vol. 6, no. S1, pp. S65-S94, 2019.
[http://dx.doi.org/10.1086/701188]

[3]   A.K. Karmaker, M.A. Hossain, H.R. Pota, A. Onen, and J. Jung, "Energy management system for hybrid renewable energy-based electric vehicle charging station", *IEEE Access,* vol. 11, pp. 27793-27805, 2023.
[http://dx.doi.org/10.1109/ACCESS.2023.3259232]

[4]   M.S. Tanveer, S. Gupta, R. Rai, N.K. Jha, and M. Bansal, "Solar based electric vehicle charging station", *2nd International Conference on Power Energy, Environment and Intelligent Control (PEEIC),* pp. 407-410, 2019.
[http://dx.doi.org/10.1109/PEEIC47157.2019.8976673]

[5]   T. Chen, X.P. Zhang, J. Wang, J. Li, C. Wu, M. Hu, and H. Bian, "A review on electric vehicle charging infrastructure development in the UK", *J. Mod. Power Syst. Clean Energy,* vol. 8, no. 2, pp. 193-205, 2020.
[http://dx.doi.org/10.35833/MPCE.2018.000374]

[6]   M. Nizam, H. Maghfiroh, R. A. Rosadi, and K. D. Kusumaputri, "Battery management system design (BMS) for lithium-ion batteries," in *AIP Conf. Proc.*, vol. 2217, no. 1, AIP Publishing, Apr. 2020.

[7]   S.S. Zhang, "The effect of the charging protocol on the cycle life of a Li-ion battery", *J. Power Sources,* vol. 161, no. 2, pp. 1385-1391, 2006.
[http://dx.doi.org/10.1016/j.jpowsour.2006.06.040]

[8]   M.P. Santos, I.A.A. Garde, C.M.B. Ronchini, L.C. Filho, G.B.M. Souza, M.L.F. Abbade, N.N. Regone, V.J. Jegatheesan, and J.A. Oliveira, "A technology for recycling lithium-ion batteries

promoting the circular economy: The RecycLib", *Resour. Conserv. Recycling,* vol. 175, p. 105863, 2021.
[http://dx.doi.org/10.1016/j.resconrec.2021.105863]

[9]   A.A. Mohamed, D. Allen, T. Youssef, and O. Mohammed, "Optimal design of high frequency H-bridge inverter for wireless power transfer systems in EV applications", *16th International Conference on Environment and Electrical Engineering (EEEIC),* pp. 1-6, 2016.
[http://dx.doi.org/10.1109/EEEIC.2016.7555646]

[10]   J.H. Choi, S.K. Yeo, S. Park, J.S. Lee, and G.H. Cho, "Resonant regulating rectifiers (3R) operating for 6.78 MHz resonant wireless power transfer (RWPT)", *IEEE J. Solid-State Circuits,* vol. 48, no. 12, pp. 2989-3001, 2013.
[http://dx.doi.org/10.1109/JSSC.2013.2287592]

[11]   E. Apostolaki-Iosifidou, P. Codani, and W. Kempton, "Measurement of power loss during electric vehicle charging and discharging", *Energy,* vol. 127, pp. 730-742, 2017.
[http://dx.doi.org/10.1016/j.energy.2017.03.015]

[12]   H.B. Dwight, "Skin effect and proximity effect in tubular conductors", *Trans. Am. Inst. Electr. Eng.,* vol. XLI, pp. 189-198, 1922.
[http://dx.doi.org/10.1109/T-AIEE.1922.5060774]

[13]   M. Islam, and M.A.B. Sarkar, "An efficient smart solar charge controller for standalone energy systems", *International Conference on Electrical Drives and Power Electronics (EDPE),* pp. 246-251, 2015.
[http://dx.doi.org/10.1109/EDPE.2015.7325301]

[14]   K. Shirabe, M. Swamy, J. K. Kang, M. Hisatsune, Y. Wu, D. Kebort, and J. Honea, "Advantages of high frequency PWM in AC motor drive applications," in *Proc. 2012 IEEE Energy Conversion Congress and Exposition (ECCE),* 2012, pp. 2977–2984.
[http://dx.doi.org/10.1109/ECCE.2012.6342519]

[15]   J. Sears, D. Roberts, and K. Glitman, "A comparison of electric vehicle Level 1 and Level 2 charging efficiency", *IEEE Conference on Technologies for Sustainability (SusTech),* pp. 255-258, 2014.
[http://dx.doi.org/10.1109/SusTech.2014.7046253]

[16]   S. Jeong, N.N. Dao, Y. Lee, C. Lee, and S. Cho, "Blockchain based billing system for electric vehicle and charging station", *Tenth International Conference on Ubiquitous and Future Networks (ICUFN),* pp. 308-310, 2018.
[http://dx.doi.org/10.1109/ICUFN.2018.8436987]

[17]   Guangul, F. M., & Chala, G. T. Solar energy as renewable energy source: SWOT analysis. *4th MEC international conference on big data and smart city (ICBDSC),* pp. 1-5, 2019.

[18]   A. Khatibi, F. Razi Astaraei, and M.H. Ahmadi, "Generation and combination of the solar cells: A current model review", *Energy Sci. Eng.,* vol. 7, no. 2, pp. 305-322, 2019.
[http://dx.doi.org/10.1002/ese3.292]

[19]   R. Saive, "S-shaped current–voltage characteristics in solar cells: a review", *IEEE J. Photovolt.,* vol. 9, no. 6, pp. 1477-1484, 2019.
[http://dx.doi.org/10.1109/JPHOTOV.2019.2930409]

[20]   M. Zagrouba, A. Sellami, M. Bouaïcha, and M. Ksouri, "Identification of PV solar cells and modules parameters using the genetic algorithms: Application to maximum power extraction", *Sol. Energy,* vol. 84, no. 5, pp. 860-866, 2010.
[http://dx.doi.org/10.1016/j.solener.2010.02.012]

[21]   J. Dhilipan, N. Vijayalakshmi, D.B. Shanmugam, R. Jai Ganesh, S. Kodeeswaran, and S. Muralidharan, "Performance and efficiency of different types of solar cell material – A review", *Mater. Today Proc.,* vol. 66, pp. 1295-1302, 2022.
[http://dx.doi.org/10.1016/j.matpr.2022.05.132]

[22]   K.A. Emery, and C.R. Osterwald, "Solar cell efficiency measurements", *Solar Cells,* vol. 17, no. 2-3, pp. 253-274, 1986.
[http://dx.doi.org/10.1016/0379-6787(86)90016-5]

[23]   A. Haque, "Maximum power point tracking (MPPT) scheme for solar photovoltaic system", *Energy Technology & Policy,* vol. 1, no. 1, pp. 115-122, 2014.
[http://dx.doi.org/10.1080/23317000.2014.979379]

[24]   S. Vignesh, S.N. Koundinya, K. Narayanan, G. Sharma, and T. Senjyu, "Investigation on Reliability and Cost in the Presence of Electric Vehicle Charging Station", *International Conference on Smart Grids and Energy Systems (SGES),* pp. 465-469, 2020.
[http://dx.doi.org/10.1109/SGES51519.2020.00088]

[25]   A. Triviño, J.M. González-González, and J.A. Aguado, "Wireless power transfer technologies applied to electric vehicles: A review", *Energies,* vol. 14, no. 6, p. 1547, 2021.
[http://dx.doi.org/10.3390/en14061547]

[26]   N. Shinohara, "The wireless power transmission: inductive coupling, radio wave, and resonance coupling", *Wiley Interdiscip. Rev. Energy Environ.,* vol. 1, no. 3, pp. 337-346, 2012.
[http://dx.doi.org/10.1002/wene.43]

[27]   A. Mahesh, B. Chokkalingam, and L. Mihet-Popa, "Inductive wireless power transfer charging for electric vehicles–a review", *IEEE Access,* vol. 9, pp. 137667-137713, 2021.
[http://dx.doi.org/10.1109/ACCESS.2021.3116678]

[28]   M. Abou Houran, X. Yang, and W. Chen, "Magnetically coupled resonance WPT: Review of compensation topologies, resonator structures with misalignment, and EMI diagnostics", *Electronics (Basel),* vol. 7, no. 11, p. 296, 2018.
[http://dx.doi.org/10.3390/electronics7110296]

[29]   G. Yang, and H. Liang, "Adaptive frequency measurement in magnetic resonance coupling based WPT system", *Measurement,* vol. 130, pp. 318-326, 2018.
[http://dx.doi.org/10.1016/j.measurement.2018.08.025]

[30]   Y. Gu, J. Wang, Z. Liang, Y. Wu, C. Cecati, and Z. Zhang, "Single-transmitter multiple-pickup wireless power transfer: Advantages, challenges, and corresponding technical solutions", *IEEE Ind. Electron. Mag.,* vol. 14, no. 4, pp. 123-135, 2020.
[http://dx.doi.org/10.1109/MIE.2020.3002524]

[31]   E. Koutroulis, J. Chatzakis, K. Kalaitzakis, and N.C. Voulgaris, "A bidirectional, sinusoidal, high-frequency inverter design", *IEE Proc., Electr. Power Appl.,* vol. 148, no. 4, pp. 315-321, 2001.
[http://dx.doi.org/10.1049/ip-epa:20010351]

[32]   D. Han, J. Noppakunkajorn, and B. Sarlioglu, "Analysis of a SiC three-phase voltage source inverter under various current and power factor operations", *IECON 2013-39th Annual Conference of the IEEE Industrial Electronics Society,* pp. 447-452, 2013.
[http://dx.doi.org/10.1109/IECON.2013.6699177]

[33]   P.A. Dahono, Y. Sato, and T. Kataoka, "Analysis of conduction losses in inverters", *IEE Proc., Electr. Power Appl.,* vol. 142, no. 4, pp. 225-232, 1995.
[http://dx.doi.org/10.1049/ip-epa:19951966]

[34]   F.G.G. de Buck, P. Giustelinck, and D. de Backer, "A simple but reliable loss model for inverter-supplied induction motors", *IEEE Trans. Ind. Appl.,* vol. IA-20, no. 1, pp. 190-202, 1984.
[http://dx.doi.org/10.1109/TIA.1984.4504393]

[35]   M.R. Ruman, D. Paul, A. Barua, A.K. Sarker, A. Iqbal, and S. Barua, "Design and Implementation of SPWM inverter", *International Conference on Computing, Communication, and Intelligent Systems (ICCCIS),* pp. 490-494, 2019.
[http://dx.doi.org/10.1109/ICCCIS48478.2019.8974542]

[36]   Elrajoubi, A. M., & Ang, S. S. High-frequency transformer review and design for low-power solid-

state transformer topology. *IEEE Texas Power and Energy Conference (TPEC)*, pp. 1-6, 2019.
[http://dx.doi.org/10.1109/TPEC.2019.8662131]

[37]   R. Minhaz, and P. Eng, *Transformer Design & Design Parameters.* IEEE Green Mountain Chapter of
       the IEEE Power Engineering Society, 2014.

[38]   T. Majaw, R. Deka, S. Roy, and B. Goswami, "Solar charge controllers using MPPT and PWM: A
       review", *ADBU Journal of Electrical and Electronics Engineering,* vol. 2, no. 1, pp. 1-4, 2018.

[39]   M.A. Eltawil, and Z. Zhao, "MPPT techniques for photovoltaic applications", *Renew. Sustain. Energy
       Rev.,* vol. 25, pp. 793-813, 2013.
       [http://dx.doi.org/10.1016/j.rser.2013.05.022]

[40]   N. Ashraf, G. Abbas, R. Abbassi, and H. Jerbi, "Power quality analysis of the output voltage of AC
       voltage and frequency controllers realized with various voltage control techniques", *Appl. Sci. (Basel),*
       vol. 11, no. 2, p. 538, 2021.
       [http://dx.doi.org/10.3390/app11020538]

CHAPTER 10

Hardware Design of Electric Bicycle with Solar Panel

Nitesh Tiwari[1,*], **Shivangi Agrawal**[1], **Sumit Patel**[1] and **Chandra Mohan Chaurasiya**[1]

[1] *Department of Electrical Engineering, KIPM College of Engineering and Technology, Gorakhpur (UP), India*

Abstract: Solar energy manifests as rays and heat emitted by the sun. Solar panels consist of solar cells that convert light into electrical energy. The contemporary landscape calls for innovative solutions to combat fuel dependency and environmental degradation, with a solar hybrid bicycle system emerging as a promising remedy. The escalating emission of carbon dioxide from vehicular exhausts exacerbates the pace of global warming. Concurrently, the relentless surge in fuel prices across India and globally underscores the imperative to explore alternative avenues and harness natural resources judiciously. The integration of a hybrid solar bicycle system presents a tangible opportunity to mitigate CO^2 emissions and curtail fuel expenses. The solar bicycle epitomizes an electric vehicle paradigm, leveraging solar energy to replenish its battery reserves and power its motor. Endowed with nine months of abundant sunshine annually, India stands poised to reap substantial benefits from such innovative transportation solutions. The hybrid bicycle, crafted to amalgamate solar energy and a dynamo-driven battery charging mechanism, embodies a sustainable mode of transportation. Integral to the operational framework is an accelerator mechanism facilitating motor speed regulation, thereby ensuring optimal control over power supply. This fusion of renewable energy and conventional cycling components heralds a paradigm shift in sustainable mobility solutions. By harnessing solar power and kinetic energy through the dynamo, the hybrid bicycle exemplifies an environmentally conscious mode of transport conducive to reducing carbon emissions and alleviating fuel dependency. The advent of the solar hybrid bicycle system symbolizes a pivotal stride towards addressing contemporary challenges associated with fuel consumption and environmental degradation. With India's climatic predisposition favoring solar energy utilization, the proliferation of such innovative transportation solutions holds promise for ushering in a greener, more sustainable future.

Keywords: Controller, Electric vehicle, Electric two wheelers, Hardware architecture, Hub BLDC motor, Solar based vehicle.

---
* **Corresponding author Nitesh Tiwari:** Department of Electrical Engineering, KIPM College of Engineering and Technology, Gorakhpur (UP), India; E-mail: niteshwr1994@gmail.com

Nitesh Tiwari, Shekhar Yadav and Sabha Raj Arya (Eds.)

INTRODUCTION

Solar panels, comprising solar cells that convert light into electrical energy, have served as the focal point of research exploring their application in charging electric bicycle batteries [1]. The study unveils an electric bicycle powered by a 24V, 12Ah battery, requiring 9 hours and 33 minutes to charge with a 250W DC motor. As anticipated, the solar-panel-equipped electric bicycle attains a maximum speed of 17 km/h, covering a distance of 15 km with an 80 kg load [2]. The significant energy output from sunlight solidified solar panels as a reliable alternative energy solution for tomorrow's needs, offering sustainability and potential independence from traditional power sources [3]. Introducing solar panel electric bicycles marks a paradigm shift by enabling battery charging while in motion. In instances of insufficient sunlight, battery charging can be supplemented by electrical power through a battery charger connected *via* the controller [4]. This feature not only saves money in Indian currency by reducing reliance on precious fossil fuels but also ensures operational quietness and versatility in emergency or cloudy weather conditions [5]. Hence, a solar bicycle emerges as an electric motor vehicle powered by solar energy, providing the requisite voltages to operate the motor. Numerous cities have initiated vehicle development programs centered around bicycles, with electric bicycles serving as a prominent category [6]. These electric vehicles, including solar-powered bicycles, often incorporate charging systems powered by photovoltaic panels [7]. A solar bicycle can be connected to a charging station, facilitating battery charging in a stationary state. The inception of this project stemmed from existing socio-economic factors, aiming to provide affordable and efficient transportation, especially in rural India, characterized by rugged terrain predominantly comprising steep hills. The solar-powered bicycle epitomizes the transition towards sustainable energy sources [8]. While bicycles are inherently sustainable, this project enhances efficiency and fosters awareness among the masses. The solar hybrid bicycle reduces fossil fuel usage and mitigates pollution [9]. By harnessing solar energy for propulsion, the bicycle addresses both environmental concerns and energy supply challenges in remote areas. Urban mobility issues, exacerbated by traffic congestion, fuel consumption, and air pollution, necessitate sustainable transportation solutions. Electric bicycles, particularly those powered by solar energy, offer a clean, cost-effective alternative [10]. Cycling's numerous advantages have offered an effective answer to urban mobility issues, especially for short journeys, providing sustainability and health benefits. Solar bicycles leverage India's predominantly sunny climate, exploiting renewable energy advantages and replacing conventional bikes as the mode of transport [11]. Bicycles operate by converting solar energy into electrical energy, stored in batteries to fuel the hub motor, facilitating movement without relying solely on physical exertion [12]. Solar panels mounted on the carriage will charge the battery, ensuring continuous operation even during the night [13]. The solar bicycle's working mechanism involves four stages. Solar panels initially converted sunlight into electrical energy through the photovoltaic effect, harnessing sunlight's power for electricity generation. Subsequently, a motor controller and DC boost converter regulate and amplify voltage [14]. The energy is then stored in batteries and supplied to the brushless DC motor, mounted on the rear wheel, providing efficient and quiet propulsion. Finally, the sprocket and chain drive mechanism propels the bicycle forward [15]. This research underscores the transformative potential of solar-powered electric bicycles in addressing both environmental and socio-economic challenges [16]. Through the use of renewable energy sources, such innovations are paving the way for a greener, more sustainable future in transportation [17].

METHODOLOGY

The methodology behind the electric bicycle, particularly one powered by solar energy, encompasses a multifaceted approach integrating various components and technologies to enable efficient and sustainable transportation [12]. The electric bicycle functions by harnessing renewable energy and converting it into mechanical propulsion, thus decreasing dependency on fossil fuels and lessening environmental harm. The foundation of the electric bicycle lies in its power source, which typically comprises a combination of solar panels and rechargeable batteries. Solar panels, consisting of interconnected solar cells, are strategically mounted on the bicycle to capture sunlight and convert it into electrical energy through the photovoltaic effect. These panels are often positioned on the carriage or integrated into the bicycle frame, maximizing exposure to sunlight while maintaining aerodynamic efficiency. Once solar energy is harvested, it undergoes a series of conversions and transformations within the bicycle's electrical system [15]. The solar panel-generated electrical energy is directed to a charge controller, regulating voltage and current for safe, efficient battery charging, ensuring optimal performance and prolonging battery life. This controller serves as a crucial interface between the solar panels and the battery, optimizing energy transfer and storage [18]. Simultaneously, the electrical energy is directed towards charging the onboard batteries, typically lithium-ion or lead-acid batteries, depending on the specific design and requirements of the electric bicycle. These batteries act as energy reservoirs, storing excess solar energy during periods of sunlight for later use when solar irradiance is insufficient or during nighttime operation. The charging process is managed intelligently by the battery management system, which monitors battery health, prevents overcharging, and optimizes energy utilization [19]. The heart of the electric bicycle lies in its propulsion system, comprising a motor and drivetrain mechanism responsible for converting electrical energy into mechanical motion. Electric bicycles commonly employ hub motors, which are integrated into the wheel hub either at the front or rear wheel, providing direct drive propulsion without the need for additional gears or transmission components. These motors are typically brushless DC (BLDC) motors, renowned for their efficiency, reliability, and compact design [20]. The motor's functioning is governed by an electronic motor controller, adjusting speed, torque, and power output in response to user commands and system settings. Serving as a bridge between rider and motor, it interprets inputs to regulate performance effectively. Additionally, advanced motor controllers may incorporate regenerative braking capabilities, allowing the motor to function as a generator during deceleration, thereby recovering kinetic energy and replenishing the batteries. The electric bicycle's electrical and mechanical components are interconnected through a sophisticated network of wiring, sensors, and control interfaces to ensure seamless integration and optimal performance. This integrated system enables real-time monitoring, diagnostics, and feedback mechanisms to maintain operational efficiency, safety, and user comfort. Furthermore, modern electric bicycles may feature additional smart functionalities such as GPS navigation, connectivity, and app-based control interfaces, enhancing user experience and functionality. The methodology of the electric bicycle revolves around the efficient utilization of solar energy to power an integrated electrical system comprising solar panels, batteries, motors, and control electronics. Electric bicycles, powered by renewable energy and advanced technology, provide a sustainable alternative to fossil fuel-driven transport. They promote cleaner, greener mobility options for both urban and rural areas, reducing environmental impact and offering eco-friendly transportation solutions across diverse landscapes. The block diagram of the solar electric bicycle is shown in Fig. (**1**).

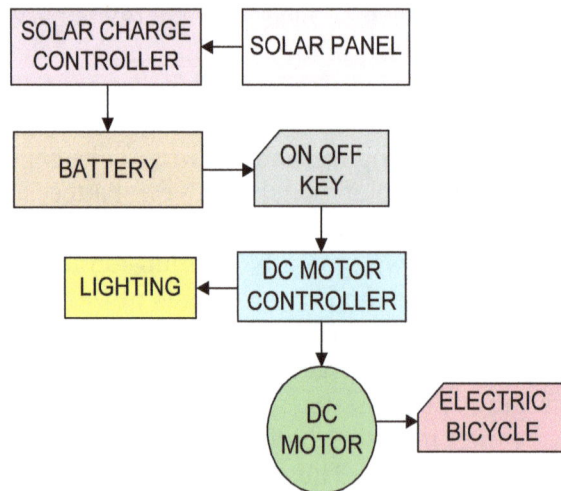

Fig. (1). Block diagram of solar electric bicycle.

CIRCUIT DIAGRAM

The circuit diagram of an electric bicycle integrated with a solar panel represents a sophisticated yet interconnected system designed to efficiently harness and utilize solar energy for propulsion. At the heart of the system is the solar panel array, composed of solar cells strategically arranged to capture sunlight and convert it into electrical energy *via* the photovoltaic effect. This energy is managed by a charge controller, which is crucial for overseeing voltage and current flow to guarantee secure and effective battery charging. The batteries, commonly lithium-ion or lead-acid, act as energy storage units, holding surplus solar energy for subsequent use in situations of reduced sunlight or nighttime operation. Connected in parallel to the batteries is the electric motor, typically a brushless DC (BLDC) motor integrated into the wheel hub, facilitating direct-drive propulsion. The motor, managed by a motor controller, adjusts speed, torque, and power output according to user input or sensor feedback. Additionally, the motor controller may feature regenerative braking capabilities, allowing the motor to function as a generator during deceleration, thus recuperating kinetic energy and replenishing the batteries. The circuit is completed by wiring and connectors, ensuring seamless communication and power transfer between the solar panel, charge controller, batteries, motor, and other auxiliary components. This interconnected network facilitates real-time monitoring, diagnostics, and feedback mechanisms to maintain operational efficiency, safety, and user comfort. The electric bicycle's circuit diagram, featuring a solar panel, represents the fusion of renewable energy, storage, and propulsion systems. It provides a sustainable, eco-friendly transportation solution, decreasing dependence on fossil fuels and minimizing environmental harm for a cleaner future. The structure of the electric bicycle is shown in Fig. (**2**). The required material for the hardware design of the wireless charger is given in Table **1**.

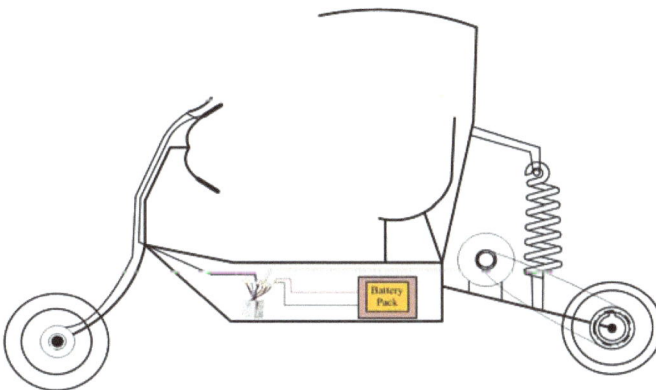

Fig. (2). Structure of electric bicycle.

Table 1. Required material for hardware design of wireless charger.

S. No.	Component Name	Rating
1.	Solar panel	60W
2.	Solar charge controller	24V 20A
3.	Dc motor	24V/250W
4.	Controller	24V/250W
5.	Battery	24V/12Ah
6.	Throttle	4V
7.	Lighting	-
8.	Boost Converter	10V
9.	Jumper wire	-

MATHEMATICAL MODELLING

Mathematical modelling of various components of solar-based electric bicycle is given below:

Mathematical Modelling of DC Drive

The motor controller plays a crucial role within the system, responsible for regulating the power delivery and propelling the BLDC hub motor. It facilitates diverse speed control of the hub motor by converting DC voltage from the battery into adjustable amplitude and frequency alternating voltage. Comprising MOSFET transistors and a small microprocessor, it is adept at detecting malfunctions through the motor hall sensors and throttle. Moreover, it incorporates protective features against excessive current and under-voltage, serving as vital safeguards for the system. The DC motor is famous worldwide in the world of machines. It can spin things around and move back and forth when connected to wheels or cables. Inside, there is a part called the armature that spins because of electricity and another part called the rotor that can move by itself. Together, they make the motor do its magic, helping things move in all sorts of machines, from toys to cars. The torque and current are both proportional to each other and are given in Eq. (**1**).

$$T = K_t i \qquad\qquad (1)$$

The electro-motive force e is associated with the rotational velocity by given Eq. (**2**):

$$e = K_e \dot\theta(t) \tag{2}$$

Based on the previous diagram, the following equations can be derived from Newton's law combined with Kirchhoff's law as given in Eqs. (**3** and **4**).

$$j.\theta(t) + b.\dot\theta(t) = K_e.i(t) \tag{3}$$

$$L.\frac{di(t)}{dt} + R.i(t) = V(t) - K. \ \dot\theta(t) \tag{4}$$

With the help of L.T., the whole modelling Eqs. (**5**) and **6**) can be written in terms of operator(s).

$$(Js + b).\theta(s) = K.I(s) \tag{5}$$

$$(Ls + R).I(s) = V(S) - K.\theta(s) \tag{6}$$

From Eq. (**5**), we get Eq. (**7**):

$$\boldsymbol{I(s)} = \frac{(Js+b).\theta(s)}{K} \tag{7}$$

Substituting Eq. (**7**) into Eq. (**6**) to get Eq. (**8**):

$$\frac{(Ls+R)(Js+b).\theta(s)}{K} = V(s) - K.\theta(s) \tag{8}$$

From Eq. (**8**), we get Eq. (**9**):

$$\frac{\theta(s)}{V(s)} = \frac{K}{(Ls+R)(Js+b)+K^2} \tag{9}$$

Mathematical Modelling of Lithium-ion Battery

Lead acid batteries have long been favored for electronics due to their popularity and safety. Despite slightly lower energy density compared to lithium batteries, lead acid is deemed safe when charged and discharged with care. Its advantages make it the preferred option for solar-assisted bicycles, offering reliability and suitability for prolonged usage, aligning with the demands of sustainable transportation powered by solar energy. Under various operating modes, cell temperatures are predicted, and heat release is analyzed under different current loads by the mathematical model of a lithium-ion battery. The model's core comprises a heat transfer Eq. (**10**) essential for thermal management, utilizing Fourier's law of thermal conductivity to calculate conductive heat transfer. This aids in comprehending and managing the battery's thermal behavior, guaranteeing efficiency and safety.

$$q = -Knn\frac{\partial T}{\partial n} \tag{10}$$

Newton's law for the convection heat transfer is given by Eq. (**11**):

$$q = h.\Delta T \tag{11}$$

The rate of heat flow per unit area between a surface and a material is represented by q. The convection film coefficient is denoted by h, and the temperature difference between the surface and the material is denoted by ΔT. Stefan-Boltzmann law is used to describe the radiation as shown in Eq. (**12**):

$$q = \sigma.\varepsilon.Ai.Fij(Ti^4 - Tj^4) \tag{12}$$

The rate of heat flow from surface I to surface j. ϵ: Emissivity, which measures how well a surface emits thermal radiation. σ: The Stefan-Boltzmann constant, used in calculations involving thermal radiation. Ai: The area of surface iffy: The view factor, indicating how much radiation from surface i reaches surface j. Ti: The absolute temperature of the surface it: The absolute temperature of the surface for a very small volume. The heat conduction equation is shown in Eq. (**13**).

$$\rho c\frac{\partial T}{\partial t} + Q - K\nabla^2 T = 0 \tag{13}$$

The density of the substance is denoted by ρ, while its heat capacity is represented by c. Temperature is indicated by T and time by t. The rate of internal heat generation per unit volume is referred to as Q. The specific thermal conductivity tensor is symbolized by k. The temperature Laplacian, which describes the rate of change of temperature in a region, is given as $\nabla^2 T$.

Biota and Fourier numbers are crucial in mathematical model optimization and updating frequency, determining the connection between body temperature difference and surface temperature difference based on a dimensionless ratio:

$$B_s = \frac{h\Delta x}{K},$$

The average heat transfer coefficient h, the average width of the element Δx, and the average thermal conductivity K define the Biota Number Bs. The Fourier

Number is a key factor in heat transfer analysis, showing how quickly temperature changes spread through a material compared to heat diffusion. It is crucial for understanding heat transfer in different systems as shown in Eq. (**14**):

$$F = \frac{4K\Delta t}{\rho C (\Delta x)^2},$$

(**14**)

The Fourier Number F is determined by the average thermal conductivity K, Δt is the time frame, ρ is the density of the substance, C is the heat capacity, and Δx is the average width of the element .

HUB MOTOR CONTROL CIRCUIT

In the world of electric vehicles, the hub motor stands as a silent powerhouse, revolutionizing the way we think about propulsion systems. Compact, efficient, and versatile hub motors have emerged as a key technology driving the transition towards electric mobility. Let us delve into a comprehensive explanation of hub motors, exploring their design, function, applications, and impact on the automotive industry. A hub motor is an electric motor housed within a wheel hub, directly propelling the wheel's rotation for propulsion. Unlike traditional internal combustion engines, which require complex drivetrains consisting of transmissions, differentials, and axles, hub motors eliminate the need for many of these components, simplifying vehicle design and improving efficiency. The design of a hub motor can vary depending on the specific application and performance requirements. However, most hub motors consist of several key components, including the stator, rotor, housing, bearings, and wiring. The stator is the stationary part of the motor, typically mounted inside the housing and containing coils of wire arranged around a central core [21].

The rotor, on the other hand, is the rotating part of the motor, connected directly to the wheel hub and surrounded by the stator coils. When electric current is supplied to the stator coils, a magnetic field is generated, which interacts with the magnetic field produced by the permanent magnets in the rotor. This interaction creates a rotational force known as torque, which causes the rotor to spin. By controlling the magnitude and direction of the electric current supplied to the stator coils, the speed and direction of the motor can be precisely regulated. One of the primary advantages of hub motors is their compact and integrated design, which allows them to be easily incorporated into a variety of vehicle types, including bicycles, scooters, motorcycles, and even cars. By placing the motor directly inside the wheel hub, hub motors eliminate the need for bulky and complex drivetrain components, such as engines, transmissions, and differentials, resulting in a more streamlined and efficient vehicle architecture. Furthermore, hub motors offer significant performance benefits compared to traditional propulsion systems. Their direct-drive configuration eliminates energy losses associated with mechanical drivetrains, resulting in higher overall efficiency and energy conversion. Additionally, hub motors provide instant torque delivery and precise control over vehicle dynamics, enhancing acceleration, handling, and braking performance.

Hub motors also offer greater design flexibility and packaging efficiency, allowing vehicle designers to optimize weight distribution, interior space, and aerodynamics. Electric vehicles equipped with hub motors can take advantage of regenerative braking, which recaptures kinetic energy during deceleration and feeds it back into the battery, further improving energy efficiency and extending range. Another key advantage of hub motors is their potential for modularization and scalability. By using multiple hub motors distributed across the vehicle, designers can achieve All-Wheel Drive (AWD) or torque vectoring capabilities, enhancing traction, stability, and performance in various driving conditions. Hub motors offer versatility by accommodating various power levels and vehicle sizes, rendering them ideal for diverse applications. From nimble electric bicycles to robust electric trucks, their adaptability ensures efficient propulsion across a broad spectrum of transportation needs. In recent years, hub motors have gained traction in the automotive industry as automakers seek to electrify their vehicle fleets and meet increasingly stringent emissions regulations. Electric vehicles equipped with hub motors offer numerous advantages, including improved efficiency, performance, and reliability, as well as reduced maintenance requirements and operating costs. Furthermore, hub motors are well-suited for emerging mobility trends, such as autonomous vehicles and shared transportation services, where compactness, efficiency, and reliability are paramount. By integrating hub motors into their vehicle platforms, automakers can unlock new opportunities for innovation, differentiation, and market competitiveness. Despite their many advantages, hub motors also present certain challenges and limitations. One potential drawback is the unsprung weight they add to the vehicle, which can negatively impact ride comfort, handling, and suspension performance. Additionally, hub motors are more complex and expensive to manufacture compared to traditional drivetrain components, which can affect upfront costs and scalability. Moreover, hub motors may pose challenges in terms of serviceability and maintenance, as they are integrated directly into the wheel assembly and require specialized tools and expertise for repair or replacement. However, ongoing advancements in materials, manufacturing techniques, and motor control technology are helping to address these challenges and improve the performance, reliability, and cost-effectiveness of hub motors. In conclusion, hub motors represent a transformative technology with the potential to reshape the future of transportation. Compact, efficient, and versatile hub motors offer numerous advantages over traditional propulsion systems, including improved performance, efficiency, and design flexibility. As electric vehicles continue to gain momentum and evolve, hub motors are likely to play an increasingly prominent role in driving innovation and sustainability in the automotive industry. The Hub motor controller circuit is shown in Fig. (**3**).

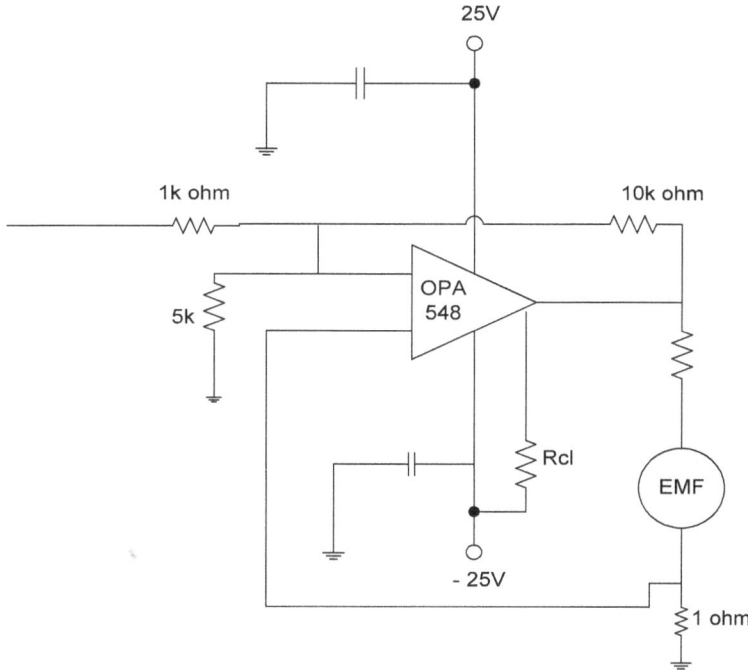

Fig. (3). Hub motor controller circuit.

SOLAR PANEL

Think of the solar panel as a sun-powered electricity generator. It takes sunlight and turns it into electricity, which gets stored in a battery. Now, imagine the solar panel as a puzzle, where each piece affects how much electricity it can make. The bigger the puzzle (or panel), the more electricity it can produce. Also, the better the quality of the pieces (or platelets), the more efficient it becomes at making electricity. So, depending on how big the panel is and how good its pieces are, it can make more or less electricity. This also means that the time it takes to charge the battery can vary because some panels can make electricity faster than others. In the summertime, solar panels come into their own, harnessing the abundant sunlight to generate clean and renewable electricity. These technological wonders, commonly observed on rooftops or in expansive solar farms, are pivotal in our shift towards sustainable energy. They symbolize progress towards cleaner, renewable power sources for a greener future. As the sun rises high in the sky during the summer months, its rays beam down with greater intensity and duration, providing ample opportunity for solar panels to soak up the energy they need to function.

The key to this process lies within the solar panels themselves, where a fascinating interplay of physics and engineering unfolds. At the heart of a solar panel lies the photovoltaic (PV) cell, a small unit comprised of semiconductor materials, most commonly silicon. These cells are what make solar panels tick, as they're responsible for converting sunlight into electricity through a process known as the photovoltaic effect. Imagine each solar cell as a tiny powerhouse capable of generating electricity when exposed to sunlight. When sunlight, composed of photons, strikes the surface of the solar cell, it sets off a chain reaction within the semiconductor material. The photons transfer their energy to electrons in the material, knocking them loose from their atomic bonds and creating a flow of electricity. This flow of electrons is directed by the internal structure of the solar cell, which is carefully engineered to facilitate the movement of charge. In a solar cell, the semiconductor material is doped with impurities to establish a p-n junction, forming a boundary between areas with distinct electrical characteristics essential for generating electricity from sunlight. This junction acts as a one-way street for electrons, allowing them to flow in a specific direction when liberated by sunlight. As electrons move towards the n-type (negative) region of the semiconductor, they leave behind positively charged "holes" in the p-type (positive) region. This separation of charge creates an electric field across the solar cell, generating a voltage difference between the two regions. This voltage difference drives the flow of electrons through an external circuit, creating an electric current that can be harnessed to power electrical devices. But the magic of solar panels doesn't stop there. To capture as much sunlight as possible, solar panels are designed with efficiency in mind. Each solar panel consists of multiple solar cells arranged in a grid-like pattern, maximizing the surface area exposed to sunlight. Additionally, the top layer of the solar panel is made of tempered glass or special plastics, which protect the solar cells from environmental damage while allowing sunlight to pass through unimpeded. The design and placement of solar panels are also critical factors in maximizing their efficiency. Solar panels are typically installed in locations with ample sunlight exposure, such as rooftops, open fields, or solar farms.

The orientation and tilt angle of the panels are carefully adjusted to optimize sunlight capture throughout the day and across different seasons. In the summer, when the sun is high in the sky for longer periods, solar panels can generate even more electricity than during other times of the year. But what happens when the sun isn't shining as brightly or when clouds obscure its rays? Despite their reliance on sunlight, solar panels are surprisingly resilient and can still generate electricity under less-than-ideal conditions. Even on cloudy days, diffuse sunlight can still penetrate the atmosphere and reach the surface of the Earth, providing enough energy to keep solar panels ticking over. Furthermore, advancements in solar panel technology have led to the development of innovative solutions to enhance their performance and reliability. For example, some solar panels are equipped with tracking systems that adjust their orientation throughout the day to maximize sunlight exposure. Others incorporate microinverters or power optimizers to improve energy harvest and mitigate the impact of shading or uneven sunlight distribution. The benefits of solar panels extend beyond their ability to generate clean and renewable electricity. Solar panels use sunlight to make electricity, reducing the need for dirty fossil fuels. This cuts greenhouse gases, fighting climate change by keeping the Earth cleaner and cooler.

They also contribute to energy independence and security, as sunlight is freely available and abundant in most regions of the world. Moreover, the widespread adoption of solar panels creates economic opportunities and drives innovation in the renewable energy sector. Solar energy installations create jobs, stimulate economic growth, and attract investment in local communities. Solar panels offer consistent electricity for homes, businesses, and industries, diminishing reliance on centralized grids and fossil fuels, thereby fostering energy independence and sustainability across diverse sectors. Solar panels exemplify human creativity, utilizing solar energy to illuminate a sustainable future for posterity. They epitomize innovation, offering hope for a brighter tomorrow through renewable energy solutions. As we bask in the warmth of summer sunlight, let's not forget the role that solar panels play in powering our homes, businesses, and communities with clean and renewable energy. With continued advancements in technology and widespread adoption of solar energy solutions, the sky's the limit for the potential of solar power to transform our world. The block diagram of the solar panel-based system is shown in Fig. (**4**).

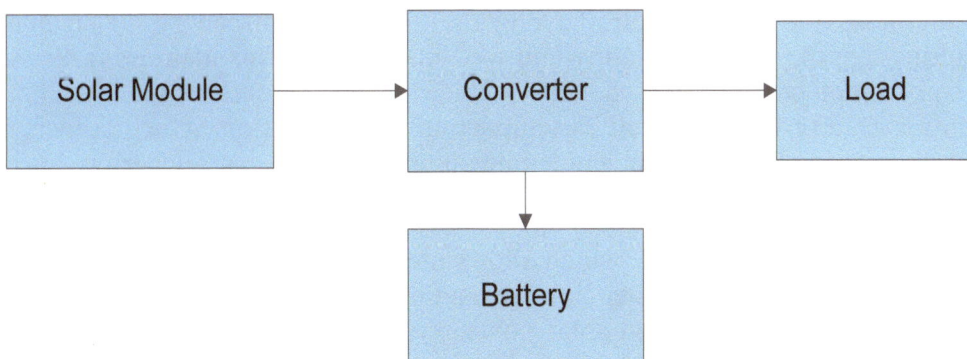

Fig. (4). Block Diagram of Solar Panel based System.

SOLAR CHARGE CONTROLLER

In a solar hot water system, an electronic device manages the circulating pump to enhance heat extraction from solar panels. It directs the working fluid through panels to the heat exchanger at the thermal store. Heat transfer occurs as the solar panel temperature surpasses the water temperature in the heat exchanger. Overheat protection is triggered by halting the pump when the store hits its maximum temperature. Periodic cooling activates by turning on the pump when the store exceeds the panel temperature, ensuring system efficiency and safety. A solar charge controller acts as the guardian of a solar power system, managing electricity flow among panels, batteries, and loads to ensure peak performance and longevity. This exploration delves into solar charge controllers' intricacies, functions, types, and importance in maximizing solar energy system efficiency and reliability. Solar power systems rely on solar panels to capture sunlight and convert it into electricity. Yet, variations in output occur due to factors like sunlight intensity, temperature, and shading. These variables influence the efficiency of energy conversion, impacting overall system performance. Without proper regulation, this variability can lead to overcharging or undercharging of batteries, potentially damaging them and compromising the overall performance of the system. This is where the solar charge controller steps in. Acting as a smart regulator, the charge controller monitors the voltage and current output of the solar panels and adjusts the charging process to ensure that batteries receive the optimal amount of charge without being overcharged or depleted. Essentially, it acts as a traffic cop, directing the flow of electricity to where it is needed most within the system. One of the primary functions of a solar charge controller is to regulate the charging voltage and current supplied to the batteries. Most batteries have specific charging requirements, and exceeding these limits can lead to reduced battery life or even permanent damage. The charge controller prevents overcharging by disconnecting the solar panels from the batteries once they reach full charge, thereby protecting the batteries from excessive voltage or current. Furthermore, the charge controller plays a crucial role in battery management, ensuring that they remain healthy and well-maintained. This includes tasks such as equalization charging, which helps balance the charge levels of individual cells within a battery bank, as well as temperature compensation, which adjusts the charging voltage based on ambient temperature to optimize battery performance.

In addition to battery management, some charge controllers offer advanced features such as load control, which allows users to connect DC loads directly to the controller for automatic switching on and off based on battery voltage. This is particularly useful in off-grid solar power systems, where energy consumption needs to be carefully managed to avoid draining the batteries unnecessarily. Solar charge controllers, PWM and MPPT, offer distinct advantages and suit different solar power system needs. PWM controllers are cost-effective and suitable for smaller systems, while MPPT controllers maximize efficiency by tracking the solar panel's maximum power point, ideal for larger installations. WM charge controllers are the more traditional and cost-effective option, suitable for smaller solar power systems with relatively low voltage and current requirements. They work by rapidly switching the solar panel's output on and off, effectively reducing the voltage supplied to the batteries to match their charging requirements. While PWM controllers are simpler and less efficient than MPPT controllers, they are still widely used in off-grid and small-scale solar installations. On the other hand, MPPT charge controllers are the more advanced and efficient option, capable of extracting the maximum power from solar panels under varying environmental conditions. MPPT controllers employ advanced algorithms to track the solar panel's Maximum Power Point (MPP), optimizing voltage and current for enhanced energy extraction and maximizing solar energy harvest. This results in higher efficiency and energy yield than PWM controllers, making MPPT controllers ideal for larger solar power systems and grid-tied installations. When selecting a solar charge controller, it is essential to consider factors such as system voltage, current capacity, battery type compatibility, and desired features. Additionally, choosing a reputable and reliable manufacturer can ensure the longevity and performance of the charge controller over its operational life. Solar charge controllers are pivotal for solar power systems, overseeing electricity flow between panels, batteries, and loads for optimal efficiency. They regulate and manage the process, ensuring reliable performance by preventing overcharging and maximizing power utilization. Whether it is PWM or MPPT, these intelligent devices help ensure that solar energy is harnessed and utilized effectively, contributing to a more sustainable and resilient energy future. The block diagram of the solar charge controller is shown in Fig. (**5**).

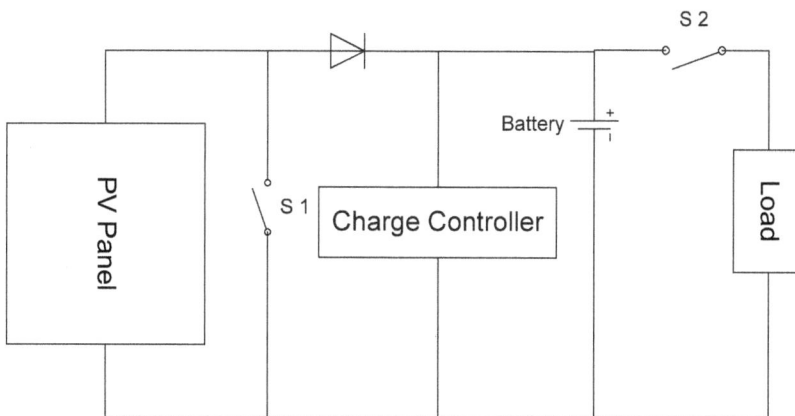

Fig. (5). Block Diagram of Solar Charge Controller.

HARDWARE

The hardware diagram for an electric bicycle with solar power outlines each component's role, including solar panels, charge controller, battery, motor, and throttle, facilitating efficient energy conversion and propulsion. Let us delve into it. At the heart of the system is the solar panel. This device captures sunlight and converts it into electricity through a process called photovoltaic conversion. Solar panels consist of semiconductor solar cells, often silicon-based, where sunlight energizes electrons, generating an electric current. This process, known as the photovoltaic effect, forms the basis of solar energy conversion. The size and efficiency of the solar panel determine the amount of electricity it can generate. The electricity generated by the solar panel is not always consistent due to variations in sunlight intensity and weather conditions. To manage this variability and ensure optimal charging of the battery, a charge controller is employed. The charge controller manages solar panel output, adjusting voltage and current to protect the battery from overcharging or undercharging. It also includes features like temperature compensation to maximize battery lifespan and efficiency. A hardware diagram of the electric bicycle with a solar panel is shown in Fig. (6).

Fig. (6). Hardware Diagram of the Electric Bicycle with Solar Panel.

Solar panel-generated electricity is stored in a battery pack, enabling utilization at a later time for various applications. The battery pack serves as an energy reservoir, allowing the electric bicycle to operate even when sunlight is not available, such as during cloudy days or nighttime. Lithium-ion batteries are preferred for their high energy density, lightweight, and longevity in electric bicycles. The battery pack's capacity dictates the bike's range and duration of electric assistance. The motor controller regulates power to the electric motor, converting battery DC voltage to three-phase AC to efficiently drive the brushless DC (BLDC) hub motor. It adjusts AC voltage amplitude and frequency to control speed and torque, integrating features like regenerative braking for energy recovery. The throttle serves as a user interface, enabling riders to manage speed and acceleration. Through rider input and system requirements, the motor controller optimizes power delivery. This comprehensive setup not only enhances the bike's performance but also promotes sustainability, as it efficiently converts and manages energy, offering a cost-effective and environmentally friendly transportation solution. It is typically mounted on the handlebars and connected to the motor controller. By twisting or pressing the throttle, the rider can increase or decrease the power output of the motor, similar to how a throttle works in a traditional internal combustion engine vehicle. This provides intuitive and responsive control over the electric assistance provided by the motor. In addition to the primary components, the electric bicycle with solar power may incorporate various safety features to protect the system and ensure reliable operation. These features can include overcurrent protection, overvoltage protection, and temperature monitoring to prevent damage to the components. Additionally, built-in diagnostics and fault detection systems may be implemented to detect and address any issues that arise during operation, enhancing the overall safety and reliability of the electric bicycle.

The hardware diagram also includes the wiring and connections that link the components together to form a complete electrical system. High-quality wiring and connectors are essential to minimize power loss, ensure proper communication between components, and maintain system integrity. Proper insulation and routing of wires are also important to protect against damage and ensure safety. Finally, the hardware diagram may depict the mounting and integration of the various components onto the electric bicycle frame. This includes mounting brackets, fasteners, and other hardware to securely attach the solar panel, battery pack, motor controller, throttle, and other components to the bicycle frame while ensuring proper weight distribution and balance. The hardware diagram of an electric bicycle with solar power illustrates the integration of key components such as the solar panel, charge controller, battery pack, motor controller, throttle, safety features, wiring, connections, mounting, and integration. Together, these components form a sophisticated electrical system that harnesses solar energy to provide sustainable and efficient propulsion for the electric bicycle, reducing reliance on fossil fuels and mitigating environmental impact.

CONCLUSION

In conclusion, the integration of solar panels into electric bicycles represents a remarkable stride towards sustainable transportation. These innovative vehicles offer a plethora of benefits, both for individuals and the environment. By harnessing solar power, electric bicycles with solar panels provide a renewable energy source that diminishes reliance on fossil fuels and mitigates greenhouse gas emissions. This eco-friendly mode of transportation not only fosters cleaner air but also contributes significantly to global efforts in combating climate change. One notable advantage of electric bicycles with solar panels is their capacity to extend the range and duration of electric assistance. Unlike traditional electric bicycles, which are dependent solely on battery power, these bicycles can recharge while using solar panels. This feature not only extends their range but also diminishes the necessity for frequent stops for recharging, rendering them suitable for various applications, from commuting to recreational riding and long-distance touring. Electric bicycles provide an affordable and eco-friendly alternative to traditional transportation, reducing costs while promoting sustainability and environmental stewardship. Despite the initial higher investment compared to traditional bicycles, the long-term savings on fuel and maintenance costs offset the upfront expenses. Moreover, the utilization of solar energy reduces or eliminates the need for grid electricity, further trimming down operating expenses and minimizing the environmental impact of the bicycle. As solar technology advances and becomes more affordable, electric bicycles with solar panels are poised to become more accessible globally, promoting the widespread adoption of clean and renewable transportation solutions. In urban settings, these bicycles have the potential to revolutionize mobility and address pressing issues such as traffic congestion and air pollution. Electric bicycles provide convenient, eco-friendly transportation, promoting sustainable travel choices. This reduces traffic congestion, enhances air quality, and benefits public health by encouraging active lifestyles. As a result, electric bicycles with solar panels emerge as a promising solution to foster cleaner and healthier cities, ushering in a future where sustainable transportation is the norm.

AUTHORS' CONTRIBUTION

Nitesh Tiwari: Analyzed and interpreted the data.

Shivangi Agrawal: Study conception and design, and wrote the paper.

Sumit Patel: Study conception and design.

Chandra Mohan Chaurasiya: Wrote the paper.

REFERENCES

[1]   A. Asrori, "The design and Performance Investigation of Solar E-Bike using flexible solar panel by different battery charging controller", *International Journal of Mechanical and Production Engineering Research and Development,* vol. 10, no. 3, pp. 14431-14442, 2020.

[2]   2. Apostolou, Georgia, Angèle Reinders, and Karst Geurs. "An overview of existing experiences with solar-powered e-bikes." *Energies 11.8,* 2129, 2018.

[3]   S.A. Hamoodi, A.A. Abdullah Al-Karakchi, and A.N. Hamoodi, "Studying performance evaluation of hybrid e-bike using solar photovoltaic system", *Bulletin of Electrical Engineering and Informatics,* vol. 11, no. 1, pp. 59-67, 2022.
[http://dx.doi.org/10.11591/eei.v11i1.3298]

[4]   R. Cong, R. Martinez, M. Casilang, and P. Vong, "Electric bicycle system," 2010.

[5]   N. Hatwar, A. Bisen, H. Dodke, A. Junghare, and M. Khanapurkar, "Design approach for electric bikes using battery and super capacitor for performance improvement", *16th International IEEE Conference on Intelligent Transportation Systems (ITSC 2013),* pp. 1959-1964, 2013.
[http://dx.doi.org/10.1109/ITSC.2013.6728516]

[6]   T. Suresh, T.D. Subha, C. Surendra Kumar, and T.D. Subash, "A study of novel technique - solar powered bicycle", *Mater. Today Proc.,* vol. 43, pp. 3595-3602, 2021.
[http://dx.doi.org/10.1016/j.matpr.2020.09.827]

[7]   S. Suripto, G.A.W. Utomo, K. Purwanto, K.T. Putra, M.Y. Mustar, and M. Rahaman, "Design and Analysis of Solar-powered E-bike Charging Stations to Support the Development of Green Campus", *Journal of Electrical Technology UMY,* vol. 6, no. 2, pp. 85-93, 2022.
[http://dx.doi.org/10.18196/jet.v6i2.16543]

[8]   A. Asrori, Y. Winoko, S. Subagiyo, P. Udianto, and I. Eryk, "Design and development of hybrid solar e-bike for sustainable green transportation", *Journal of Applied Engineering Science,* vol. 21, no. 4, pp. 1139-1147, 2023.
[http://dx.doi.org/10.5937/jaes0-45297]

[9]   J.R. Babu, M.R. Nayak, and B. Mangu, "Design And Simulation of Hybrid Electric Bicycle Powered by Solar Photovoltaics to Reduced Co2 Emissions", *Journal of Optoelectronics Laser,* vol. 41, no. 3, pp. 267-280, 2022.

[10]   M. Kumar, A. Kumar, A. Kumar, A. Ranjan, and A. Kumar, "Design and Fabrication of Solar Bicycle", *Invertis Journal of Renewable Energy,* vol. 9, no. 1, pp. 21-27, 2019.

[11]   C. Sivapragash, C. Shankar, M. Nageena, B. Reetha Devi, and K. Kiruthiga, "An innovative solar powered electric bicycle", *Journal of Chemical and Pharmaceutical Sciences ISSN,* vol. 974, p. 2115, 2015.

[12]   L. Vijayan, R. P. Shamil, U. S. Momin, Mahammad Athavulla, and Y. Rao. "Free energy electric bicycle."., *Int. J. Eng. Res. Technol. (Ahmedabad),* vol. 7, no. 8, pp. 1-7, 2019,

[13]   B.A. Sudhir, B.T. Chandrakant, B.O. Prakash, and P.D. Chandrakant, "Design and Fabrication of Solar Electric Bicycle", *Journal of Thermal and Fluid Science,* vol. 3, no. 2, pp. 53-58, 2022.

[14]   R. Shende, N. Karkade, G. Kuchankar, R. Bhoyar, T. Kamde, G. Ghotekar, and V. Bisen, "Design and Fabrication of Solar Operated E-Bicycle", *International Journal of Research in Engineering, Science and Management,* vol. 4, no. 5, pp. 231-234, 2021.

[15]   M. Sankar, Reddi, T. Pushpaveni, and V. Bhanu Prakash Reddy. "Design and development of solar assisted bicycle.".*International Journal of Scientific and Research Publications,* vol. 3, no. 3, pp. 452-457, 2013.

[16]   K. Abou Saleh, and R.V. Murali, "Design, Analysis and Development of Solar-Powered Electric Bi-Cycle for domestic use", *European Journal of Engineering and Technology Research,* vol. 4, no. 2, pp. 54-58, 2019.

[17]   P. Reddy, "Rampulla, KS Shivani Gowda, S. Charitha, and R. Mahalakshmi. "Review and Redesign of Pedal Energy-Solar Power Augmented Hybrid Bicycle", *Third International Conference on Smart Systems and Inventive Technology (ICSSIT)*, pp. 376-380, 20202020.

[18]   F. Fogelberg, "Solar powered bike sharing system with electric bikes - An overview of the energy system and the technical system design," 2014.

[19]   H. Patange, M. Govli, S. M. A. Mahdi, and V. Mehetre, "Solar EV charger for e-bikes (cycle)," 2023.

[20]   F. D. Oliveira Rodrigues Maruco, L. G. Veraldo, M. Martins, and P. de Lima Bianch, "Renewable energies: sustainability by installation of photovoltaic panels and urban mobility by electric bicycle electronics," in *Advances in Human Factors, Sustainable Urban Planning and Infrastructure: Proc. AHFE 2017 Int. Conf. Human Factors, Sustainable Urban Planning and Infrastructure*, Los Angeles, CA, USA, Jul. 17-21, 2017, vol. 8, pp. 310–317, Springer International Publishing.

[21]   Z. Taha, J.M. Sah, R. Passarella, A.R.G. Raja, N. Ahmad, Y.H. Jen, T.T. Khai, Z. Kassim, I. Hasanuddin, and M. Yunus, "A solar vehicle based on sustainable design concept", *Proceeding of. The IASTED international Conference on Solar Energy*, pp. 16-18, 2009.

Conclusion and Future Scope

Nitesh Tiwari, Shekhar Yadav & Sabha Raj Arya

Chapter 1, "A Review of Emerging Research Trends and Opportunities in Harnessing Solar Energy for Electric Vehicles", discussed how Electric vehicle (EV) and solar energy integration have advanced significantly, tackling the dual problems of sustainable energy production and transportation. Knowledge of photovoltaic (PV) technology, energy conversion efficiency, and storage systems has advanced significantly in academia. Research has concentrated on optimising the integration of solar energy into EV powertrains and charging systems, as well as increasing the power output of solar panels through technologies like perovskite and multi-junction cells. Notwithstanding these advancements, issues like solar energy's erratic nature and the shortcomings of current energy storage systems are still being researched.

The commercialisation of solar-powered electric vehicle technology is accelerating from an industrial standpoint. Businesses are investigating hybrid solutions that blend conventional grid-based charging with renewable energy sources and solar-integrated charging stations. Products like mobile solar charging stations and car solar roofs have started reaching niche markets. However, more advancements and financial investments are needed to scale these technologies to satisfy mass-market demands and guarantee economic viability.

Socially, popular and governmental support for solar-assisted EV solutions is being driven by the growing awareness of environmental sustainability and the advantages of renewable energy. Adoption rates are rising as a result of financial incentives and policies supporting renewable energy. However, obstacles like the absence of extensive infrastructure for charging and the expensive upfront costs of solar-integrated systems still prevent universal access, especially in developing nations.

Future Directions in Harnessing Solar Energy for Electric Vehicles: Insights from Emerging Research Trends

Research in the upcoming years will probably concentrate on removing the technological obstacles that presently prevent the integration of solar and electric vehicles. It will continue to be a top goal to increase PV cell efficiency using cutting-edge materials like perovskite and quantum dot-based cells. Solar energy is now more feasible for automotive applications because of these technologies, which offer increased energy yields and reduced prices. Furthermore, it is anticipated that the creation of predictive energy management systems that use artificial intelligence (AI) and machine learning would dynamically optimise energy use to overcome the unpredictability of solar power. Additionally, hybrid energy solutions that integrate solar energy with other renewable resources like wind or hydrogen are expected to become more popular to enhance energy availability and dependability.

In the industrial sector, the emphasis will shift to increasing production capacity in order to more economically produce solar-integrated EV components. The secret to guaranteeing smooth integration without sacrificing performance or design will be lightweight, flexible, and long-lasting solar panels made especially for automobiles. Advancements in modular solar charging stations that can operate in both off-grid and urban settings will serve a wider range of users. In autonomous EVs, where self-sufficient energy systems are necessary for prolonged operations, industries will also investigate the use of solar energy.

The shift to solar-powered EVs will necessitate strong legislative frameworks and extensive public education from a sociological perspective. It is anticipated that governments will play a significant role in promoting the use of solar-assisted EVs through the implementation of regulations, tax breaks, and subsidies. To increase the knowledge of these technologies' long-term cost savings and environmental advantages, educational programs will be required. Ensuring that these solutions are accessible in underserved and rural areas will be crucial in facilitating their equitable adoption across socio-economic divides. The urban-rural divide will be lessened with the support of community-driven renewable energy projects and partnerships between public and private organisations.

A revolutionary change to create sustainable energy and transportation systems is presented by the combination of solar energy with electric vehicle technologies. The industrial sector is responsible for converting these developments into scalable, market-ready solutions, while the academic community continues to tackle basic issues pertaining to efficiency, storage, and control. Socially, fair access, encouraging legislation, and public involvement are all necessary for solar-EV systems to succeed. A cleaner, more sustainable, and renewable-powered transportation ecosystem will become a reality when these factors come together, ensuring a more efficient and environmentally friendly future.

Chapter 2, "Introduction to EV Motors", explores how the demand for environmentally friendly transportation options has propelled substantial advancements in the field of Electric Vehicle (EV) motors. Many motor technologies, such as brushed DC motors, brushless DC (BLDC) motors, induction motors, and Permanent Magnet Synchronous Motors (PMSMs), have been the subject of in-depth scholarly investigation. Efficiency, torque performance, and compatibility for particular EV applications are just a few of the distinct benefits that each type of motor offers. In order to precisely regulate speed and torque, significant advancements have also been achieved in our understanding of motor control systems, including Direct Torque Control (DTC) and Field-Oriented Control (FOC). Nevertheless, reducing heat losses, increasing energy efficiency, and addressing material dependencies such as using rare earth metals in magnets remain difficult tasks.

With an emphasis on mass production and modular designs, EV motors have improved in efficiency, dependability, and affordability from an industrial standpoint. Compact designs, improved thermal management, and higher power densities have all been made possible by manufacturing techniques and materials developments. By creating alternative motor designs like Switching Reluctance Motors (SRMs), industry leaders are attempting to lessen reliance on rare earth elements. However, there are still issues with these inventions' scalability and incorporation into cost-sensitive sectors.

Socially speaking, the increasing popularity of EVs has raised awareness of motor technology as an essential part of sustainable mobility. Demand has been fuelled by government policies and subsidies, as well as public knowledge of the environmental advantages of EVs. However, researchers and producers are under tremendous pressure to develop quickly while maintaining affordable costs for the general public because of social expectations for affordability, range, and performance.

Future Directions in Electric Vehicle Motor Development: Insights from Emerging Trends and Technologies

Academic research in the upcoming years will probably concentrate on improving EV motor performance and efficiency even more. Research on new materials, like high-temperature superconductors and sophisticated composites, may result in innovations that improve thermal performance and lower energy losses. In order to reduce system weight and improve compactness, a major area of study will also be the development of integrated motor-inverter systems. Enhanced modelling and simulation methods powered by AI and machine learning will be anticipated to optimise motor design and control schemes for particular driving circumstances, improving performance in various applications.

Concerns about cost and sustainability will be addressed as manufacturers work to improve motor designs for mass-market adoption. With developments in switching reluctance and ferrite-based motors, efforts to lessen or completely eradicate reliance on rare earth materials will accelerate. It is anticipated that the shift to next-generation motor technologies, like axial flux motors, which provide great power density in a small package, will quicken. In order to ensure optimal performance across segments, industries will also increasingly concentrate on developing motors specifically designed for specialised EV applications, such as driverless vehicles, two-wheelers, and heavy-duty trucks.

Social acceptance of EVs and related motor technologies will be contingent upon further cost reductions and accessibility enhancements. Policies that support clean energy and mobility, like financing for research into sustainable motor technology and incentives for EV adoption, will be essential. Public support and a move away from internal combustion engine vehicles towards Electric Vehicles (EVs) can be generated *via* educational efforts that emphasise the economic and environmental advantages of EV motors. Achieving fair mobility solutions will need to ensure global access, especially in developing nations.

EV motor development is at the nexus of industrial adaptability, technological innovation, and societal change. Performance gains will be fuelled by scholarly research into improved materials, motor architectures, and control systems. Manufacturers are in a good position to concentrate on sustainability, cost reduction, and scalability. The adoption rate will be influenced by social factors such as public knowledge, policy backing, and equal access. The next stage of EV motor development will be shaped by the joint efforts of manufacturers, researchers, and legislators, paving the way for cleaner, more sustainable, and efficient transportation in the future.

Chapter 3, "Field Oriented Speed Control of BLDC Motor for Practical Drive Cycle", discusses how in Electric Vehicle (EV) applications, Field-Oriented Control (FOC) for brushless DC (BLDC) motors has emerged as a component for attaining accurate speed and torque control. Understanding the mathematical modelling, vector control concepts, and real-world application of FOC has advanced significantly from an academic standpoint. Studies have indicated that FOC enables the separation of torque and flux components, resulting in improved dynamic performance under variable drive cycles, smoother operation, and increased efficiency. However, issues like sensor accuracy, computational complexity, and noise management continue to exist, requiring more research into sophisticated control algorithms and hardware improvements.

The use of FOC in the industrial sector has made it possible for BLDC motors to satisfy the exact torque delivery, quick acceleration, and energy efficiency demands of EVs. To ensure scalability and cost-effectiveness for mass production, industries are currently concentrating on merging FOC algorithms with real-time digital controllers and sophisticated sensors. However, the expense and complexity of the system are increased when FOC implementation relies on precise sensors like rotary encoders or Hall-effect sensors. The development of sensorless FOC methods, which lessen hardware dependence while preserving control accuracy, is still underway.

The usage of FOC in BLDC motors is essential for improving EV users' driving experiences from a social standpoint. The overall dependability and appeal of EVs are influenced by the smooth and effective performance of motors during realistic drive cycles. FOC-based motor control systems must change to meet the public's increasing demands for more performance, greater range, and lower costs. However, there are difficulties because of the intricacy of FOC and the requirement for highly qualified technical knowledge for upkeep and troubleshooting, particularly in less developed areas.

Advancing Field-Oriented Control in BLDC Motors: Future Directions for Practical Drive Cycles

In order to increase efficiency and lessen implementation difficulties, future research will probably concentrate on improving FOC algorithms. The development of adaptive control systems that can optimise FOC parameters in real-time for changing drive circumstances is anticipated to be aided by emerging technologies like artificial intelligence and machine learning. In order to reduce hardware dependencies, work will also focus on improving sensorless control methods by using model-based estimators or back-EMF detection. Hardware-in-the-loop (HIL) technologies and sophisticated simulation tools will also make testing and validating FOC techniques easier across a range of drive cycles.

The next stage in the industrial process will be to incorporate FOC algorithms into small, powerful motor controller devices. Manufacturers will concentrate on creating affordable sensorless FOC systems that reduce system complexity without sacrificing accuracy. There will also be a greater focus on reducing controllers' size, improving temperature control, and increasing dependability in challenging working environments. In line with industrial trends towards greater efficiency, the use of wide-bandgap semiconductors in motor controllers, such as Silicon Carbide (SiC) and Gallium Nitride (GaN), is anticipated to improve performance while lowering energy losses.

By enhancing motor performance and cutting costs, the development of FOC technology in BLDC motors would encourage wider EV adoption from a social standpoint. Accessibility will be accelerated by policies that encourage research and development in cutting-edge motor control technology and provide incentives for the manufacture of EVs. For the technology to be adopted fairly, educational programs that teach technicians and engineers how to implement and maintain FOC will be essential. Furthermore, the public's acceptance and use of FOC systems will be improved by their simplification through intuitive interfaces and diagnostics.

An important development in enabling effective, accurate, and high-performance EV motor systems is the field-oriented control of BLDC motors. Ongoing scholarly investigations into sensorless approaches, adaptive algorithms, and sophisticated modelling techniques will keep pushing the limits of FOC capabilities. Industrial advancements in cost optimisation, power electronics, and motor controllers will guarantee the scalability and viability of FOC solutions. Socially, incorporating FOC technology into common EV uses will require extensive education, legislative support, and streamlined system designs. By working together, these initiatives will guarantee that FOC stays at the forefront of EV motor control, advancing a sustainable and effective transportation future.

Chapter 4, "Phase Shifted Full Bridge Converter-based Battery Charger for Fast Charging of Electric Vehicles", discusses Phase-Shifted Full-Bridge (PSFB) converters, a major development in power electronics, are used in battery chargers for Electric Vehicle (EV) fast charging.

PSFB converters are extensively researched from an academic standpoint because of their capacity to minimise switching losses through soft-switching approaches like Zero-Voltage Switching (ZVS) and achieve high efficiency and power density. Because these converters can adjust to different input-output circumstances, which is essential for quick EV charging, they have been extensively studied. Nevertheless, there are still issues with integrating bidirectional capabilities for vehicle-to-grid (V2G) applications and refining control algorithms to guarantee reliable operation under dynamic load situations. Additionally, research into improving Electromagnetic Interference (EMI) performance and thermal control is still ongoing.

From an industrial standpoint, PSFB converters are used more frequently in commercial fast-charging stations because of their excellent efficiency and power-handling capacity. In order to accommodate the various charging needs of EVs, industries have concentrated on standardising designs to provide modular and scalable systems. Significant obstacles still exist, though, including the expense of high-performance components, the intricacy of PSFB design, and the requirement for wide-bandgap semiconductors like Gallium Nitride (GaN) and Silicon Carbide (SiC). Furthermore, maintaining compatibility with changing international charging standards (such as CCS and CHAdeMO) presents difficulties for broad adoption.

From a societal standpoint, PSFB converter-enabled rapid charging infrastructure is essential for lowering range anxiety and promoting EV adoption. The user experience is much improved by the shorter charging periods, which increases the public's interest in EVs. However, the upfront costs of setting up fast-charging stations and the unequal infrastructure distribution, especially in underprivileged or rural areas, highlight the necessity of public-private partnerships and policy changes.

Future Trends in Phase-Shifted Full-Bridge Converter Technology for Fast EV Charging Applications

Future scholarly investigations will probably concentrate on improving PSFB converter performance. This involves incorporating adaptive control techniques to optimise real-time performance and improve ZVS functioning under a greater range of load circumstances. One of the main areas of research will be the development of bidirectional PSFB converters to facilitate V2G applications and the incorporation of renewable energy. Furthermore, investigating cutting-edge materials for transformer cores and passive parts will increase system efficiency and minimise its size. Another option for resolving certain operational issues may be hybrid topologies that combine PSFB with alternative converter designs.

Wide-bandgap semiconductors like SiC and GaN will be used more frequently in industry to improve PSFB converter efficiency and dependability while lowering heat production. These materials make higher switching frequencies and smaller designs possible, which are essential for next-generation fast chargers. In order to ensure compatibility with a wide variety of EVs, industries will also prioritise modular and adaptable PSFB-based chargers that can accommodate different power levels. Industrial advancements will also heavily rely on integrating sophisticated communication protocols for dynamic load balancing and real-time monitoring.

The pricing and accessibility of PSFB-based fast chargers will determine their social success. It will be necessary for policymakers to implement incentives and subsidies to promote the installation of fast-charging infrastructure, especially in developing regions. Public awareness campaigns can increase the acceptability of EVs by emphasizing the convenience and environmental advantages of fast charging. In order to meet societal demands, it will also be crucial to guarantee fair access to charging stations through thoughtful location and inclusive infrastructure design.

The phase-shifted full-bridge converter is one of the most important technologies for providing dependable and effective fast charging for electric vehicles. Developments in hybrid designs, materials, and control systems will fuel continued innovation in academia. Thanks to the industrial use of scalable designs and wide-bandgap semiconductors, PSFB chargers will be easier to integrate into standard infrastructure. Socially, the advantages of fast charging will be available to everyone through well-thought-out policies and awareness-raising initiatives. Combined, these initiatives will create a future where quick, effective, and environmentally friendly charging options facilitate the global shift to electric vehicles.

Chapter 5, "Introduction to Power Electronics Converters", discusses that the foundation of contemporary energy systems is power electronics converters, which provide effective energy conversion and control for various uses, such as industrial automation, electric vehicles (EVs), and the integration of renewable energy sources. Many power electronic converters, such as DC-DC, AC-DC, and DC-AC converters, have been the subject of in-depth scholarly investigation. These investigations aim to reduce losses and system complexity while increasing efficiency, power density, and dependability. The performance of converters has been greatly improved by innovations like soft-switching techniques, wide-bandgap semiconductors (such as Silicon Carbide (SiC) and Gallium Nitride (GaN)), and sophisticated control algorithms. However, issues with cost-effectiveness, Electromagnetic Interference (EMI), and thermal management still exist, particularly for high-power applications.

Power electronics converters are used extensively in the industrial sector to supply power for industrial machines, electric vehicle charging infrastructure, and renewable energy systems.

Strong and small converter systems that can function in a variety of load and environmental circumstances have been successfully created by industries. Because of their versatility and simplicity of integration, scalable and modular converter designs are becoming increasingly popular. Notwithstanding these developments, manufacturers are still forced to innovate while balancing cost and performance due to the growing demand for converters in high-efficiency applications.

From a social standpoint, the use of power electronics converters has greatly aided in the broad deployment of electrification and renewable energy solutions, tackling issues like energy security and climate change. Greener energy consumption patterns have been made possible by incorporating power converters into EVs and renewable energy sources. However, problems like cost and availability of cutting-edge converter technologies in underdeveloped areas underscore the necessity of inclusive approaches to guarantee fair advantages.

Future Directions in Power Electronics Converters: Advancements for Sustainable Energy and Electric Mobility

Future scholarly investigations will probably concentrate on improving converter performance and efficiency using innovative materials and designs. Compact designs, lower thermal losses, and higher switching frequencies will all be made possible by wide-bandgap semiconductors like SiC and GaN. Furthermore, the creation of multipurpose converters that are capable of performing several energy conversion jobs in a single unit will become more popular. Dynamic optimisation and fault-tolerant operations will also be made possible by advanced control approaches that make use of Artificial Intelligence (AI) and machine learning, especially in applications related to renewable energy and electric vehicles.

In the industrial sector, the goal will be to increase the output of high-efficiency converters while cutting expenses. This entails creating standardised designs that serve a variety of uses, ranging from industrial-grade machinery to home renewable energy systems. Innovations in cooling technologies and component designs will be fuelled by efforts to increase the longevity and dependability of converters, particularly in demanding working settings. Additionally, in order to make installation and maintenance easier in large-scale applications, companies are anticipated to investigate plug-and-play and modular converter architectures.

In terms of society, including power electronics converters into commonplace energy and mobility systems will be essential to promoting sustainable development. The deployment of efficient converters in EVs and renewable energy systems will be accelerated by policies and incentives that support their use. More acceptance may result from public awareness initiatives highlighting how power electronics improve system performance and reduce energy waste. Addressing issues of affordability and accessibility by making focused investments in R&D, manufacturing, and infrastructure development for underprivileged areas would be equally crucial.

The development of sustainable energy and transportation systems depends on power electronics converters. Academically, advancements in materials, designs, and control methods will drive the next generation of converters. Scalable, affordable, and dependable industrial solutions will promote broad use in a variety of applications. Socially, all facets of society will benefit from new technologies thanks to inclusive legislation and awareness campaigns. Power electronic converters will keep playing a revolutionary role in enabling a more efficient and environmentally friendly future as research, industry, and society come together.

Chapter 6, "An Adaptive Passivity-based Controller for Battery Charging Application: The Lagrangian Framework", discusses Improved performance, stability, and adaptability in dynamic environments provided by the development of adaptive Passivity-Based Controllers (PBC) for battery charging applications, especially within the Lagrangian framework. This represents a significant advancement in the control of power electronic systems.

Although PBC's use in battery charging is relatively new from an academic standpoint, it has shown promise because of its ability to handle external disturbances and system uncertainties. Utilising energy conservation concepts, the Lagrangian approach provides a strong foundation for creating resilient and efficient controllers. Current scholarly research aims to enhance these controllers' real-time adaptability by enhancing their design to accommodate changes in battery properties and charging circumstances. To improve charge profiles, there is also a continuous endeavour to integrate PBC with other cutting-edge control techniques like neural networks and Model Predictive Control (MPC). However, issues with real-time implementation and computational complexity still need to be looked into further.

The use of adaptive PBC in battery chargers is still in its exploratory stage in the industrial sector, with an emphasis on verifying the theoretical findings in real-world settings. Industries are experimenting with incorporating PBC into current charging systems to increase the longevity and efficiency of batteries, especially in Electric Vehicles (EVs) and renewable energy storage systems. More accurate control over charging profiles may be possible with this technique, which could result in better system performance, less battery wear, and more economical energy use. However, the Lagrangian-based PBC approach's intricacy and high processing power requirements may prevent it from being widely used in cost-sensitive markets.

Socially speaking, the use of adaptive PBC in battery charging has a lot of promise to improve the longevity and performance of battery-based systems, which are essential to the expanding EV and renewable energy industries. These technologies can potentially enhance user experience by lowering charging times, increasing battery life, and improving energy efficiency if they are broadly adopted. However, the intricacy of these systems might necessitate larger upfront expenditures for specialised knowledge and gear, which would prevent general adoption, particularly in less developed areas.

Advancing Adaptive Passivity-Based Controllers for Battery Charging: Future Directions and Applications

In order to increase the adaptive PBC algorithms' real-time applicability without sacrificing speed, future scholarly research in this area is probably going to concentrate on making them even simpler. To improve its resilience and computational efficiency, research will probably also look into hybrid control strategies that combine adaptive PBC with other approaches like fuzzy logic or reinforcement learning. Furthermore, there will be an effort to create adaptive PBC frameworks that can function with a greater range of battery chemistries, increasing these controllers' adaptability in various applications (such as solid-state, lithium-ion, and alternative battery technologies).

In the industrial sector, adaptive PBC integration into commercially accessible battery charging systems, particularly in EVs and large-scale energy storage solutions, is probably going to become more popular. To ensure that these controllers can be used in low-cost, high-volume manufacturing situations without compromising efficiency, manufacturers will concentrate on optimising the computational burden. Hardware developments like the usage of microcontrollers and Digital Signal Processors (DSPs) will contribute to the affordability and accessibility of these systems. Energy Management Systems (EMS) that use adaptive PBC for optimal charging will also be the focus of industrial efforts. This will help the grid function more efficiently overall, especially in applications like vehicle-to-grid (V2G) systems.

By extending battery life, cutting down on charging times, and increasing overall energy efficiency, adaptive PBC for battery charging systems has the potential to significantly benefit consumers from a societal perspective. These advantages would help EVs and renewable energy sources become more widely used. However, resolving the technical complexity and guaranteeing cost is necessary for social adoption to be widely accepted. The priorities will probably be training employees to install and maintain these cutting-edge charging systems and raising awareness of their long-term advantages, such as lower energy consumption and battery replacement costs. Governments and the commercial sector should work together to offer incentives for advancing and incorporating these technologies into energy infrastructure, particularly for sustainable energy solutions and green mobility.

A viable avenue for enhancing the effectiveness, stability, and versatility of battery charging systems is the creation of adaptive passivity-based controllers within the Lagrangian framework. Academically, the emphasis will be on investigating hybrid control strategies and improving algorithms for real-time applications. The focus of industrial efforts will be on keeping these systems cost-effective while streamlining their implementation. Socially, incorporating these sophisticated controls will enhance the user experience and sustainability of EV and renewable energy systems. Adaptive PBCs will be crucial in developing battery charging technology, promoting the use of cleaner energy sources, and improving the efficiency and lifespan of battery-based systems as long as research, business, and social initiatives are coordinated.

Chapter 7, "Vehicle-to-Grid (V2G) Battery Charging System for Electric Vehicles", discusses an inventive method of incorporating electric cars (EVs) into the larger energy ecosystem: Vehicle-to-Grid (V2G) technology. V2G systems facilitate bidirectional power flow by enabling EVs to both charge and discharge energy back into the grid, increasing the power grid's resilience and flexibility.

In recent years, V2G research has advanced significantly from an academic standpoint. The development and improvement of the bidirectional chargers, control schemes, and communication protocols that enable V2G interactions between EVs and the grid have received the majority of attention. To guarantee the effective, dependable, and secure operation of V2G systems, researchers have investigated various Energy Management Systems (EMS), sophisticated algorithms, and real-time optimisation strategies. In order to optimise the use of clean energy, integrating energy storage devices and renewable energy sources with V2G has also emerged as a crucial research topic. Numerous scholarly obstacles still exist, nevertheless, including the requirement for reliable grid stabilisation methods, real-time monitoring, and resolving problems with battery deterioration brought on by repeated discharging.

With few commercial solutions, mostly in pilot projects or particular locations, V2G systems are still in the early phases of broad deployment from an industrial standpoint. Bidirectional charging infrastructure is currently being developed, although there are several technological obstacles, including high installation costs, the requirement for grid infrastructure changes, and standardisation problems. To integrate them into smart grids and microgrids, a number of automakers and energy businesses are investigating V2G-enabled EVs and charging systems. However, worries about battery life, the complexity of energy management, and regulatory frameworks have hampered widespread adoption.

V2G technology can potentially change how people engage with energy systems from a social standpoint. Stabilising grids with renewable energy might help the entire energy transition and give EV owners an extra revenue stream through energy sales to the grid. However, obstacles like public awareness, governmental permission, and the economic viability of bidirectional charging infrastructure must be overcome before widespread adoption occurs. Social concerns about the effect on EV battery life and the dependability of V2G technology in emergency situations must also be addressed to boost public confidence.

Future Trends in Vehicle-to-Grid (V2G) Technology: Advancements and Opportunities for Smart Energy Systems

Academic research in the future is probably going to concentrate on enhancing the stability and efficiency of V2G systems by optimising charging/discharging cycles to minimise battery degradation and using sophisticated control algorithms. The development of intelligent energy management (EMS) or hybrid systems that can balance the demands of the environment, EV owners, and the grid will be prioritised. Furthermore, real-time optimisation and predictive maintenance will be made easier by the incorporation of machine learning and Artificial Intelligence (AI) into V2G systems. The use of V2G to integrate more dispersed renewable energy sources and improve grid resilience is also expected to be further researched, especially in light of increasingly decentralised energy systems.

In the industrial sector, the shift to V2G will concentrate on enhancing the infrastructure required to facilitate bidirectional charging, such as creating scalable, affordable, and effective bidirectional chargers. Significant work will be done to improve V2G systems' interoperability so they may be easily integrated with current communication networks and grids. Furthermore, issues like battery longevity, energy storage efficiency, and smooth microgrid integration will need to be addressed by V2G systems. In order to further balance energy supply and demand, enterprises will seek to optimise V2G applications in fields like fleet management, where fleets of electric buses or delivery trucks can act as mobile energy storage units.

V2G technology has the ability to change how energy is distributed and consumed in society completely. By lowering the overall cost of ownership, individuals can sell extra energy back to the grid, which can encourage the adoption of EVs. However, the creation of precise legal frameworks that facilitate V2G transactions and provide consumer rights will be necessary for widespread adoption. Efforts must be directed towards educating consumers about how to optimise their EVs for grid involvement and increasing public knowledge of the advantages of V2G. Furthermore, regulatory backing and funding for the required infrastructure (such as bidirectional chargers and grid upgrades) will be crucial for achieving large-scale implementation.

Vehicle-to-grid (V2G) technology has the potential to revolutionise the energy and electric vehicle industries by providing solutions for renewable energy integration, grid stabilisation, and extra revenue streams for EV owners. V2G research will keep developing academically, with an emphasis on minimising battery degradation and improving energy management systems. The creation of affordable infrastructure, interoperability, and microgrid integration will fuel adoption in the industrial sector. Socially, V2G might democratise energy consumption and serve as a link between the power and transportation industries. As industry, society, and research work together, V2G may emerge as a crucial technology for building a more robust and sustainable energy future.

Chapter 8, "IoT Based Floor Cleaning Electric Vehicle Robot with Live Streaming Camera", discusses an important development in automation and smart technology, which is the combination of Internet of Things (IoT) technology with robotic systems, such as electric car floor-cleaning robots with live streaming cameras. In order to provide more effective and user-friendly robots for both commercial and household applications, these systems integrate autonomous mobility, Internet of Things connectivity, and real-time video streaming.

Developing autonomous navigation algorithms, increasing the energy economy, and strengthening the integration of IoT devices for remote monitoring and control have been the main focus of academic study in this field. These systems' usage of live streaming cameras enables real-time feedback, which is crucial for the robot's navigation system as well as users. The focus of current research is on improving sensor networks for more precise environmental sensing and investigating machine learning methods to enhance robot decision-making and adaptability. Nevertheless, there are still obstacles to overcome in order to get the best possible battery life, multitasking capabilities, and reliable communication systems that can manage massive volumes of data from cameras and sensors.

From an industrial standpoint, the market for floor-cleaning robots is expanding due to the increased interest in automation for cleaning in both homes and businesses. Users may remotely monitor and operate the robots thanks to the substantial added value of integrating IoT and live streaming capabilities. Data security, system cost, hardware durability, and battery life are issues that industries must deal with. Manufacturers are striving to create more dependable, reasonably priced robots with improved cleaning capabilities and longer operational lifespans. IoT deployment also brings with it cybersecurity and data privacy issues that need to be resolved to maintain customer confidence.

IoT-based floor-cleaning robots have several social advantages, including lower labour costs and more convenience in day-to-day living. Users can follow the cleaning operation in real-time by using live streaming to remotely monitor the robot. Data security and privacy are issues, though, particularly when live-streaming features are used. Making sure the technology is available and cheap for various socioeconomic groups is another social concern, since some users may not be able to afford advanced robotic systems at this time.

Future Directions in IoT-Based Robotic Systems: Advancements in Autonomous Floor Cleaning and Real-Time Monitoring

Enhancing the autonomy and intelligence of floor-cleaning robots will probably be the main focus of future academic research. Robots will be able to adjust to various cleaning conditions thanks to developments in machine learning and Artificial Intelligence (AI), increasing productivity and lowering the need for human intervention. In order to guarantee dependable, low-latency data sharing between robots and user devices, research will also concentrate on improving IoT-based communication protocols. Furthermore, extending the operational period and sustainability of these robots would require the development of energy-efficient algorithms and improved battery management systems. The study will examine ways to improve privacy safeguards, lower data overhead, and improve video quality with low latency in relation to live streaming and user engagement.

More sophisticated robots with enhanced cleaning skills, like better navigation in challenging areas (like under furniture or in confined spaces), are expected to become the norm in industry. In order to provide smooth automation and remote control, manufacturers want to incorporate these robots into smart home systems. Additionally, greater attention will be paid to cutting expenses without sacrificing functionality, lowering the cost, and expanding the accessibility of IoT-based cleaning robots. Industries may add more sophisticated features, including voice control, customised cleaning modes, and connectivity with other smart home appliances, to enhance the user experience. More secure systems and user-friendly interfaces that enable users to regulate and manage data flow efficiently will be developed as a result of the growing concern over data privacy.

Socially, the widespread deployment of IoT-based cleaning robots has the potential to drastically alter how individuals approach domestic chores, as automation results in more labour and time being used efficiently. Customers may become more productive as a result, particularly older or disabled people who would find manual cleaning physically taxing. However, open policies and strong security measures will be required to address privacy concerns associated with live streaming and real-time surveillance. Additionally, as with any cutting-edge technology, the societal issue of guaranteeing equitable access to these gadgets will need to be resolved, especially in less wealthy regions where access to them may be limited. Attempts to raise awareness and offer adoption incentives, like eco-friendly features or energy savings, could aid in bridging the divide between various social groups.

Chapter 9, "Hardware Design and Modelling of Solar-based Wireless Electric Vehicle Charging Station", discusses an important step towards more convenient, effective, and sustainable energy solutions the creation of solar-powered wireless Electric Vehicle (EV) charging stations. These systems offer a more environmentally friendly option to conventional charging infrastructure by combining Wireless Power Transfer (WPT) technology with renewable energy from solar panels.

The design and modelling of these systems have advanced significantly from an academic standpoint. In order to guarantee a steady and dependable energy supply, research has concentrated on increasing the efficiency of wireless power transfer, optimising solar power generation capabilities, and refining control algorithms. Another significant area of scholarly investigation has been the incorporation of these elements into a smooth, user-friendly charging station. Furthermore, a practical strategy for scaling these systems has been developed through the modelling of energy flow, power management, and the influence of environmental conditions on solar generation. Despite developments, there are still issues with maximising energy loss during transmission and increasing the effectiveness of wireless charging over greater distances.

Wireless EV charging stations powered by solar energy are still in the prototype or early commercial stages from an industrial standpoint. These technologies are being tested and developed by a number of businesses and research institutions with the goal of integrating them with the current EV infrastructure. One significant benefit is the solar component, which lessens reliance on the grid and gives EVs a more sustainable energy source. However, the price of solar panels, wireless power transmission devices, and the system architecture present difficulties. Furthermore, securing a steady energy supply is challenging because of the weather-related unpredictability of solar power, necessitating storage technologies to ensure continuous operation. Industries are concentrating on lowering the cost of these systems while increasing the efficiency of power conversion and transfer as the technology advances.

Solar-powered wireless EV charging stations provide several social advantages, especially when it comes to environmentally friendly transportation. By utilising clean, renewable energy, these technologies have the potential to lower the carbon footprint of electric vehicles significantly. Furthermore, wireless charging is more convenient because it does not require physical connections, which may enhance user experience. However, significant infrastructure investment and public education regarding the features and advantages of wireless charging are necessary for the broad adoption of such systems. Furthermore, social fairness concerns could surface if only wealthy areas or people have access to this cutting-edge charging technology.

Advancements in Solar-Powered Wireless Charging Systems for Electric Vehicles: Future Trends and Opportunities

Enhancing the effectiveness of wireless power transfer is probably the main goal of future scholarly studies on solar-powered wireless EV charging stations. These systems' scalability and feasibility will improve as long-distance energy transfer efficiency rises. In order to overcome the intermittent nature of solar energy, research will also probably focus on optimising hybrid systems that integrate solar energy with other renewable energy sources (such as wind or grid electricity). To guarantee that the energy produced by solar panels is usable when needed, more sophisticated energy storage technologies will also be essential. From the modelling standpoint, efforts will continue to be directed towards refining prediction algorithms and simulating diverse environmental situations better to manage variations in the supply of solar electricity.

Efforts in the industrial sector will probably focus on improving wireless power transmission technology to make it more reliable, efficient, and affordable for commercial use. Enhancing wireless charging efficiency will be significantly aided by developments in materials science, such as the creation of more effective resonant inductive coupling materials. Better energy management and distribution will also be possible with the incorporation of smart grid technology, increasing the systems' flexibility in response to fluctuating demand and solar availability. To even out the variations in the power supply from solar energy, energy storage devices like sophisticated batteries and capacitors must be used. On a broader scale, the industry will concentrate on the infrastructure required to implement the extensive deployment, including collaborations with energy suppliers and municipalities.

Wireless EV charging stations powered by solar energy have the potential to revolutionise the social acceptance of electric automobiles. These technologies could promote wider use of electric vehicles, help cut carbon emissions, and create a cleaner environment by making EV charging more sustainable and easier. Furthermore, a preview of the future of smart cities where transport and energy systems are smoothly integrated may be offered by the combination of solar energy with wireless technology. However, the availability of these systems in less developed or financially resource-constrained locations may be restricted by the substantial initial investment needed for infrastructure. Governments and private businesses may need to work together to develop funding and incentive schemes to guarantee fair access to new technologies. To encourage acceptance and adoption, the general public must also be made aware of the ease and environmental advantages of solar-powered wireless EV charging.

An intriguing nexus of wireless technology, renewable energy, and environmentally friendly mobility is the creation of solar-powered wireless EV charging stations. Research in academia will keep concentrating on improving energy storage technologies, optimising hybrid energy systems, and increasing the effectiveness of wireless power transfer. From an industry perspective, the focus will be on increasing cost-effectiveness and optimising the infrastructure for wider implementation. The social benefits of these systems in lowering emissions and encouraging sustainable mobility are obvious, but widespread adoption will need to overcome obstacles relating to infrastructure, cost, and public awareness. As these technologies advance, they could drastically alter how people travel in the future, making it more convenient, ecological, and energy-efficient.

Chapter 10, "Hardware Design of Electric Bicycle with Solar Panel", discusses an emerging field of innovation combining efficient transportation and renewable energy sources: the hardware design of electric bicycles, or "e-bikes," with integrated solar panels. By employing solar panels to charge the battery, these systems seek to increase the range of electric bicycles, potentially decreasing their dependency on conventional power sources and increasing their sustainability.

From an academic standpoint, the main goals of this field's study have been to improve power management systems, optimise energy conversion efficiency, and better integrate solar panels with e-bike power systems. To create intelligent charging systems that maximise performance, much research has focused on comprehending the energy dynamics between the solar panel, battery, and motor. To increase the effectiveness and longevity of these systems, research also looks at different battery technologies, such as solid-state or lithium-ion batteries. Nonetheless, there are still issues with the solar panel's capacity to produce enough electricity in various environmental circumstances and the incorporation of affordable and lightweight components into the e-bike's design.

Electric bicycles with solar panels are still in the prototype or early commercial stage of development from an industrial standpoint. Large-scale adoption may be hampered by the expense of adding solar panels and batteries to e-bike systems, as well as the extra weight and space these parts need. Nonetheless, businesses are becoming more aware of the potential of solar-powered e-bikes, particularly in markets that prioritise clean mobility and sustainability. Scaling these systems to offer workable solutions for daily usage while preserving performance and cost-effectiveness is still a challenge. Furthermore, the viability of these e-bikes for wider commercial manufacturing depends on developments in energy-efficient power management systems and lightweight solar cells.

Adopting solar-powered electric bicycles has several social advantages, especially in metropolitan settings and places with lots of sunlight. These e-bikes can lessen reliance on fossil fuels and are an eco-friendly substitute for conventional forms of transportation. Socially, these bikes could increase access to reasonably priced and environmentally friendly transportation, particularly in underdeveloped nations. However, as solar-powered e-bikes may now be too costly for many users, there are obstacles to guaranteeing fair access to these vehicles. To promote adoption, it will be essential to raise knowledge and understanding of the financial and environmental advantages of solar e-bikes. Government incentives and the availability of charging infrastructure could also encourage their broad usage.

Future Trends in the Hardware Design and Optimization of Solar-Powered Electric Bicycle Systems

Future scholarly investigations will probably concentrate on enhancing the efficiency and integration of solar panels in e-bike systems. The focus will be on increasing the solar panels' power production without appreciably raising the bike's weight or price. An important field of research will be the study of hybrid energy systems, such as those that combine solar power with regenerative braking or other renewable sources. Additionally, important developments in energy storage technologies will be made, especially the creation of high-capacity, lightweight batteries. Investigating smart charging technologies that optimise solar energy usage throughout the day and optimising power management algorithms that guarantee the effective use of solar energy will also become important study areas.

On an industrial level, the emphasis will probably move to making solar-powered e-bikes more affordable, scalable, and user-friendly. Manufacturers will concentrate on creating more affordable and efficient e-bikes that are lighter and more robust as solar panel efficiency increases and battery technology advances. It will be crucial to incorporate cutting-edge power management technologies that can adjust to changing solar conditions and maximise battery charging. Innovation in the industry will also be fuelled by creating small, integrated solar panels that do not detract from the bike's usefulness or appearance. In parallel, businesses might focus on developing the infrastructure—such as solar-powered charging stations needed for the broad use of solar-powered e-bikes, especially in urban and rural regions.

Socially speaking, solar-powered electric bicycles have the potential to completely transform urban transportation by providing a more sustainable and cleaner substitute for conventional automobiles. Lower carbon footprints and less urban pollution may result from this. Solar-powered e-bikes have the potential to greatly increase the affordability and accessibility of clean transportation in areas with plenty of sunshine. Combining solar power with electric bicycles may help promote more ecologically friendly travel practices, especially among customers who care about the environment. Government regulations, subsidies, and incentives will be necessary to guarantee that these technologies are available to a wide range of people, including those living in rural areas and those with low incomes. Campaigns to raise public knowledge of the advantages of solar-powered e-bikes, such as their financial and environmental benefits, will also be essential in promoting adoption.

An encouraging step towards more environmentally friendly and effective urban transportation is the hardware design of electric bicycles with solar panels. In order to make solar-powered e-bikes more feasible and accessible, academic attention will move to improving solar panel efficiency, creating better battery technology, and streamlining power management systems. From an industrial perspective, increasing these e-bikes' cost-effectiveness, scalability, and battery integration are crucial to their broad acceptance. In terms of society, switching to solar-powered e-bikes has major environmental advantages, especially in lowering urban pollution and dependency on fossil fuels; nevertheless, issues with accessibility and price will need to be resolved. Solar-powered electric bicycles have the potential to play a significant role in the sustainable transportation environment as long as research and industry improvements continue.

SUBJECT INDEX

A

AC 46, 65, 185, 187
  induction motors 65
  motor drive 46
  voltage 185
  wave 187
Adoption 24, 33, 93, 95, 223, 224, 225, 226,
    230, 234, 237,
  accelerated 93
  broad 226, 234
  equitable 223
  mass-market 224
  promoting 237
  promoting EV 226
  social 230
  support EV 33
  wider EV 225
  widespread EV 95
  worldwide 24
Aerodynamics 211
Algorithms 216, 230
  advanced 216
  sophisticated 230
Amplitude 52, 189, 207
Analysis 139, 143
  comparative 139
  comprehensive 143
Angle based 72, 76, 77, 79
  control system 72
  positioning 76
  strategy 77, 79
Applications 30, 31, 37, 38, 48, 49, 66, 68, 69,
    86, 87, 124, 210, 222, 224, 228, 229,
    230
  automotive 222
  charging 124, 229
  high-efficiency 228
  large-scale 228
Arduino 161, 163, 166
Asynchronous motors 27

Automation 66, 156, 172, 173, 178, 227, 232,
    233
  domestic 156
  industrial 66, 227
  smooth 233
Automobiles 24, 93, 222, 235, 236
  electric 235
  engine 24
Average 123, 129, 188, 209, 210
  dynamics 123, 129
  energy loss 188
  heat transfer coefficient 209
  inductor 129
  width 209, 210
Awareness campaigns 229
Axial flux motors 224

B

Battery 23, 24, 29, 72, 78, 95, 103, 105, 106,
    110, 111, 112, 114, 115, 132, 135, 139,
    140, 145, 152, 154, 202, 215, 217, 218,
    219, 231, 232, 237
  controllers 95
  degradation 95, 145, 152
  deterioration 152, 154, 231
  galvanic isolation 95
  health 95
  integration 237
  life 29, 231, 232
  load 132, 135, 139, 140
  longevity 231
  management 215
  pack 23, 24, 72, 78, 217, 218
  performance 215
  power 219
  reference voltage 103
  reserves 202
  voltage 105, 106, 110, 111, 112, 114, 115,
    215
Bidirectional 37, 55, 56, 57, 96, 143, 144, 147,
    152, 153, 230, 232

Nitesh Tiwari, Shekhar Yadav and Sabha Raj Arya (Eds.)